Contents

Small School, Giant Dream

A Year of Hoosier High School Hoopla

Raymond Moscowitz

For Barbara and David

Small School, Giant Dream
A Year of Hoosier High School Hoopla

Littleguy   Enterprises
Box 255
Wabash, Indiana 46992

Library of Congress Catalogue Card Number: 90-91797

ISBN 0-9627117-0-5

Foreword

You are about to read a book on Indiana high school basketball and the way it consumes most small towns across the state at tournament time.

Ray Moscowitz has captured very eloquently all of the emotion, high spirits and heartbreak surrounding Northfield High School game by game through its memorable 1989-90 season.

This is a heart-pumping story about a small school with big dreams built around talented 6-10 and 6-9 twins Joe and Jon Ross, the Chay brothers who fled Laos with their family, Brad Hampton and an underrated supporting cast.

Coach Steve McClure put it all together much the way Marvin Wood steered tiny Milan to the 1954 state championship against mighty Muncie Central. It remains the single most memorable shocker in 80-year state tourney history.

This is a David and Goliath story that would be possible in just two other states where one class basketball is the rule. Some would have you believe that all of the best basketball is wasted on the big inner city schools. Don't try to peddle that sLuff past Milan and Northfield.

Northfield accepted every challenge in a thrill-packed season. Game after game the believers grew. You have to admire Coach McClure's young lads the way they battled from behind when they had to.

Coach McClure, every inch a class guy, said it best in a team prayer: "Father, we thank you for the neat times we've had and for the lessons. If there is any guilt on any of these young men's minds, just erase it right now. Just shine your light on them and spread your love amongst this team as you have all season."

Amen. Amen.

Bob Williams
Executive Staff, IHSAA;
Indianapolis Star Columnist, 1943-84

Preface

Steve McClure, basketball coach at Northfield High School, has my deepest appreciation. From the day I proposed this book to him to the final day of the season, he cooperated fully. Yet, he never tried to influence my reporting and writing.

I also appreciate the cooperation of assistant coaches Steve Desper and Harold Christie, Northfield Athletic Director Jim Kaltenmark, Principal William Neale and Metropolitan School Corporation Superintendent David Herbert.

I owe much thanks to people at Nixon Newspapers, Inc. John R. Nixon, president; John E. Mitchell, executive vice president, and John W. Stackhouse, vice president for finance, not only encouraged me throughout the season, but allowed me time and resources as needed.

Others at Nixon Newspapers who have my deepest appreciation are J. David Tipton, marketing director; Deborah M. Huff, internal accountant; Emil Milker, controller, and Ruby Hendrix, executive assistant.

My thanks also go to Bill Brooks and Howard Hewitt, managing editors of two of the Nixon newspapers, for reading the manuscript and making suggestions. *Wabash Plain Dealer* photographer Harold Chatlosh provided all photos, including those on the cover. Steve Leininger, advertising manager of the *Peru* (IN) *Daily Tribune*, contributed creative input. Barbara Tipton, whose background is in advertising, proofread the manuscript.

My greatest thanks go to my wife, Barbara. She not only nudged me into launching the project, but also transcribed several hours of tape and, as a former copy editor, made important editing suggestions.

Ray Moscowitz

Chapter 1: **The Dream Unfolds**

It is 3:15 in the afternoon on Monday, October 16, 1989, and the pungent aroma of fertilizer peppers the nostrils as it wafts from the fields surrounding Northfield High School in rural Wabash County, Indiana, population 36,000.

For students scurrying to their cars in the parking lot adjacent to the school's two gymnasiums, it is just another Indian summer afternoon, a time to head for part-time jobs, fast food places, crops in the fields, or home for chores and study.

But for 38 young men inside the practice gymnasium, it is not just another day. Like the outdoors, the air is not normal. It is a stomach-turning mixture of excitement, nervousness, wonder and anticipation that can be unsettling for youngsters who dream of being the next Hoosier Hotshot -- Johnny Wooden, Oscar Robertson, Larry Bird, Rick Mount, George McGinnis, Steve Alford.

It is the first day of basketball practice sanctioned by the Indiana High School Athletic Association -- the IHSAA. And in two weeks, 26 of the young men will experience a letdown that will range from a searing of the psyche for perhaps 48 hours to rock-bottom self-esteem that, to some degree, might never go away. Those 26 young men will be told that for this year, at least, they will not be a direct part of something so integral to Indiana, it is like a second religion in the Hoosier state. They will have been cut from making the varsity basketball team.

For the Northfield Norsemen candidates this year, rejection will carry an extra sting. It will mean not being part of a team representing one of Indiana's smallest schools -- 382 students -- with a legitimate chance to repeat the "Milan Miracle" of 1954. That's when Bobby Plump's 15-foot, last-second jump shot gave tiny Milan -- 162 students; 73 boys -- a legendary 32-30 triumph over mighty Muncie Central.

Shortly before opening day, *Hoosier Basketball Magazine*'s preseason edition hit the stands with Northfield ranked No. 9 in the Top 50. In his roundup article, Editor/Publisher Garry H. Donna wrote about the Fort Wayne Semistate, "If the (Marion) Giants are watching in Fort Wayne rather than playing next March 18 (actually, the 17th), they'll probably be watching Northfield represent the Marion Regional." And a week after tryouts have concluded, the Associated

1

Press' preseason poll has Northfield No. 10 -- the first time one of Wabash County's five high schools has achieved such lofty status.

The high expectations are based on some outstanding talent returning from last season's team. That squad recorded a 23-2 mark, was ranked No. 16 in the final poll and won the Sectional tournament before losing in the Marion Regional title game to the unbeaten, No. 1-ranked Giants.

Northfield's preseason publicity is generated by the returning "Twin Towers," 6-10 Joe and 6-9 Jon Ross. In September they announced that Notre Dame won the recruiting war, and they would make it official November 8, the first day of the college signing period.

But as Coach Steve McClure starts the season on this pleasant, mid-October day, he knows he has much more than the towering Rosses. They will be complemented up front by Brad Hampton, a 6-5, 190-pound junior who grew two inches over the summer and has displayed excellent all-around skills. McClure's backcourt will be blessed by Peck and Noi Chay, who, as infants, fled Laos with their family in 1976 after the communist takeover. Then there's Troy Miller, who can pop from the outside, and Nathan Winegardner, a "gym rat" who has grown up on the Northfield hardwoods while his father has coached, taught history and served as vice principal at various times in the last 22 years.

So for Northfield, winning the state championship is not far-fetched, not an impossible dream. It would be the culmination of a season that offers major goals along the way: winning the Wabash County championship, grabbing another Three Rivers Conference crown, repeating as Sectional champions, nabbing the school's first Regional title -- most likely against mighty Marion -- and triumphing in the Semistate.

But now, on this first day of a five-month season, those achievements are far from McClure's mind as he moves around the floor in a dark blue pullover shirt and tan shorts. He is focusing on the task at hand: finding the best combination of 12 players.

Now in his fourth year with a record of 56-14, he knows the kids well. Most of them have taken part in basketball clinics and camps he has conducted at the elementary and junior high levels. When he calls for partner drills, the candidates know exactly what he wants.

"Get into good habits, boys," he shouts over the soft din and squeaking shoes as the candidates pair up to practice their passing. "Fundamentals, form ... use your legs, follow through."

McClure ends the 45-minute session and gathers the hopefuls in a sitting position at center court. Standing over them, he is not an imposing figure -- 180 pounds on a stocky, 5-10 frame topped by a balding head -- but the youngsters' eyes and ears send a strong message of respect.

His speech features phrases, rather than sentences, and his tone is thick with a Southern Indiana/Larry Bird twang, some words getting cheated out of a letter. He tells them what they can expect for the next two weeks. And then he mentions the high hopes for the team, noting that the Ross twins' photos are on the cover of the North edition of *Hoosier Basketball Magazine*, featuring Eric Montross of defending state champion Lawrence North. (The South cover features Damon Bailey of Bedford North Lawrence, ballyhooed since the eighth grade when he was mentioned in *Sports Illustrated*.)

"It's three-fifty a copy for anyone who wants one," McClure tells the sprawled gathering. "I have a bundle in my truck. You can see me after practice if ya wanta buy one." He does not need to apologize for not providing free copies, because while coaching varsity boys basketball in Indiana is something special -- to some, almost God-like -- it doesn't necessarily mean great financial reward.

"We're not goin' to keep people who can't contribute to the Northfield basketball program," McClure says as he concludes his remarks. "That's not fair to you." Then, to help provide a soft landing later for those who don't make the varsity, he adds, "You will always be part of the Northfield program. You're part of the team."

McClure divides the group for the first official scrimmage of the year -- Ross against Ross, Chay against Chay -- and positions himself at a balcony rail where he can look down on the play. After several minutes, he's asked what he's searching for.

"We number one look for attitude. A kid with a good attitude's goin' to be able to play for us because he'll be able to learn, and, you know, basketball's a teachable sport. And if we can get a kid with a good attitude who's happy out here, who loves to play the game, he'll pay the price to be a good player. We can work with that."

Attitude is what McClure is all about. It is the one ingredient that controls everything else in a man who was once a cocky, all-around athlete turned wild, boozy college student and now, at 37, talks about God "dropping this team into my lap."

He glances over at assistant coach Steve Desper to point out a move made by Matt White, a 6-5 ninth-grader, then resumes talking about what he's looking for: "Of course, you know, we want to see what their grades are. We check that closely, the midterms and reports, try to keep a contact with the teachers. We want them to be sound students so we don't have to worry about them academically. Then we look at ability. You know, it's nice to have the combination of a good attitude, good academics and good ability. That's the three A's there, and with good ability, they can obviously help us."

From a pure basketball standpoint, the two coaches are looking for team play, defense and hustle. During a break for substitutions, McClure shouts from above, "If you want to make the team, play some defense and handle the ball."

The two Rosses resume battling each other inside and McClure resumes the conversation while keeping his eyes below. "The kids are going to be a little bit nervous, it's goin' to be hard for them to look good offensively," he points out as the scrimmage takes on a tone of playground freelancing. "But, you know, we're lookin' for people who would be able to play a role -- a good ball handler, a person who could come in and give you good defense, a good passer. This year with the Ross twins we want to get the ball inside a lot, so we want clever passers, people who can just fit that role."

Among those looking for a role is Scott Kunkel, already a hero of sorts in Wabash County. Now a 16-year-old, 6-2 sophomore, Kunkel was a hard-throwing lefthander in 1986 when the City of Wabash's Little League team won the state championship and came within a game of reaching Williamsport.

How will he feel if he doesn't make the varsity?

"If I work as hard as I can and I don't make it, I won't be disappointed," he says shyly. "If I don't work hard, and I don't make it, then I'll be disappointed in myself."

In a few months, those same words could apply to the team McClure puts together. If the squad doesn't work hard and come close to its full potential, the air next spring in Wabash County will be heavy not only with fertilizer, but also disappointment. If the Norsemen work hard, though, and reach their potential but don't succeed, the disappointment might sting less. But more important, if the hard work results in rewards that look so promising this autumn day, the

Norsemen could find themselves in front of perhaps 40,000 people inside the Hoosier Dome in Indianapolis on March 24, hoping to repeat Milan's storied feat.

And if that should happen, wonderful *deja vu* could await Steve McClure's parents. It would be 36 years since they drove from a speck on the terrain, Bright, Indiana, to the nearby Milan Country Club for a celebration marking a triumph forever etched in Hoosier high school basketball lore. There would be one difference, however: Youngest son Steve, who was 15 months old when Milan made the map, would be in the center of things, instead of having diapers changed at Grandpa McClure's house.

It is 3:15 in the afternoon on Monday, November 20, and the warmth and blue skies of Indian summer have given way to the cold and slate gray skies that signal the dawn of winter.

Inside the main gym, the Norsemen start their sixth week of practice with calisthenics and shooting around before Steve McClure arrives from White's Institute, 9.3 miles away, where he teaches physical education and health. Then, as usual, the varsity and junior varsity teams form a tight huddle at center court, pile their hands and say a prayer.

The huddle disbands as Randy Keaffaber, who like Scott Kunkel was a star pitcher on a Wabash Little League state championship team, strolls into the gym. On this Monday, Keaffaber, who played guard and forward last year for Northfield, is home for Thanksgiving from Indiana State University, which he attends on a baseball scholarship. McClure spies him and they hug warmly.

While the squad goes through a variety of drills simultaneously, McClure says, "These are drills that are programmed at junior high on up, and it gives us a bond. And, you know, when the younger kids come in and watch the varsity practice they can identify with it. The better we can be fundamentally, the better we're goin' to be as a team. And I think the key in high school sports is to not beat yourself. Like I just saw a kid shoot a lay-up wrong. I've got to go correct that. 'Kay?"

Now, as the varsity and junior varsity prepare to scrimmage, the JayVee players shed their shirts. McClure gathers his squad at one free-throw line, while Steve Desper, who coaches the junior varsity, does the same at the other.

5

At 5-10, McClure is almost buried among the players as he explains what he wants, stressing defense: "Think good defensive principles. Get off the ball weak side; man-to-man defense on the strong side, zone on the weak side on any defense we're playin'. But the biggest thing I can see is jumpin' to the pass with your hands up. Every time. That'll make the defense much more effective. Now if we're in (defense) 5, just stack the guards. 'kay? The quickest guard comes up first, then the next quick, and just stack it up so we can get a little disguise goin'. And our best trap will be right across the 10-second line."

"Right across the 10-second line?" Brad Hampton asks.

"Right across the 10-second line. That way they can't throw it back."

McClure switches to offense: "We want turnovers to the minimum. We want you to have good shots for the situation that you're in. Imagine you're startin' off the game right now, and obviously you want to get the lead. Take shots that will get you the lead; don't come down and start crankin' it. Get the ball inside. On the fast break, if you've got the lane, do it; otherwise set up your early offense. And on early offense, we need to see some X cuts. Normally the best time to run that is on a score. Any questions?"

As play begins, McClure is relieved to see Hampton on the floor, with his shatter-proof goggles securely in place. Twelve days earlier, it appeared as if the tough junior forward would be out for a month with a dislocated left shoulder. McClure, who was returning from a press conference in Indianapolis for the Associated Press' Top 20 teams, saw Hampton get injured just as he walked into the gym. It occurred in a scrimmage as Hampton went in for a layup, got bumped accidentally by a trailing player and fell heavily to the floor. But now the right-handed youngster is not showing signs of discomfort as he works the boards and moves easily with and without the ball.

McClure teaches from midcourt, shouting out a steady stream of advice, reminders and encouragement. Harsh criticism is missing -- for now. "What're we doin'?" he yells. "Make sure we're organized. Keep it movin' ... *gooood*, good job."

As the team heads for the water fountain, he says, "We stress not havin' a lot of turnovers, and we're doin' a good job. And we're reactin' well on defense. We're switchin' from man-to-man to zone each time we come down the floor; we want to confuse the offense. The kids have to think out there."

6

Keaffaber, the alum, has been watching the scrimmage intently. He's asked how his freshman year under McClure's predecessor differed, if any, from the three under McClure. "My freshman year," he begins without hesitating, "the players just wanted to play for themselves. They weren't out there for the school and the pride. They just wanted to play, not really to win. Coach McClure came in here and brought in a whole new attitude. You know, you put the team first, you put yourself last. He has a religious background, and we always had a team meeting, and everybody just got along real well. That was the main thing that was different between my freshman and senior years, team unity and how we got along."

McClure blasts his whistle to halt play and reposition players. He puts the 6-10 Joe Ross at guard. Why the big man outside? "In case of foul trouble. See, this doesn't allow the opposing team to post-up a big man in foul trouble. You can do this with the Rosses because they move so well."

They not only move well, they exhibit a court presence that indicates strong intelligence for the game -- an intelligence transferred from the classroom, where they also shine. "Yes, they are intelligent players," McClure says. "They want to learn; they want to get better. They are much better than last year "

Suddenly, McClure shouts out, "What're we doin'!?" as the varsity moves into an offensive position. "Move it! move it! move it! Reverse it!" And Noi Chay finds himself with an open 15-footer that goes in and out and back in again on Hampton's tap.

"Last year and in previous years, we just tried to put in our system, both offensively and defensively," McClure says. "And there's been a lot of just basic teaching goin' on. Now we feel we have a group, and we have carried over some veterans, which is unusual at a small school. We see we have basics in one area, so now we're tryin' to refine things. And the kids are mentally ready for that, as well as physically, 'cause they're wantin' to learn. I'd say right now -- there's a beautiful play -- there's good teamwork, they're learnin' to pivot and stop and look for each other. And those're the things we didn't have in the program a few years ago. So we're pleased with progress that we're makin'. We're seein' it in all the groups comin' up."

McClure's program, like most at all levels, is a game of numbers. He uses five basic offensive patterns, and he defends with five formations.

Offensively, the numbers relate to patterns, including one that isolates Joe or Jon Ross in the low post. Or a number might mean getting the ball to Jon in a certain area; and if he doesn't have his first option, go into a basic pattern in which anyone has a chance to score.

Defensively, his teaching is more specific. If he yells "3," he wants a 3-2 zone, three players being out high. Conversely, a "2" calls for two defenders being up. A "1" is a 1-3-1 zone trap, one person being up high. McClure's "4" is man-to-man, and the "5" is a match-up arrangement that can vary from game to game.

"The kids got to know that if I say 4, 4, 4, we're runnin' number four offense, we're gonna press man-to-man full court," McClure explains. "So the kids have to be students of the game. Sure. And, see, we try and make it as simple as possible so that we don't take away from their aggressiveness and that."

The scrimmage ends and McClure gathers the varsity at midcourt for a brief critique. "You did okay on defense," he says, scratching his mustache. "But still, I want to see you get those hands up every time the ball is passed. Consciously and subconsciously, you're forcin' them further out, and it gives you more time to react, 'cause the first thing they're goin' to look at are your hands. They're not goin' to look at the basket. Offensively, you're doin' some good things. The only thing I could say right now is when we're in a half-court situation, don't be afraid to reverse it. Couple of times you punched it in a little too soon. Most of the time, they (the Rosses) are big enough, you can get it in. I mean, if you see a lot of defense, reverse it away and we'll see what comes from the weak side. Then when it comes back to you, you've either got a shot or a little better angle. You get the defense movin' a little bit. Make the defense move more. 'Kay? Anybody got any questions or comments? 'Kay. Rinse out."

Kunkel has made the varsity. But as he heads for the drinking fountain he's a "skin," having played with the junior varsity during the scrimmage. Although listed on the official varsity roster, he will play mostly junior varsity. Under IHSAA rules, a player is allowed 80 quarters, which is equivalent of all 20 regular-season games. Kunkel, junior guard Troy Baer and sophomore forward Ryan Dubois will play up to three full quarters of the junior varsity game that precedes the varsity contest, then be available for one full quarter of varsity play if needed.

Kunkel feels he played well during the two-week tryout period, but he's not satisfied. "If I had played then the way I'm playing now, I'd have made it," he says softly with only a hint of disappointment in his voice. "I see things now. My game has come a long way." There is no bitterness in his tone, only simple truth, which is not surprising from the bright youngster.

For McClure, basketball is more than team play. Basketball is *family*, an integral part of growing in life for those who play the game. As the season develops, he will consciously coalesce his people into a unit with all the familial trappings -- love, sharing, crying, working out differences, looking out for each other, and bonding far beyond X's and O's.

As the family knits together, its motto for the year -- worn on practice jerseys -- will constantly ring out: "Forward march!"

And Steve McClure, the low-key, easy-going "daddy" in the dawning days of the season, will change, alternating between a patient papa and a fiery father while riding the emotional waves that come from coaching 12 teenagers.

•••••••••

Five Indiana high school basketball champions? For now, no.

The IHSAA has a football orgy in November, crowning five champions over a two-day period inside the Hoosier Dome. The number of male boys enrolled determines the divisions; 5A schools are the largest.

Basketball is something special. When a move was made a few years ago for class basketball, it gained little support. Milan's feat has not been repeated for 35 years, but more often than not, a Milan-like team -- such as Northfield or Loogootee in southern Indiana -- comes along, making the symptoms of "Hoosier Hysteria" even more pronounced.

Folks who oppose divisional play often mention "The Spirit of '76," referring to tiny Argos, just below South Bend in Marshall County. On January 16, 1981, the Argos Dragons bettered the state's longest regular-season winning streak, breaking Madison's mark of 61 set from 1960 to 1962. Argos, a school with less than 200 students, went on to win 76 straight before Glenn ended the Cinderella run almost a year later with a 58-50 triumph on December 17, 1981.

During the run, Argos won a staggering 94 games while losing only four. The victories included four Sectional titles and, in 1979, a storied trip to the state finals. Three games are played on the final day of the season, two during the day and the championship contest that night. Every little burg -- and probably some large communities too -- was pulling for Argos, which went into the finals at Indianapolis' Market Square Arena with a 28-0 record. But the Dragons, who had given away height all year long, couldn't match Anderson's size in the early game and fell 74-64.

"...but the Dragons played well enough to convince a sellout crowd of more than 17,000 that they were not out of place," Bob Williams wrote in his book, *Hoosier Hysteria*. Williams' account continued:

"Several metropolitan dailies and even *Sports Illustrated* sent their writers and photographers to record one of the most unbelievable chapters in Hoosier Hysteria since Milan's Cinderella team. ...

"Coach (Phil) Weybright and Principal Stephen Keith told how adult fans appeared to get a lot more worked up over the long winning streak than the youngsters."

Adults and youngsters alike get worked up when Sectional time rolls around the last week of February. A fever for which there is no cure spreads throughout the state. Nothing is more intense, including the pulse-pounding excitement of the Indianapolis 500 race. Practically nothing stops the populace from filling tiny gyms that seat a few hundred to the world's largest high school arena, the 9,335-seat New Castle facility.

Even snowstorms can't stop the faithful. The weather has been relatively mild in recent years, but for a time, a major blast of winter seemed to accompany Sectional play. It was not unusual for folks to bundle up, pile onto a tractor and plow through snowdrifts to reach the Sectional site.

While youngsters talk today about the Eric Montrosses, Damon Baileys and Ross twins, old-timers recall with precision yesteryear's storied coaches -- Marion Crawley, Bill Green, Everett Case, Glenn Curtis, Cliff Wells -- and storied players -- "Fuzzy" Vandivier and the "Wonder Five," the Van Arsdale Twins, Bill Garrett, Marion Pierce, and Clyde Lovellette, not to mention the Woodens, Robertsons and Mounts.

Outsiders -- the Sophisticated Slickers whose world is glass and steel and marble -- may laugh at the country bumpkiness of it all, ridiculing the Cinderella syndrome that permeates from the Ohio River to Lake Michigan as winter steams toward spring. But insiders -- from CEO's to folks who man the steel and auto lines -- know that high school basketball is the glue that holds Indiana together.

In 1924, Irwin S. Cobb, one of America's best writer-historians of the time, called Indiana "the most typically American democracy." And as the last decade of the 20th Century unfolds, Cobb's words still ring with truth as Indiana emulates the nation in forging economic development, dealing with problems in education, fighting the evil of drugs, adjusting to decreased agrarian power, and struggling with religious change. But high school basketball remains constant.

Howard Hewitt, a native Hoosier who is managing editor of the *Frankfort Times* and formerly its sports editor, puts it well: "High school basketball in Indiana is more than an extra-curricular activity. It's a way of life for many Hoosiers. Many live for those morning-afters to discuss strategy. To second-guess the coach. It's a time to lament your team's poor free throw shooting. It's also a time to pat your buddy on the back, because his strapping lad scored the winning basket."

Bill Brooks, another Hoosier who is managing editor of the New Castle *Courier-Times*, and a former sports editor elsewhere, illustrates Hewitt's words. Brooks tells a story about Bruce Firchau, who coached in Illinois for several years before coming to Plainfield, where Brooks was newspapering.

Forty minutes had passed since Firchau had won the Brownsburg Sectional in his first season, and the veteran mentor was only beginning to calm down. "He was not fully prepared for Hoosier Hysteria," Brooks recalled. "After this particular installment in the history of Indiana basketball, Firchau and I retreated to a corner of the locker room, and he took several deep breaths to gather himself."

Brooks continued: "Firchau grew up on Chicago's south side, close enough to East Chicago (Indiana) to know about Hoosier basketball. And as a child, he remembered reading about Milan's stunning victory. So when he got the Plainfield offer, he accepted partly out of curiosity, to discover what all the fuss was about."

He discovered, all right. In the locker room that night, Firchau told Brooks: "After the big pre-Sectional dinner hosted by a parent of a senior team member, we -- the men -- all went into the living room and the boys went outside. The fathers took turns telling me how to set up my defense against our arch-rival Brownsburg.

11

"As they talked, I looked outside and saw snow on the ground. I could see the boys out in the barn, and there was a rim inside. They were playing ball.

"I had to pinch myself and say, 'Wow, this is happening to me.'"

Firchau's experience reminded Brooks that such "near-religious fervor" does not occur everywhere. "Boys do not play inside barns when the snow is too deep to play on the surfaced court that dots so many homesteads," Brooks pointed out. "Where, except maybe in the inner cities of New York, Chicago and Detroit, do boys shovel snow to play ball in hooded sweatshirts and gloves? And where else do thousands and thousands of fans and fanatics crowd into gymnasiums that rise from our landscapes like cathedrals?"

Can high school basketball be *that* serious? the Sophisticated Slickers ask. Don't those hicks have more to worry about?

Well, yes, it *can* be that serious -- as serious as brawls at soccer matches, bottle-throwing at major league baseball stadiums and ugly taunting at football fields. And yes, Hoosiers have more important things to worry about. But high school basketball is the ultimate escape from those worries, the great equalizer among the masses.

For Northfield Norse fans, the 1989-90 season promises to be one of the best escapes ever.

Chapter 2: Rough Road to Maturity

William McClure was livid. "Go to your room!" he ordered.

Steve McClure was deflated. He trudged off, his bubble of joy leaking fast.

Moments earlier, 11-year-old Steve had burst into the house, exclaiming, "You'll never believe what I did! I swam across the Ohio River!"

Bill McClure's anger rose after getting the details of his youngest son's adventure. "You put yourself in real danger," he said, pointing out that Steve could have become tired and drown, gotten hung up by a barge, or been endangered by other craft. At the least, he should have taken an inner tube along or something similar for safety.

"*Boy*, I was crushed," Steve McClure recalls 26 years later. "Here I was, braggin' and really proud of that. And Wilbur Rule -- I love that guy and his family -- my father's roommate at Purdue -- was down for the weekend to see it."

The river swim had begun, as most things do for an 11-year-old, as a lark.

"Me and this guy were down at the boat dock, and I thought he was Tarzan," McClure continues. "I thought he was the greatest swimmer to ever hit the waters. And I said, 'J.D., you want to swim across the river?' And he said, 'Sure.' "

So the youngsters swam about three-quarters of a mile across the murky Ohio from Rising Sun, Indiana, to Rabbit Hash, Kentucky.

"Rabbit Hash, yes," McClure says with a smile. "That's what it's called, and there's like two general stores there." The smile widens as he pauses. "Yeah, I was raised in the sticks."

Some folks would say he still lives in them.

The leaves have made their autumn escape, tumbling from intermittent trees that hug the narrow county roads naked against the flat, harvested fields.

Five houses sit clustered by themselves along a half-mile stretch of County Road 100 West, just off 200 North, seemingly standing guard over the barren soil of late November. Like scores of houses that dot both the urban and rural landscapes of Indiana, three of the five have orange hoops attached to white backboards supported by black iron poles in driveways.

One of those three houses -- a ranch built of flagstone and slabs of wood stained in deep brown -- is home for Steve and Lisa McClure and their three children.

Inside the modern home built by students from the Upper Wabash Vocational School, McClure sits in an old, stuffed wing chair the day after Thanksgiving and talks easily about his river swim and other events in his life.

Unlike the serene, comfortable living room, McClure's life at times was a wild roller coaster ride until Lisa and the Lord applied the brakes.

At Rising Sun High School, McClure was an all-around athlete, a tough, wiry kid earning 15 letters out of a possible 16 in basketball, baseball, track and cross country. He makes a point of noting that he missed getting his 16th monogram only because knee surgery in April 1969 kept him out of track his sophomore year.

Despite his athletic skills, no meaningful scholarship offers came his way, so McClure, who had been leaning toward Purdue anyway, enrolled there. Family roots played a part, too, his father and two older brothers having preceded him to West Lafayette, Indiana. And his mother, who had attended Indiana University at Bloomington, made it "official," insisting, "You are going to Purdue; you won't get an education at I.U."

McClure laughs. "I have a lot of fun telling my Indiana University friends how I ended up at Purdue."

Once he got there, though, a different kind of fun his first two years almost ruined him for life.

Before freshman registration, he had talked things over with his parents and decided that the job market didn't look promising for a straight physical education major. He loved to work with tools and build things when he was younger, so he decided to major in industrial management.

But after his first semester, physical education won out anyway when he began developing aspirations to coach. By then, he was a "walk on" for the baseball team, confident he could make it as a pitcher.

"I'd had some interest in professional baseball," he recalls, leaning forward in his chair, "and I could throw the ball over 95 miles an hour. I didn't have a curve ball, and didn't think I needed one, being able to throw that hard."

14

The Purdue coaches thought differently. He did not letter his freshman and sophomore years, and when it came time to take the team picture, he declined to be in it, feeling he had not been given a chance to contribute. In fact, he never pitched in a varsity game, but once threw a three-hit shutout against the varsity for the second team.

McClure admits that not succeeding on the Purdue baseball team was tough. He felt he had worked hard, spurred on by great family support. Older brother Mike was still on campus at the time.

McClure had another reason for giving up on baseball: He was behind academically. But increased study time did not necessarily replace the hours he spent on the baseball diamond. Instead, he drank more.

His drinking had started before college. "I was drinkin' a lot of beer and just, you know, I guess rambunctious," he says in a level voice. "Just figured, if you're goin' to college you have to be wild and you have to kind of fit the mold. And I'd listened to some of the stories my brothers had told me. And I guess I was just there for the good time, just, you know, the social activities that normally take place there. But I don't remember breakin' the law or anything like that."

McClure lived at the Kneale House, a co-op similar to a fraternity, including pledgeship. And, like the heavy drinking that can take place in fraternity houses, the beer flowed freely at Kneale. McClure remembers getting drunk often.

His weekly routine revolved around pizza and brew. Monday night was a house meeting. "You wanted to get kind of drunk before you went to those," McClure recalls, " 'cause they're boring. Wednesday night was pizza and pitcher night at the Caboose. And then maybe go to school a bit on Thursday. Friday and Saturday were the weekend, and, of course, college students are supposed to party on the weekends. Sometimes on a Friday and Saturday we'd drive from West Lafayette to Illinois and bring back a case of beer." McClure and friends would occasionally drive over on Sundays, too, because the sale of alcoholic beverages on the Sabbath was illegal then in Indiana.

So Steve McClure, the trim, 170-pound athlete in high school became a flabby, 200-pound ex-jock in college.

"It got to the point," he volunteers, "to where I felt I needed to have a drink all the time. At football games we'd sneak in liquor, and sometimes, you know, almost have to be carried out."

McClure admits he was "bordering on alcoholism."

15

He looks back and sees "how dumb" his pizza and beer diet was. "I certainly don't want my kids (his own and his basketball boys) to do it. I really feel bad that my kids see all the drinkin'. And I feel even worse that, you know, 20 years ago, or 15, whatever it was, that was me."

The summer before his junior year, he told his parents he knew his behavior was leading him down a dangerous road. He wanted to change, but didn't know how.

His parents owned a mortuary, and as McClure grew up, he watched how his dad related to people under stressful situations. Steve recalls: "Here's a loved one that's been lost laying in a casket and you've got cryin' family and all, and I just used to sit back and watch Dad and he was, you know, very skilled at relatin' to people."

His mother, who was a nurse, "is probably one of the toughest people I know as far as patience and stayin' the steady course."

Toughness and patience, indeed.

There was that time, not too many years after the Ohio River swim, of another lark. Bored, McClure and friends decided to ride around in the huge station wagon his dad used for the ambulance business then provided by funeral homes.

Looking for something to do, McClure and his pals started taking bird baths and yard ornaments to see how many they could swipe without getting caught. They could swipe plenty, they found out. So they drove to Grants Creek Bridge, which sits along the Ohio River.

"We just stood up there and started throwin' stuff in the crick," McClure says. "Gosh, we even took some from family friends. We didn't even know what we were doin', you know, 'cause when we finally got caught, I had to answer to some very dear people."

The answering came after the police called on William McClure the next morning. Upstairs in the funeral home, Steve lay "scared to death," but thinking, "Dad doesn't lie to me, so I'm not gonna lie to Dad."

McClure and his friends wound up paying a fine and were ordered to replace what they had taken and dumped into the Ohio.

He looks back: "We had a friend -- we called him Spazz -- his name's Bobby Anderson -- and his family ran a restaurant and boat dock on the river. And he had scuba equipment. The police said if we could get ahold of the stuff and bring it back in good shape, that would be fine.

"That was somethin', scuba divin' in muddy water. We took turns goin' down, and I think Bobby was the only one who'd ever been down. Of course, I felt like I was gonna drown."

The youths retrieved most of what was taken, but they had to hunt around southern Indiana to find replacements for items that were broken in the fall.

"I have the highest respect for my parents, for what they've done with three boys," McClure says, a bit choked up. "We weren't exactly angels."

But they were William and Jean McClure's sons, for sure, and when they came to them troubled, like Steve did after his sophomore year, the toughness, patience and understanding they had shown through the years rose to the fore again. And as they had done in the past, they counseled him, striving to get him on the right track before he began his junior year at Purdue.

Along came Lisa Custer.

On an autumn day in 1973, McClure and his good friend, Chris Smith, went to a campus dance. He saw an attractive coed in the crowd. "There is my wife," he told Smith.

Intrigued, Smith investigated. The attractive young woman was Miss Custer, a sophomore who had graduated from Northfield, where she had been a cheerleader.

Smith made the introduction.

McClure's first words were, "Will you marry me?"

The answer would have to wait, understandably, until after several dates, when Lisa posed a question of her own: "Do you believe in God?"

"Suddenly, it awakened in me a spiritual consciousness that had been buried for years," McClure says, leaning back in the cushy chair.

He began to settle down, and by taking some summer classes was able to get his degree in four years. His grade-point average rose steadily, and in his last semester, he made the Dean's List, achieving a 5.7 average out of 6. That mark boosted his cumulative average to 5.0.

Lisa's words had steered him back to church, where he could see that while athletic success had come his way, failure as a person had tagged along.

Failure in marriage almost came next.

In August 1976, after dating for almost three years, Steve and Lisa said their vows and soon launched teaching careers.

In November 1976, Steve and Lisa said their goodbyes, starting a separation that came within two weeks of resulting in divorce.

"I filed, essentially," McClure recalls without prompting. "I had no desire to see her. I didn't even want to talk to her on the phone."

Family -- that ingredient so central to McClure's life -- was just as central to his new bride's. She had not planned on "teaching forever" and thought about farming near her parents. But Steve, with his streak of independence, wanted to live between his and her family homes.

The situation between the newlyweds became strained after Lisa learned that her mother was seriously ill with pneumonia. A deep depression set in after the pneumonia, prompting Lisa to spend large amounts of time at the family home on Rural Route 6, just north of the Wabash city limits. The McClures were living close by -- in a trailer situated on the ground now occupied by the McClure house.

"I felt she should have been with me more," McClure says, looking back. "But she was so drawn to her mother. And so we were two strong-willed people going off in different directions."

McClure moved to an apartment in Marion, just south of the Wabash County line. It was not far from Oak Hill High School, where he got his first job out of Purdue in 1975, teaching physical education and coaching minor sports. Lisa, who was teaching part-time at Southwood Elementary in southern Wabash County, moved in with her parents. So the McClures were close -- geographically.

As winter stalked the countryside, depression stalked McClure as he went home each night to the small, empty apartment, again confused and looking for answers. He would look for those answers again, he decided, with his parents during the Christmas break.

And then something odd happened. On December 22, Steve and Lisa McClure had separate automobile accidents. Lisa was returning home from Southwood Elementary in her 1972 Datsun when a fender-bender occurred a quarter of a mile from her parents' residence. Some four hours later, Steve's Buick Opal was struck by a car pulling out from a side street in Aurora, Indiana, a small town less than 15 miles from his parents' home in Rising Sun.

Neither was hurt. And neither knew about the other's accident. It was Farm Bureau Insurance who got the news to them. After receiving calls from each, the company wondered if a mistake had been made before learning that yes, the rare had occurred, both McClures were in accidents just hours apart.

"Those accidents, that made me think," McClure recalls. "God's gettin' our attention. I had thought my family would fill the void; it didn't. I was about to call it quits."

McClure was not contemplating suicide. "No, no," he says. "I was just startin' to lose worth for life."

So he prayed in earnest.

"Our vows were said in the presence of God," McClure continues. "We had got within two weeks of the divorce. I asked myself what I really wanted to do. I desperately turned to God and said, 'Help, I need you.' "

Meanwhile, Lisa had been trying to see him, but he had "just shut her out, cold."

McClure asked God to "take me now or get somethin' workin' with Lisa."

God got something working in early January 1977.

On a typically cold and snowy day, they managed to get off from teaching and drove around the countryside to see if they could work their problems out.

"We knew our marriage had hit rock bottom. But we knew that with God's help we could work things out," he remembers.

A month later, Brady, their first child, was conceived.

"She seduced me," McClure says, a grin covering his face. "It was the blizzard of '77; there was no school. We were in that small apartment at Turtle Creek in Marion. She put on a new bathing suit and said, 'What do you think?' Well, I knew she wasn't goin' swimmin'."

Lisa laughs at that, says she doesn't recall those details, but then turns serious and adds, "I remember thinking that if it didn't work out, I still wanted a part of him for the rest of my life."

Before getting married, McClure had been offered the job of coaching seventh-grade basketball at Oak Hill for the 1976-77 season. Jack Keefer, who would go on to win the state basketball championship in 1989 with Lawrence North, made the offer in the spring of McClure's first year at the school.

McClure jumped at the chance. He had been coaching wrestling, which he enjoyed, but he had never participated in the sport, and, too, he wanted to work with Keefer, who had built a strong reputation.

The opportunity to work with Keefer didn't materialize, though, because Keefer was offered the job at Lawrence North, a brand-new school in the Indianapolis area.

Another excellent opportunity came along three years later, however, when McClure got the assistant coach's job at Oak Hill with Glenn Heaton, who would become a piece of sad irony in McClure's life.

After three years with Heaton, McClure decided to quit coaching.

"For the sake of my family," he says, remembering those days. "We were gonna have our third kid. We did, in fact, in August '82. And it was really rough, 'cause I was really gettin' into coaching, I enjoyed the kids at Oak Hill."

But instead of quitting cold turkey, McClure decided to keep coaching junior high football, which lasts only six weeks, and assist Terry Lichtenberg, the new varsity coach.

McClure laughs: "We never got beat in football at Rising Sun. Of course, we didn't have a team."

Lichtenberg had a team, though, and he proceeded to win the state's 1A championship -- for the smallest schools -- his first year. McClure got his first taste of being a real winner.

Another taste came later -- after Glenn Heaton's wife, Nancy, told him he would make a great head basketball coach, to which he replied: "Never. I'll never be a basketball coach."

In 1985, having spent 10 years at Oak Hill and growing restless, he cast his eyes elsewhere. But not at White's Institute, a school for troubled youths, mostly from outside of Wabash County. At any one time, about 125 students live and learn there until they are ready to return home.

When White's notified him about a teaching position, he thought, No way. Then he thought about his own checkered past and figured that perhaps he could help some of the youngsters there relate to life better.

And he thought about Lisa. She had taught summer school at White's, and he remembered that the pay was good and she got 90 minutes for lunch.

"*Hey*," he says, "the kids were human beings. You know, all you think about White's is a bunch of hoods and it's ugly and a bunch of rejects work there. It's quite to the contrary -- it's a super place with super people."

McClure also liked the idea of getting into the Metropolitan School District of Wabash County, which administers the partly private White's. He was living in his current house, three minutes from Northfield, and driving about 50 miles 'round trip each day to Oak Hill. White's would mean getting on the same schedule as his young family; they'd have spring break at the same time.

So when Lew Curless, the principal, asked him to interview, he agreed, "because my wife was encouragin' it. And I thought, at least I'm gonna look."

By the time the interview ended, he was ready to "grab a pencil and wantin' to sign," even though he had not been offered a job.

A job offer was almost a given, though, and McClure signed to teach physical education and health and coach eighth-grade basketball and junior high track.

He coached the eighth-graders with a legend -- Clyde Lovellette, the 6-9 Hoosier great who had also found his way to White's and later would be elected to the Basketball Hall of Fame.

The Northfield basketball job became available in the spring of 1985, a year after McClure moved to White's. He had no thought of applying, perhaps feeling a little gun shy after two unsuccessful attempts earlier for head coaching jobs. He had lost out at Wabash High and nearby North Miami High, the latter telling him he didn't have any experience. By then, he says, he was not consumed with wanting to be a head basketball coach, "and besides, White's was spicin' up my life enough as it is."

But deep down, he knew he was rationalizing his feelings for not applying. He had, in fact, seen some Northfield games, living so close, and he could visualize himself at the Norsemen helm. He knew he had to try to stretch himself.

"I could see that our family was settling in the Wabash area, which is something I said I would never do," he says. "I didn't feel like you need to live by either set of parents. I guess I'm very independent. I felt that with my abilities and God behind me, I could do about anything. You just grow where you're planted."

So McClure applied and prayed, figuring his chances were a longshot at best. After all, he'd been out of varsity coaching for three years, and to think that someone would gamble on a guy now mentoring eighth graders, well...

"But there again," he says with a bit of awe, "when the Lord wants you in somewhere, he'll handle all the details."

McClure became one of three finalists, along with Monte Moffett and Steve Desper. McClure felt that Desper should have the job, because he'd paid his dues at Northfield over several years. But Desper would lose out and continue as assistant coach and teach math. Moffett would later get the job at Southwood, which is also in the Metropolitan district.

McClure went into the job with great support from his wife. "She knew it would be good for me just to go ahead and accept a challenge like that whether it worked out or not," he recalls.

So as the 1986-87 school year opened, McClure found himself doing what he told Nancy Heaton he would never do: be a varsity basketball coach in Indiana.

Northfield had not won a Sectional since 1970, when Lisa McClure was a cheerleader. And McClure was not thinking Sectional as he greeted his hopefuls on opening day.

But the team would jell around a great shooter in Chad Fordyce en route to a 15-5 regular-season record going into the Huntington Sectional. The Norse would draw a bye and then open tournament play by defeating Wabash 72-63. That triumph would put Northfield in the championship game against Huntington North, coached by Glenn Heaton, who had left Oak Hill for a brief stop at Greenfield before moving on again.

Northfield would score a 54-52 victory in overtime, and McClure would think, "My God, we've won this thing." And he would experience powerful mixed emotions -- the thrill of victory and the agony of Heaton's defeat. And he would worry that Heaton would feel heat at Huntington, a basketball-rich school.

Mostly, though, as he hugged Lisa in the tumult, Steve and Lisa McClure would experience a crest in their lives -- a personal victory over adversity.

For the McClures, the biggest victory had already been won -- Jesus Christ on the cross.

"You know," he says softly, "basketball is nothing but a coffee break in life. And yet it's somethin' we want to give 100 percent to. Sure, basketball's important to us, but there's other priorities. For instance, this job was given to me by God. There's no doubt about it.

22

I see basketball as a tool where you can help kids prepare for challenges that they're going to meet later down the road."

If his kids are better persons after a season, he doesn't care if the team goes 0-20, he says. "I'll feel like a success. And you're always gonna have people who will doubt what you're doin', who's gonna question you."

He smiles. "One thing I get a kick out of this year, a lot of people are comin' up and they tell me they have high expectations for this year's team. And the only question I always ask is, do those same people have high expectations of themselves? And, you know, it doesn't always work that way. You got a lot of losers puttin' pressure on these kids."

McClure, once a loser himself, will put pressure on them too -- the pressure to play hard, play smart, and, most important, grow as individuals in the process.

•••••••••

Steve McClure inherited some quality players when he arrived at Northfield, but more importantly he inherited an extraordinary person in an ordinary guy named Steve Desper.

A slight man at 5-9 and 170 pounds, Desper is a bookish-looking 36. His dress is far from flashy, his glasses plain, his demeanor rather quiet away from the basketball court. In short, he looks and acts like a teacher, with a certain seriousness and quiet intelligence about him -- which is why he is still at Northfield High School after 15 years and not coaching somewhere else.

As the odd man out in the three-man contest for Northfield's head coaching job, it would have been understandable -- expected, in fact -- if Desper had departed, because losing out to McClure and Moffett wasn't the first time he had been denied the top job.

In fact, he essentially had the job in the summer of 1980 for the 1980-81 season, only to be knifed, although he's too nice a guy to use that word.

The third son in a family of four children, Desper was born in Columbia City, Indiana, to strict parents "who made sure you toed the line." The family moved later to nearby Kendallville, near Fort Wayne. He attended East Noble High School, where he participated in basketball, golf, tennis and cross country. He excelled at golf, and the

Ball State University golf team benefitted from it in 1973 and '74. Today he plays with a three handicap.

After earning a bachelor's degree in math in 1975, Desper got his first and only teaching job that fall at Northfield. He also received the assistant varsity basketball coach's job, working with Bob Denari. A master's degree in secondary education from Ball State and a family, including a son and daughter, would come later.

When Denari was replaced by Harold Christie, Desper continued as the assistant. And when Christie was replaced by Randy Unger, Desper stayed put. The top job, however, was his, on an interim basis, for the 1979-80 season, while Unger took a year's sabbatical.

Desper guided a team with average talent to an 8-13 record and a Wabash County Tournament championship that Northfield had not since won again going into the 1989-90 season. When Unger decided not to return, Desper appeared to have the job on a permanent basis. Before starting his summer job as a general laborer at Salamonie State Forest, not far from his Wabash home, Desper signed a contract that didn't have "interim" in it.

But Unger changed his mind, and the Metropolitan School Board had not signed the contract with Desper's signature on it. After talking to Unger at seven o'clock one night, school officials went to the state forest the next afternoon at 1:30.

Desper recalls the visit: "I was told by the president of the school board that they had received phone calls from some people in the community, and Mr. Unger had numerous relatives and friends in the community supporting him, that they really wanted him to return. So the school board made a phone call to him, asked him if he would change his mind, and he decided yes, he would change his mind and return."

Desper was very disappointed, but after a few days he realized that the game is for the kids, not for him, and the important thing was to keep the program going in a strong direction.

So Desper agreed to assist Unger, who stayed for two more seasons before leaving. But Desper was denied again. The board hired Gary Baker, who stayed for four years, with Desper as his assistant.

When Steve McClure got the job, he visited Desper and asked, "What's the deal? Can we work together?"

24

And, not surprisingly, Desper said, "Sure, we can work together." And that was that, because, quite simply, Desper is a teacher first, a coach second.

He admits that while he occasionally thinks about coaching varsity basketball, he does not do so with intensity. And it's easy to believe him after he ticks off the reasons for staying at Northfield: He's allowed to teach very academic courses; Principal William Neale is a great man to work for; Wabash is an excellent place to raise a family, and McClure, whom he likes "very, very much," treats him with a great deal of respect.

McClure, he says, is "by far the best psychologist I've ever seen with teen-age kids. He truly understands what's going on in their minds and he is able to read their personalities very well. He learns how to deal with each one individually to get the most out of their talent."

And the talent this season is the best Desper has seen in his 15 years. He believes the Ross twins will be productive players at Notre Dame, but will need more physical strength if they're going to rebound at the major-college level.

Aside from the Rosses, he sees Brad Hampton as the ideal high school forward at 6-5. "He's extremely quick and a tremendous defensive player. That is a great asset to the two big guys. We have different kinds of people at guard. Steve can play combinations that fit just about any type of style that needs to be played."

Desper's job on the bench is to watch how the game is progressing and make suggestions.

When the game is over, he turns to his own kids. "I really enjoy time with my family probably more than anything else," he says. "I love working with my kids with their homework and playing little games with them, to see them develop.

"You know, if you're going to be a teacher, you have to be a pretty good psychologist. And it's fun to see kids grow up and see their personalities change."

All of which perfectly complements Steve McClure's philosophy.

Chapter 3: Opening Tough

Two hours before the season opener on December 1, the black of an autumn night is punctuated by whirling lights of emergency vehicles helping to direct traffic descending from the countryside onto the Northfield campus.

In past years, it's been easy to park near the gyms as the junior varsity game tips off at 6:30. But now, at 6:45, an attendant directs cars past the filled Northfield parking lot to Sharp Creek Elementary School, which sits adjacent to the high school.

Aside from the hoopla swirling around the Ross twins, other factors account for the early arrivals who want to be assured a seat in a facility that holds 2,200 on a first-come, first-served basis. The game is not only the delayed season opener, it's the Three Rivers Conference tip-off, pitting the Norse against an outstanding Whitko team, which is already 3-0. Secondly, more adult season tickets have been sold at Northfield this year than in any of the last 10. And, finally, Northfield is the only Wabash County school playing at home this Friday night.

It's possible that the originally scheduled season and conference opener, set for November 22 against country cousin Southwood, would have attracted a capacity crowd, too. But one thing's for sure, tonight's throng in the refurbished Norse gym is the largest since last season's Wabash County Tournament championship game against Manchester, which also plays in the Three Rivers Conference.

Steve McClure doesn't say so -- he's not the kind -- but deep down, he probably wishes he were opening against a decent Southwood Knights squad tonight instead of an outstanding Whitko team.

The Southwood football team forced an unexpected change. Improving sharply late in the season, the Knights came within one game of playing for the 1A championship before falling to eventual champ, Bremen. Some of the basketball players were key football performers, so the Knights were in no condition for the scheduled pre-turkey day clash. These situations are not unusual at small schools in Indiana, and McClure understands and accepts the fact.

Still, as the standing-room-only crowd overflows the gym, spilling into a school hallway, McClure's intensity level and tightness can be felt as he returns from the locker room for the second half of the junior varsity game.

The looseness McClure displayed in practice is missing, replaced by a "game face" that even his first pair of glasses, just 11 days old, can't hide. But his demeanor this evening is no surprise, because while he has tried to act normal going into a season that doesn't figure to be normal, the pressure to win -- especially at the high school level in Indiana -- can't be brushed aside. And now come Whitko's Wildcats, with four starters and seven lettermen returning from a team that went 20-4 last year before losing the Fort Wayne Regional championship game in overtime.

Before strolling back to the court, McClure spent a few minutes alone in the locker room, writing with speed and fury on the blackboard. When the 12 varsity players arrive, they will see in the middle of the board:

Winners
Expect
To
Win!

On each side of those words McClure has printed:
<u>OFFENSE</u>
-- Early: Push it at them.
-- #3 vs. man: X cut.
-- #2 vs. zone (#4 also).
-- #1 vs. man or zone.
-- #5 vs. man.
<u>DEFENSE</u> The key!
-- #5 communicate and be active.
-- #2 find the shooters and nothing inside.
-- #1 aggressive. Guards pressure the ball.

As the junior varsity battles Whitko in a tight game, the varsity players leave with 4:37 left in the third quarter for the locker room. They get a monstrous cheer as they move out of the bleachers from behind the players' bench, which is actually the first row of seats.

By now, people have been scrambling over each other to find a seat in the packed gym, which lost about 150 seats during a summer renovation project.

The jockeying for seats, the deafening crowd, the honking scoreboard, the blaring Northfield band, the growing heat, the tantalizing aroma of popcorn, the leaping cheerleaders, the limping old folks, the prancing toddlers, and the hanging banners send a simple message: Welcome to Indiana high school basketball.

There's hootin' and hollerin' as the varsity players enter the small locker room, and a few pound a mass of metal that backs a set of six empty, three-foot lockers. On the metal backing, words painted in white against a royal blue background remind everyone every day:

19 Huntington 87
Sectional Champs

Marion Regional
Champs 198?

Fort Wayne Semi-State
Champs 198?

Indiana State
Champions 198?

"Take your time getting dressed," Brad Hampton says, nonchalantly scratching his short red hair. "We've got plenty of time." But within minutes, the 12 are ready and starting to bounce balls on the concrete floor, except for the Ross twins, who stretch their arms up to the ceiling, trying to loosen up.

Minutes later, McClure walks in, looking almost professorial in his light-colored glasses. He's wearing charcoal slacks and the team's royal blue, V-neck sweater from last year. Under the sweater is a white shirt and red tie. Dark socks and black loafers complete his attire.

He gathers his troops into a tight circle for prayer. "Father, it seems like a while; on the other hand, it seems like yesterday. We just thank you for blessing us with the talent and with each other. Just help us, Father, on each step we take. We're witnesses for a lot of people, and hopefully we can project your image throughout life and in our attitude."

Before moving to the blackboard, McClure tells his troops, "Be patient. You know, sometimes in the first game of the year, you're goin' to want to do a whole season in three minutes. It's a long game, 32 minutes. Just make sure on each possession, you come out and give it the best you can do. If someone loses the ball into the bleachers, don't worry about it. Just come back on to defense."

The coach turns to the blackboard and begins to elaborate on what he's written earlier. He wants X cuts and back screens. He wants people to look for Jon Ross, and "if it's not there, screen and we'll get you something." He wants them to look for the weak-side lob, because he expects Whitko to overplay a lot.

On defense, he says, "I expect you to play great. We have to play great on this end before we can play great anywhere else. They'll come out, they'll hit a few, they'll miss a few. Just make sure it's our defense they're beatin'."

McClure turns to Whitko's top players, starting with Steve Nicodemus, a lean, 6-3 junior with a soft, left-handed jumper. "He likes to play on the right wing and drive in to the left side," McClure notes. Then he turns to Chad Patrick, the coach's son, a 6-0 senior who is deadly from three-point range. "He likes to go to his right. Make him go left. Just make 'em do some things tonight they haven't done. 'kay?"

Then he concludes: "You're winners and you should expect to win tonight. Now it's time to go up the ladder. Go out and mentally tune in. Defense is the key to the game."

And they leave for the court with a whoop, seemingly loose and up, but taking along a batch of nervousness that's impossible to avoid or disguise.

As the Northfield band goes from "Rockin' Robin' " to "Satin Doll" while the teams warm up, McClure chats with his counterpart, Bill Patrick, natty in a dark suit. Each man wants to win, of course, and yet, like almost all of their brethren, they will defend each other, knowing they're part of a special breed whose futures rest to a significant degree in the hands of teenagers.

Shortly before co-captains Hampton and Jon Ross go to center court to meet the officials and Whitko's captains, the court announcer tells the crowd: "There will be an Adult Booster Club bus taking fans to Athens, Ohio, for the game Saturday, December 16. Watch the *Plain Dealer* for details." He has referred to Northfield's accepting an invitation to play in the McDonald's-Days Inn Classic, a one-day event in which 14 teams will play seven games on the Ohio University campus.

But now it's game time in Speicherville, Indiana, population 40.

McClure chooses Troy Miller and Peck Chay for his guards to go along with the twins and Hampton up front.

Joe Ross gets the first tip of the season, and seconds later, brother Jon gets loose inside for the first hoop, bringing the first ear-shattering roar. Whitko fails on its first offensive possession, and Peck comes down with the ball, drives the middle, pulls up, hits a short jumper. Seconds later, Hampton converts a follow underneath and Miller a free throw. It's seven-zip, Northfield. A rout in the opener over an outstanding team?

No way. Chad Patrick eases his father's concern by hitting a trey, and the Wildcats begin clawing their way back into the game. As they do, McClure's concern grows. Joe Ross has picked up two quick fouls, and the Norse are forgetting the coach's words: "Defense is the key."

As the first quarter fades, McClure moves Joe Ross outside on defense, trying to protect him, and thus losing rebound strength. And so, after the first eight minutes of the season, the quick Norse lead has dissolved into a 17-17 deadlock.

Two minutes and 14 seconds into the second quarter, Joe Ross picks up his third foul, forcing McClure to move Miller to forward and rotate Nathan Winegardner and Noi Chay with Peck Chay at guard.

We're going to get measured early, McClure figures.

And then something rare occurs. McClure is called for a technical, which did not happen at all last season and only once in each of his other two years. It is a bad call, coming on top of another bad one. The first call, whistled right in front of McClure, was made on Noi after he cleanly stole the ball, only to lose it right back and then be charged with reaching in. The official missed an obvious elbow to Noi's midsection, and McClure was hardly off the bench to complain before the other official called the "T."

It's Whitko playing with confidence now, forging into an eight-point lead with less than two minutes remaining before intermission. The Norse cut it to two, but Whitko answers with a field goal and a free throw for a 36-31 halftime advantage.

In the locker room, McClure is contained, but clearly not happy. He's bothered by his team giving up the baseline, and yet, he notes, Whitko is getting easy shots outside by getting Northfield to pack its defense. "I can remember at least three times they've driven the base line, then kicked it out for three pointers," he scolds.

"What're we doin' givin' 'em the baseline in the first place? Is that a defensive philosophy we just put in tonight? You got to concentrate. You're foulin' people 50 feet from the basket. You're jumpin', you're outta position. You know better than that!"

He calms. "We came out and moved the ball the first five possessions and scored every time   And then we started throwin' it up. We quit movin'. We just stood still. How many -- what're the two things we want you to do?"

Brad Hampton speaks up: "High post and X cuts."

And McClure answers his own question, too: "High post, low post, and X cuts. Let's question how many times we did that."

An uneasy mumbling follows, and then McClure shouts at the top of his voice, "Why!!?"

Dead silence.

"No thinkin' out there," he begins anew. "You're not even playin' hard. This time of the year you should be playin' hard. It's kind of hard to ask you to play smart, but you're not even playin' hard. You're more concerned that he's tearin' me up, he's all over me. Well, you're not movin'. X cut, guys, X cut. We have done a shoddy job of runnin' our offense and have 31 points. What're you gonna do when you start workin' in five-man units? You'll tear 'em up."

Things do not go well in the opening minutes of the third quarter. Joe Ross picks up his fourth foul after only a minute and 13 seconds. Whitko's five-point halftime margin grows to eight at 43-35.

Then Miller and Jon Ross go to work, one outside, one inside, and suddenly the Norse surge into a 44-43 lead on a run of nine straight points. Patrick's three-pointer stops the binge, but with 59 seconds left in the quarter, he's called for his fourth foul and has to come out. So does another starter, Todd Darley, 16 seconds later.

McClure's squad holds a 49-47 margin to open the fourth quarter -- with Joe Ross still on the bench. The two teams trade baskets when they're not being sloppy with the ball. Jon Ross is working hard inside, and it's paying off against the smaller Wildcats, who are tiring and fouling. He converts six free throws to keep Northfield in the game.

With 5 minutes and 50 seconds left, Joe returns. McClure's thinking, This is it.

Northfield clings to a slight lead as the clock winds down. At 1:01 and the Norse on top, 65-61, Whitko calls timeout. The Wildcats have set up a play, but it goes awry, and with 47 seconds left, the

Norse are in control. Whitko fouls the wrong guy -- Miller. But he misses the front-end. However, Joe nabs the rebound, is fouled and converts his first free throw. Whitko hits a final three-pointer, but it's not enough -- Northfield 69, Whitko 64.

In the locker room, the players almost collapse on the benches before McClure walks in, removes his glasses, towels his brow and starts talking about character.

"You proved the system works," he tells them, referring to his program -- belief in God, unity, an upstanding life in times of good and bad. "You build character in kids," he continues, referring not necessarily to himself, "because a lot of teams would have wilted in these circumstances, playin' a team as good as they are. And they played a great game, guys."

He swabs his brow again before starting anew: "You had presence of mind to hang tough when you had to. We know where we're goin' now. Now we just improve and improve and improve ... every game."

He shifts to fundamentals, starting with surrendering the baseline, and as he does, Jon Ross scolds, "Listen up!"

"I know it will be taken care of," McClure says about the baseline problem, taking a positive approach. "Concentration, isn't it? Concentration."

Then he quickly shifts again: "But the thing is, guys, your character, your talent will take you a long ways. But I'll tell you, that was tough. We love tough games like that. I hope you loved this tonight."

Jon Ross and Troy Miller had to love the night, finishing with 27 and 20 points respectively, Ross getting key buckets inside and dropping in his free throws, Miller hitting clutch three-pointers in the third quarter.

After sending his team to the showers, McClure comments on the way to a radio interview: "We stayed focused. We opened some doors for Whitko, but we hung together and got it down. Our guard play was adequate, but yet, I'm concerned. But they showed they have character."

Sitting next to game announcer Bill Rogge of Wabash FM station WKUZ, McClure tells listeners that "getting the big lead was the worst thing that could happen to us. It got us to relax."

Rogge, a former teacher and coach who is an institution in Wabash, says Northfield won the game with just one man, referring to

Joe Ross' foul trouble. McClure neither agrees nor disagrees, instead praises his team's character.

After the interview, it's mentioned that Rogge apparently forgot Hampton is 6-5 and played inspired basketball. McClure just smiles.

The game has been over for almost 45 minutes, but people still mingle around. The gym lights flash off and on, signaling them to leave. They have stayed, one senses, to savor the win as long as they can -- and perhaps to avoid as long as possible the stinging cold winds coming off the surrounding fields.

Seventeen hours later, still glowing from the successful struggle with Whitko, the Norsemen board a school bus for a 45-minute trip to Caston High School, a non-conference foe that has split its first four games.

As the players get settled, well-known sportscaster Don Fisher is heard above the clamoring, giving play-by-play of the Indiana-Kentucky college contest that's being waged before more than 40,000 fans in the Hoosier Dome.

But the talk is not about Bob Knight's Hoosiers, the stirring Whitko win or Caston's Comets. The talk is about shoes -- Troy Miller's and Peck Chay's. Each player has had a pair stolen, and a high school wrestling team is suspected.

During the day, Northfield hosted the five-school, county wrestling tournament. When the basketball players arrived shortly after four o'clock, as the meet ended, to shoot around in street clothes, Miller found his practice shoes missing from his locker. The situation was even worse for Chay. His *only* shoes were gone.

What is particularly galling for Miller is he had just bought the like-new low-cuts from Nathan Winegardner and worn them one time. He hadn't even paid for them, but they were in his locker.

The shoe talk fades as the bus winds through mostly country roads that provide classic views of rural life: narrow blacktops, harvested fields, patches of woods, munching cattle, ramrod silos, red barns, tractors and their kin.

In stark contrast to Friday night, only a scattering of fans is on hand for the junior varsity contest at Caston, situated a mile from Fulton, population 400. The school is a consolidation that brought to an end the basketball lives of high schools in Fulton, Metea, 12 Mile and Grass Creek.

McClure has worked over the blackboard in the visitors' locker room by the time the varsity arrives to get dressed. His message in the middle reads:

Will We Move
Upward
Tonight?

His instructions are basic. On offense, "take what they give you," and "make them play some 'D'," and "guards start offense and then be attackers." On defense, he's more specific. If he calls 21, he wants the sidelines contested. If he calls 32, he wants Joe and Jon up. And he wants to deny the baseline.

Peck Chay loosens up in the locker room in his brown street shoes. He'll wear junior varsity player Scott Bumgardner's game shoes. Those shoes might have extra heat in them in the wake of Desper's stinging remarks after his team has dropped a one-point game.

McClure, alone with his team, picks up on Desper's comments. "The JayVee needs to see a winning performance from you guys, because they came over with their heads you know where."

He asks that they commit fewer than 10 turnovers, pointing out that they had 14 Friday night against Whitko. "It's goin' to be tough out there," he says. "They're goin to be like little gnats. They'll press."

Gnats, indeed. Caston's tallest player is 6-3.

"I imagine they're goin' to be all over our guys," he continues, referring to the twins and Hampton. "Let's be above that crap and not lose our control."

Before turning them loose, he reminds: "Stop the baseline. They (Whitko) got 11 points last night off the baseline. Make sure we improve."

The team is greeted by a crowd that has swelled to about 800 in a gymnasium slightly smaller than Northfield's. McClure follows his team, sans glasses, which need minor repair. He's wearing a gray sweater over dark gray slacks.

He opens with the same starting five against Whitko. And it takes just 16 seconds for Hampton to open the scoring with two free throws after getting hammered underneath. Jon Ross rejects a shot moments later, bringing some oohs and aahs. But as the first quarter winds down, the Norsemen appear out of synch.

McClure's team is dominating play inside, as expected, and Caston is showing the press, as expected. What's not expected is the score at the first stop: Northfield 14, Caston 13, thanks to Peck Chay's 12-footer at the buzzer.

Caston continues to play with inspiration, Northfield off kilter. And so at the half it's only 31-25, Northfield -- much closer than anticipated. The margin would have been greater had the Norse shot better from the line. They got the chances, what with the smaller Comets hanging all over the twins and Hampton.

In the locker room, just off the gym, McClure has to shout to be heard over a spirited Caston band, situated in a corner of the bleachers. "When they go into a zone, you stand around," he says with a bit of exasperation. "You just stand there and pay for it. You gotta move. You're probably tired from them hanging on your jersey. Well, you just stand there and let them do it. I would too if I could get away with it. But if you move, you'll be fine."

On defense, he tells them they "just have to be comin' and comin and comin'. Just keep contestin' the shots. They're hittin' well. We've had some pretty good pressure on the shots they've hit. Mentally, though, guys, you just gotta do it."

McClure wants to employ all of his defenses tonight as part of his teaching for the long haul. He wants to achieve an adequate level of execution in one formation before moving to another. But if his team is not mentally attuned, he can't keep changing. "We have to stay with a defense long enough that you learn to play it, and then we try somethin' else."

Switching his tack as he does often, McClure turns psychologist again: "You thought, man, they're a bunch of fish, a bunch of runts. We beat 'em 20 last year and played like crap, so let's play like crap this year and beat 'em 10.

"Well, he (Caston coach Kent Adams) is in there saying, 'We're only five, six points down, you keep doin' this, you keep at 'em, you get 'em irritated and do all that stuff. ... '

"And your fate will be just like the JayVees. Right now, you're not a whole lot ahead of schedule, the way the JayVees was tonight. You're just kinda goin' through the motions. You gotta learn to play with your heart, guys, sooner or later. You might as well learn to do it early in the season, so learn to do it now."

Caston's Monte Babb, a scrappy, bespectacled six-footer short on bulk, doesn't look like a player, but he is. He opens the second half with a trey and is fouled, but he misses the free throw, so it's 31-28.

McClure has started the second half with Noi Chay and Nathan Winegardner at guard. That combination finished the first half, having played well together through much of the second quarter. But Winegardner soon draws his fourth personal, so the backcourt becomes Chay and Chay. And Allen Strait, a lean, 6-2 senior, is given his first playing time of the season, replacing Hampton. It's still a tight game, with Northfield ahead by only two points at one point, but McClure has chosen to experiment in this non-conference contest -- something he would not do in a Three River Conference game.

The third quarter ends at 44-40, and Caston coach Adams has to be feeling good. But a bad omen occurs just a minute and 14 seconds into the final quarter. Babb draws his fourth foul and has to sit. A minute later, two free throws by Joe Ross give Northfield its biggest lead, 52-42, and one thing is obvious: The Norse's height has begun to wear on Caston, now being whistled for foul after foul.

The lead goes to 13 on a short Hampton jumper. Any thoughts of a rout are doused, however, as the home team battles back to 57-50. But Caston's hopes for an upset fade at 3:11 with the score still 57-50 when Babb fouls out after scoring 15 points and playing pesky, tireless defense. Still, Caston cuts it to two, 60-58, at 2:45. But Chad Pugh, another starter who hit for 15, fouls out, and so will Matt Bingle and Bryan Albright. And Todd Boldry and Steve King will finish with four.

Noi Chay has played an outstanding game, which prompts one to wonder where Troy Miller was all night. After a spectacular game against Whitko, he has missed his first four shots and been ineffective in the little time he has been on the floor. Were his missing shoes on his mind? To some degree, yes. After all, losing a pair of $94 basketball shoes is no small matter for a high schooler.

The final is 67-59 -- Miller hustling for a rebound, getting fouled and converting the free throws to wrap it up.

Jon Ross has played another outstanding game, getting 20 points. Brother Joe has improved on his Friday night performance, although fouling out again, this time with less than two minutes remaining. And the twins have been a force on the boards, combining for 25 rebounds. Hampton has pitched in with 10 more. And Noi Chay has given McClure some joy, coming off the bench for 16 points and playing a steady all-around game. But there's no joy over two other stats -- 19 turnovers and a pathetic 26 of 45 shooting at the free throw line.

In the locker room, McClure goes to the board and writes:

Whitko	Caston
US	US

McClure asks, out of a possible five points, with five being the highest, how would they rate themselves? They give themselves a two against Whitko, and McClure chalks in the number to the right of "US." They give themselves a 0 against Caston, and McClure chalks that in, too.

"Out of a possible ten," he says, "we got only 20 percent. Why did we not get five's?" Silence.

"You can't be happy with 20 percent," he continues after a pause. "I'm not happy with 20 percent. You know, it's always good to win, but I appreciate the way you feel right now." He knows they are disappointed in the way they played.

He's not through softening the situation. "Right now we're a good ballclub," he continues. "They played a great game. They hit some runners, they threw 'em in. And you have to accept, guys, they are goin' to come at us like a bunch of packs of wolves. Every opportunity you have to play someone else, they are goin' to give you everything. Be thankful for it."

Then he asks the question of the night: "How many of you wanted to beat 'em 40 tonight?"

Almost every hand goes up.

"See, right there is the problem," he responds. "You want to beat 'em 40. Is that a good goal to set, beat 'em 40, when we can get all our bench people in? I like that, playin' everybody. But we're not out to beat anybody 40. We're not out to please anyone but ourselves. And I don't think we're real pleased with ourselves."

Outside the locker room, McClure greets his wife, who has driven over with the children, and then answers questions.

"Caston played very inspired basketball tonight," he comments. "They were up for us and went all out for 32 minutes. But their intensity was negative a lot. It wasn't necessary for them to foul the way they did."

What do you like after this weekend, after two games? he's asked.

"Just playin' games. It's probably a typical first week. You know, we're a team that expects a lot of ourselves as individuals and collectively, and it takes time to put things together. A lot of little things have to fall in place to go from bein' good to bein' great. And right now we're just a good basketball team."

He likes close ball games, he says -- sounding like he means it -- because they test a team's character and ability to concentrate when the game's on the line.

Was there anything in particular that disturbed him?

"Yeah," he begins quickly. "It's very frustrating as a coach to sit there and watch your team play a mentally dead ballgame. Because if your mind's dead out there, your body's dead. And I think that was pretty much the case tonight. It was a non-conference game, we looked too much at the opponent. The kids look at the roster and see they're short, they look at their record and see they're 500 or so. You know, kids aren't dumb. They see all that. They read the paper. We were focused on the wrong things tonight."

Is there any one player he likes after two games?

"Oh, it's hard to single them out, because I love all the kids. But I just have to take my hat off to Brad Hampton right now. He's comin' off an injury, he's layin' his body on the floor, he's standin' in the path of someone dribblin' wide open for 84 feet and takin' a charge, even though he didn't get the call."

Is there anybody he's unhappy with?

He responds without mentioning names, instead talks about the team playing better mentally.

Did the free throw shooting bother him tonight?

"Very much. There again, we hit 'em when the game's on the line, we miss 'em when it's not. Again, that indicates it's a mentally dead night."

McClure spots David McKee, superintendent of the Caston School Corporation. He is an old friend of Lisa McClure's, having formerly been assistant superintendent for the Metropolitan School District of Wabash County schools.

While the McClures and McKees visit, the players start reappearing from the locker room, hair wet, clothes tossed on.

Jon Ross plops down on the front row of bleachers.

Was it rough out there tonight? he's asked.

"A little. They (the smaller players) get away with a lot with the officials. They just feel sorry for them. I'm not saying the officials

38

aren't fair. But for the big man, it's so hard to do anything, because they're watching you and they're not even watching the little guy. So it's really rough, it really is."

He prefers playing against big people, he adds. "The officiating is more even. It's a better game."

Jon spots his brother waving to him near the basket. A Caston girl -- perhaps 5-3 -- wants her mother to take a picture of her between the "Towers." They oblige good naturedly.

Does that happen often?, Jon's asked as the team starts out of the building for the bus. "No," he smiles, giving the feeling he's happy it doesn't.

Hampton's parents are on the bus; their van has developed mechanical problems. Coincidentally, they have brought along brown-bag "dinners" consisting of a ham sandwich, snack cake and an orange. Cokes and Mountain Dew, too. It's a tradition at Northfield -- parents of team members volunteer to provide food after each road game.

The temperature has dropped even more, and the wind has gained strength, causing the bus windows to ice up, blocking out the night. But the heat is on, the food is there, the win is still a win, and the Norsemen are 2-0, with 18 to go before the Sectional opens the last week in February.

On Monday, though, McClure will bring them back to reality. He'll remind them of a few things -- X-cuts, moving without the ball, denying the baseline, mental awareness on defense.

And he just might remind them that Friday night's conference game at Oak Hill will be one of their toughest all year.

Chapter 4: Twin Towers

The difference in success and failure for Northfield basketball this season could be less than a half-mile.

The home of Bob and Andris Ross sits at the end of a steep, stony driveway off U.S. Route 24, just before the last Wabash County road. If the driveway were another half-mile east, their twin sons would be attending Huntington North, the successor to Vice President Dan Quayle's alma mater.

Northfield and Huntington North have one distinct difference: size. Huntington North, which essentially also is Bob Ross' alma mater, is five times larger than Northfield. Almost 2,000 students attend classes on one fairly modern campus. After Indiana's legislature approved school consolidation, Huntington County chose to bring all students into one corporation. In Wabash County, political interests favoring smaller schools pushed through three districts.

When Joe and Jon Ross topped six feet in the ninth grade, rumors circulated that Huntington interests had approached Bob and Andris about moving into their school corporation.

The rumors were false.

"We've never been approached by anybody to actually move into Huntington County or anyplace else," Bob says. It is the Friday after Thanksgiving, and he's seated next to Andris on a white loveseat in the family office at home. "We'd run into acquaintances that would say, 'I understand you're moving into Huntington County so the boys can go there and play.' And I would say, 'Well, I haven't told anybody.' "

There also were rumors about moving to Marion, long a Hoosier high school power, Andris points out.

Huntington and Marion -- and any other place -- never had a chance, primarily because of a cherished piece of ground the Rosses bought from Andris' parents, Fred and Lila Beghtel.

The plot was carved out of the old Beghtel farmstead, and some 20 years ago, Bob himself built a home on an acre and a half. He and Andris lived in it for two years and then sold it after Bob built another house nearby. Two years later, they repeated the process, putting them in their home of the last 15 years.

"We were never about to pick up and move off here," Andris says. "I mean, my dad farmed out here. The boys grew with Grandpa farming. Grandpa helped make the pond, you know, planted the trees."

But while the Beghtel farmstead is the prime reason for Joe and Jon playing for Northfield, it's not the only one. The quality of education ranks right up there.

"Everybody was saying, 'Well, if you came here to Huntington or Marion, look at the competition you'd be playing against,' " Bob recalls. "And that's all true. But we wouldn't consider it. We liked the (Wabash County) school systems. We liked the smallness of the schools. We always looked at education first and still do."

Quality, smallness and the Catholic environment attracted the Rosses to St. Bernard School in the City of Wabash, where the twins and their older brother attended through the sixth grade.

The importance of education is a staple in the Rosses' backgrounds.

Born just a few miles from where they now live, Bob grew up in Huntington County and, like his sons, attended a Catholic grade school, St. Peter and Paul School.

He transferred to Huntington High School for his freshman year, by now 6-1 and strongly interested in sports. He ran track and played football and basketball until his senior year when he decided not to play football and wound up getting cut in basketball.

"I always remember back," he says a bit wistfully. "I didn't play football and we went out early for (basketball) practice before the football players came out. And the first time around I was cut."

He convinced Coach Bob Straight to give him a second chance when the football players tried out. Despite standing 6-3, about the same height as most of the men in his family, Bob Ross was cut again.

"I felt down," Bob says of that time in his life. "It was hard on me; I truly wanted to play. I was crushed for a while. It took a little time getting over."

After high school, Bob enrolled at Ball State University at Muncie. He majored in math, minored in business and got a teaching license -- and, as a freshman met another freshman, Andris Beghtel. They learned that they lived less than 15 miles apart and that he was one day older.

After teaching algebra to seventh-, eighth- and ninth-graders for two years, Ross saw his future in business and joined Lincoln National Life Insurance Company in Fort Wayne for almost 19 years.

Like Steve McClure, Ross enjoys working with his hands. In his spare time, he not only built his own homes, but helped construct others, including the Huntington residence now occupied by Vice President Quayle's parents.

So when Bob Ross left Lincoln National and established a building-related company in January 1989, the pronounced career change was no surprise to friends and family. He opened Concepts, Inc., in Fort Wayne, specializing in shelving for both homes and businesses.

Unlike Bob, Andris has worked in one field -- health -- for most of her married life. After graduating from Andrews High School, just inside the Huntington County line, she earned a diploma from Ball State as a registered nurse.

She began her career at Wabash County Hospital and nursing homes before taking a job in 1973 with Vernon Manor Children's Home in the City of Wabash. She's now a regional director and Director of Nursing Home Operations for Vernon Manor's parent company, Forum Group, Incorporated, of Indianapolis.

As a management person, Andi, as she's known to family and friends, no longer practices hands-on nursing. But she is never far from it, maintaining an office at Vernon Manor, where the bittersweet of life is always with her.

In stark contrast to the Ross twins and their older, 6-3 brother Rob, the youngsters at Vernon Manor are severely ill, many dying before they reach puberty.

The extremes she sees between the physical assets of her children and those at Vernon Manor is "very frightening" to her. "Sometimes I feel like I have had such good fortune that something's going to happen," she says, a hint of tightness in her throat. "I hate to say it, but that does go through my mind.

"I feel incredibly lucky, and sometimes I say, 'How could this happen to me that I could be so fortunate and be around others who are not that fortunate?' I feel like it's a gift of God to have had children who are healthy and talented, who also have been such a joy. And I'm delighted to be able to do something for people who are less fortunate."

The twins and brother Rob have grown up with Vernon Manor. They have worked there part-time, mowing yards and doing various other chores.

"But they always take time to talk to the kids, to say hello to them," Andris says without mawkishness. "There's one young man especially that normally sits near the front of the building. And he knows when the boys are coming. And, you know, if they don't take time to go in and say hello... That doesn't sound like much, but for a teenager to bother to go in and talk to these children that really can't talk back, it takes a little extra. And they do that."

The one aspect about the Northfield basketball team that comes through immediately is that Joe and Jon are not only highly respected, but extremely well liked. They have been covered with glory, being named high school All Americans and getting splashed in magazines and newspapers, but are clearly just two of the boys. Their modesty is genuine.

"There have been many, many days when they have given me a lift," Andris says, putting her right hand to her light-colored hair. "Number one, they are very caring. I think they know from me when I've had a bad day. They'll come up and put their arms around me and say, 'How's it goin', Mom?' That's delightful, that's wonderful. To be able to share their successes when I've had a bad day, yes, that's an upper, that's a stress reliever. That's been an incredibly pleasant thing that I have."

Bob and Andris say that the twins relate to each other with the same sensitivity. It's obvious to teammates and others alike.

"First of all," Bob says, "they get along very well. They're the best of friends to each other. If one hurts, the other hurts, no doubt about it. The stories you hear about twins -- if one gets hurt the other feels it -- I think it's really true."

Like feeling pain after defeat, basketball aside. Each has sought office in student government and lost.

"They're very, very competitive," Bob continues. "But I think the competition is very positive, because they drive each other from both an academic perspective as well as athletics. Even to the degree that if one is studying, the other feels he ought to be studying."

Bob smiles his boyish smile. "If one finds out one is in here reading or something, he'll come in and say, 'What are you reading?' or 'What are you doing?' And pretty soon he grabs the books, he's studying also. And the same is true on the court. They really push each other hard."

Although the twins share much, including their mother's light hair, there are slight differences in their physical and emotional makeups.

Joe's profile has a harder edge, and, of course, there is that extra inch. The inch translates into a slight weight difference, Joe at

215 pounds, Jon five pounds lighter. Bob believes the inch difference results from Joe's breaking the femur in his right leg when he was about five years old. In the healing process, that leg became longer, which forced him to wear a lift shoe for a long time so he wouldn't walk crooked.

Their games are slightly different, too, because of the inch and early injury, Bob feels. "Joe definitely does have more of an inside game and Jon's more of an outside player and jumps a little bit higher."

Another slight difference is in their emotional makeup, Bob and Andris believe. They think that while the twins share a strong sensitivity toward people, Joe reads people better, is more tuned in to their inner feelings. "Maybe he gets some of that from his mother, with the type of work she's in," Bob says. "It's not that Jon's insensitive, it's just that Joe seems to have that extra feeling about people."

That might explain another difference. Although both enjoy the outdoors, Joe loves to be inside cooking. While Jon glories in experiencing nature and wildlife, Joe digs toiling over pots and pans.

"The boys allow Joe to cook for them," Andris says, grin wide, "because they don't like to cook that well. He does neat things. I mean, he can just read a recipe and make it look good. He can get everything done at the same time, which is pretty cool for a young man. And when he talks about what he would like to do, he thinks it would be pretty neat to have a restaurant or something like that."

The twins, in fact, will probably pursue business-related majors, but nothing's concrete -- except Notre Dame, a school whose outstanding academic credentials are overshadowed by its football dominance. And in playing for Richard "Digger" Phelps -- who, like Steve McClure, grew up in a funeral home -- they will be coached by an outspoken critic of programs that cheat and/or do little for athletes' educations.

Notre Dame, of course, was merely one of hundreds of schools that contacted the twins, starting when they were 6-5 ninth-graders.

"Iowa was the very first one, via mail," Bob recalls, "but nothing ever materialized."

Indiana's Bob Knight called, and the twins liked him very much, Bob says. In their junior year, they accepted Knight's invitation to attend a game and visit the locker room for pregame discussions. "So they had a chance to see Coach Knight in person and in action and so forth," Bob points out.

After the visit, Knight made it clear to Bob Ross that he was very interested in Joe and Jon.

Later, Knight called and asked the twins if there is any other school they wanted to attend. They said "No."

But then Notre Dame got involved. Knight called again to say that he felt IU was the best place for them and to ask why they would consider anyplace else.

"But he never actually said we've got a scholarship for you," Bob notes. "It was not too long after that that he called and Joe told him that they had put IU on the back burner and weren't looking at IU with a tremendous amount of interest."

Knight was "very straight-forward," Bob says. "I like him very much."

Along with Notre Dame, Purdue and Vanderbilt had become very interested in Joe and Jon.

"We really liked the academic program" at Vanderbilt, Andris says, recalling the visit there. "That's the number one thing that impressed us. I went away from there with the feeling that I could give my sons to those people for four years and they would make them the very best they could as a person, as an athlete."

But geography worked against Vanderbilt, situated near downtown Nashville, Tennessee. "It seemed like it was far away from home," Andris recalls. "Bob and I wouldn't be able to watch them play as much."

Geography helped Purdue, along with Coach Gene Keady, who saw the twins play more than once and who impressed Bob as an individual. Illinois coach Lou Henson impressed Bob, too. He visited the Rosses and followed up with a telephone conversation.

In the final analysis, though, school size played a key role -- as it had with the Rosses staying in a small Wabash County high school rather than attending Huntington or Marion. The size aspect put Northwestern, similar in enrollment to Notre Dame -- 10,000 to 12,000 -- in contention for a while.

"You wouldn't believe the stacks of mail," Andris says, referring to the recruiting letters.

"Every day," Bob picks up, "we'd come home and the mailbox would be stacked two to three inches (with) maybe a couple items for us as a family and the rest for basketball. The boys got to the point they wouldn't read anything."

What had been "neat" initially to them had become a bore. So Bob and Andris opened the letters and decided which were important.

Like other highly recruited youngsters, the twins wanted to sign early and finally cut off the phone calls and stacks of mail.

Bob and Andris tried to let the twins make up their own minds. But Bob admits that the boys sensed "we'd like for them to go to Notre Dame." Still, the Rosses spent much time traveling to various universities so they could get a feel for communities, campuses, coaches and professors.

The Notre Dame environment finally won out -- the campus, the people, the Catholicism, although Andris does not believe the religious aspect played a particularly major role. "It was like the frosting on the cake," she says. "That's a bonus."

Bob adds: "The thing about Notre Dame that we felt good about was that everybody made you feel at home there -- not just the staff, but anybody you ran into on campus. People would be able to pick Joe and Jon out of a crowd and just come up and start talking."

Choosing Notre Dame, which is less than two hours from the Ross home, will allow Bob and Andris to continue seeing their sons play.

Although Andris' job takes her on the road about three days a week, she and Bob have not missed any games since the fourth grade at St. Bernard's. They even attended all of the out-of-state games the twins played for an AAU team the summer before starting their senior year.

The AAU squad, led by Damon Bailey and Eric Montross, won the state AAU championship in June.

After that competition, Joe and Jon attended a one-week Big Man's Camp in Kalamazoo, Michigan, for the fourth year. They followed that up with play in a one-day, three-on-three tournament in Michigan City, Indiana. Teaming with Whitko's Chad Patrick, they won their age group, made the all-tournament team and walked off with the sportsmanship trophy.

The summer ended with the twins rejoining the AAU team for two more tourneys, one in Memphis, Tennessee, the other in Jonesboro, Arkansas. The squad finished sixth in both competitions.

And between times, the Rosses were down at Northfield for open gym, playing pick-up games against a wide variety of competition.

Says Andris: "They don't live to play pool. They don't live to play Nintendo. But, basketball -- they need a 'basketball fix' if they haven't played basketball for a long time."

Otherwise, they are typical teenagers for the most part.

Neither owns a car. They drive to school and other places in a 1983 Oldsmobile that belongs to their parents. "Somehow they worked out who gets to drive when," Bob says. "You seldom ever hear any arguments as to whose turn it is to drive."

Like most teenagers, they have healthy appetites -- very healthy. "Yes, they eat about anything," Andris says with a smile. "They'll come home from practice and eat, and then later, when Bob and I have dinner, they'll eat another full meal again."

And, like most teenagers, they don't have a great interest in non-school reading. But music, yes. Joe especially enjoys the '60s, the sounds his parents grew up on, while Jon's tastes are diversified. And girlfriends, yes.

So Jon and Joe Ross are just a couple of high school seniors -- except one is 6-10 and the other is 6-9 and they are two of the best high school basketball players in Indiana, if not the nation, for the 1989-90 season.

••••••••••

When Bob and Andris Ross are asked if their twin sons have any heroes, they pause for a moment and finally suggest one: big brother Rob.

At 6-3, he, too, is big -- even next to two guys pushing 7-0. But it's his mind and maturity, not his size, that draws the twins' adulation.

Rob will be a senior at DePauw, a small institution with a big reputation for academic quality, when the twins enter Notre Dame as freshmen.

People who have regular contact with Joe and Jon notice one thing in a relatively short time: Sibling rivalry is missing. And neither does that rivalry exist between them and Rob. On the contrary, Rob is one of the twins' biggest supporters and most trusted advisers.

Not that sibling rivalry didn't exist when they were younger. "I used to beat them up," Rob says with a smile. "I had a temper then. Now I'm their biggest fan."

As a Northfield senior, Rob started at center for Steve McClure's first team, and thus, like his younger brothers, knows the joy of winning a Sectional. He was a role player -- defense and rebounding -- on the team led by Chad Fordyce.

Size aside, Rob's talents on the basketball floor don't equal the twins'. But he is extremely intelligent -- he finished in the top 10 of his Northfield class -- and his younger brothers respect his brain power.

So while the twins get a "full ride" to Notre Dame, Rob gets one of the best academic scholarships offered DePauw students. He's in the management fellows program, with plans to work in actuarial science.

Chapter 5: Hitting the Road

It's a homecoming of sorts for Steve McClure as his troops depart the bus at 6:40 on Friday night, December 8.

Swimming is not on anyone's mind on another frigid night in northern Indiana as the Norsemen are ushered into a locker room that serves the Oak Hill High School pool. McClure thinks about swimming, though, and hatches a ploy. At the half of the JayVee game he will promise to dive in if the Norse win by 20.

Situated in a burg called Mier, a smattering of about 100 homes around the intersection of state highways 13 and 18, Oak Hill is known as a basketball school. Its most famous player is Monte Towe, a diminutive guard who led the Golden Eagles to the Semistate his senior year and then went on to North Carolina State to be part of an NCAA championship squad led by David Thompson.

Having taught and coached at Oak Hill for 10 years, McClure knows the basketball team particularly well. The Golden Eagles will start two 6-6 youngsters, Jay Kroft and Jon Carpenter, who, as seventh-graders, had Steve McClure for industrial arts and as a coach in track and football. Two other Golden Eagles have the same distinction: Ryan Jones and Rich Hogan.

And then there's Ryan Fagan, a 6-3 swingman whose father, Steve, serves as the Oak Hill trainer -- and is one of Steve McClure's best friends. Not to be forgotten is Oak Hill Athletic Director Tom Dubois, who's not only another good friend, but who happens to be Norse sub Ryan Dubois' second cousin on the paternal side.

So McClure will see familiar faces -- even his own if he wants; it's in a photo in a trophy case -- when he strolls into the gym.

McClure spots Dubois, who's standing just off the entrance into the gym, which seats 2,400. They shake hands warmly and chew the fat.

"We can sell 942 tickets tonight," Dubois tells a visitor who has tagged along with McClure. "The rest are season ticket-holders."

Dubois coached basketball from 1982-1987 at Southwood, but Oak Hill has always been his school. He was in its first graduation class in 1960, and there was something extra special about that year: the Golden Eagles defeated Marion for the Sectional crown. Oak Hill repeated as Sectional kings in 1961 and 1962. Then a big-win dry spell set in until 1971, when Towe took the school to a Regional championship before it fell in Semistate play.

Dubois is asked about this year's squad, which is 3-1 under Kevin Pearson, an Indiana All-Star who played for Marion's State Champion team of 1975. "I'd say it's the best team we've had in the last seven years," Dubois responds after thinking for a minute.

McClure's kids know only one thing: Oak Hill will be one of their toughest games all year. And the pressure they feel is evident as they pull jock straps, shorts, shirts and knee pads from their bags in the spacious pool locker room. A quietness that was missing the first two games gives one the feeling that Northfield has truly come to play tonight.

Peck Chay's $94 Air Jordans are probably gone for good, and so after pulling on his uniform, he loosens up in his street shoes. He'll wear Scott Bumgardner's game shoes again.

As the junior varsity game winds down, McClure mutters en route to the locker room, "Let's play this sucker right now." His smile can't hide the pressure he's feeling.

The blackboard tonight reads:

Be
The
Aggressor!

After the prayer, McClure begins softly by addressing individuals. He reminds Jon Ross to think about his role -- create opportunities for brother Joe. Nathan Winegardner hears about stopping the baseline. Peck Chay has a finger pointed at him and is told to play quick. The same goes for brother Noi. For Hampton, it's making sure he helps the twins on the boards.

"How are you going to grade yourselves tonight?" he asks. "Another 0? Another 2?" There is no answer; there doesn't need to be.

"Everything we do tonight is going to work. If you're the aggressor, it's all gonna work. They'll come out extremely inspired. Name one team that won't this year. And you know that that's just a fact of life. When you're up higher on a ladder than someone, they're going to do everything they can to knock it out from under you. You just keep your eyes focused on higher goals.

"They do have some big guys, they do have some quickness, but they don't have what we have -- that's tradition, that's pride, that's faith in God and in each other.

"They want to win. We're *gonna* win. We're not going to be denied."

Then they huddle, pile their hands and shout, "Forward, march!"

It's a full house as the teams trot onto the floor. The excitement that was missing at Caston a week earlier is evident, the Oak Hill band adding to the atmosphere with swinging versions of "The Stripper" and "Heartbreak Hotel."

A banner hanging over the Oak Hill section at midcourt reads:

Rowdy Crowd
Has
Eagle Pride

Fifteen minutes before game time, a fan sitting two rows behind the Northfield bench tells McClure his team seems ready to play tonight. "They got their minds on business," the coach agrees, flashing a smile.

On Wednesday, though, the team didn't have its collective mind on business. McClure became so angry after an hour of practice, he left the gymnasium in disgust. His team was practicing the same way it had played against Caston -- "without feeling and not to lose." A heated McClure told the team he didn't have anything to offer and went into the training room for 20 minutes while the players tried to keep things going -- to little avail. Instead of ending the practice, though, McClure gathered the team and talked about pressure.

"We had been in a denial state," he noted on the bus to Oak Hill, "trying to act like the pressure is not here and this and that and the other. So we just talked about some ways we can deal with it and figured we're gonna just meet it head on."

On Thursday, a teachers' meeting at White's was scheduled before school, and, as always, devotion was given before the meeting. McClure was taken by Assistant Principal Sherm Knight basing the devotion on First Corinthians 10 :13, which talks about God not giving an individual anything that the individual and God can't handle together.

McClure had the verse printed, along with some words from President Theodore Roosevelt about critics -- how they are timid and cold and know nothing about neither victory nor defeat. At lunchtime, he put the printed messages on the players' lockers.

Thursday's practice was outstanding.

Now, he hopes, the team will take what they did in practice into tonight's game.

Twenty seconds into the contest, Hampton hits a 12-foot jumper from the side. Thirty seconds later, Joe Ross gets a rebound basket. Another 30 seconds later, Peck adds a short jumper of his own. It's a quick 6-0 Northfield lead, reminding one of Northfield's fast start against Whitko -- a fast start that was not maintained.

But now McClure's team races to an 11-2 advantage in the first three minutes, forcing Pearson to call time out.

"Look for a press!," McClure shouts in the huddle, making himself heard above the crowd's din.

The quarter ends with Northfield ahead 21-10. But the first foul on Oak Hill wasn't called until 21 seconds remained, a reminder of what Steve Desper said on the bus coming over: Playing at Oak Hill "can be quite an experience."

Northfield's tenacity on defense is the strongest it has been, allowing the Norse to maintain a double-digit lead. But Joe picks up his third foul with 5 minutes and 10 seconds left. Shades of Whitko again.

"Move the ball," McClure yells as Allen Strait replaces Joe, and Desper bellows, "Patience!"

Joe's absence changes the team's chemistry. It starts to break down. Hampton tries to fix the mix. As Oak Hill starts a run, he chases Brad King, who's on a breakaway. At the top of the circle, Hampton dives from the side to knock the ball out of bounds. The Northfield bleachers erupt, and one of the regular "crazies" shouts, "Give it 125 percent, Brad."

Craig Helfrich, a sophomore guard, hits a trio of treys for the Golden Eagles. But Northfield clings to a nine-point lead 30 seconds before intermission -- only to surrender two quick baskets on two quick turnovers. So it's 31-26 at the break.

"Guys," McClure pleads in the locker room, "you can't let up on them. They'll burn ya. They're a good ball club. Find Helfrich, the little blond-headed kid. He's got three three-pointers."

McClure doesn't talk X's and O's. He sends them back to the floor a little early, seeming to sense that what he felt before the game is correct: his kids mean business, and the last few seconds of the half was a fluke of sorts.

He's right. Northfield gets three hoops in the first 46 seconds of the third quarter to open an 11-point lead and force Pearson to call time out.

"You think they're gonna come after you?" McClure asks rhetorically in the huddle.

Less than a minute later, the crowd is stunned.

With Northfield up 37-28, Hampton again dives for the ball at Oak Hill's offensive end in an effort to stop a breakaway. He misses the ball. But his face doesn't miss the hardwood, hitting flush. He rolls on his back, almost out.

Steve Fagan, McClure's good buddy, rushes to Hampton's side. After a few minutes, Fagan manages to get Hampton into a sitting position. Then Scott Kunkel and David Pefley are sent to help him off the floor, where Athletic Director Jim Kaltenmark will take charge of the situation.

McClure shifts Troy Miller to forward and goes with the Chay boys at guard. The combination works well, pushing Northfield to a 47-32 advantage after three quarters.

Joe's little left-hand hook in the opening 30 seconds of the fourth quarter makes it a 17-point margin. And Jon, remembering his instructions, feeds his brother a few seconds later for a huge stuff. He's fouled, too, and when he converts, it's 52-32. The swimming pool flashes through McClure's mind.

Almost without notice, Hampton is back on the bench, sitting next to his mentor. He's still woozy, but his toothy grin is still in place, despite a bloody, swollen lip.

Even without Hampton, Northfield has played brilliantly, methodically building to a 63-37 lead with less than 3 minutes and 40 seconds remaining. Jon fouls out 10 seconds later, but it doesn't matter.

McClure, who has been coaching like crazy all night, is still going strong at 2:35. "I don't want any fouls," he says during Oak Hill's last timeout. "No fouls!"

A few seconds later, he goes to his bench, tells Strait, Kunkel and Pefley, "I don't want no slop."

The final is 69-49, and as the players leave the gym, Joe Ross walks off with his right arm around the still-hazy Hampton. Desper, nearby, says, "Somebody will need to drive Brad home."

Inside the locker room, the squad is thinking swimming pool, remembering McClure's promise.

Inside the locker room, the squad is thinking swimming pool, remembering McClure's promise.

He's hardly inside the room before someone yells, "Get your clothes off!" And another shouts, "Yeah, tie and shoes only."

"Let me talk to you while I'm doing this," he says, removing his tie and shoes. "Hey, sky's the limit. Sky's the limit. All I'm gonna say is we got a little sloppy late. And we beat a good ball club. They're a lot better than that. And yet, you've shown that you can play your standard, not someone else's. With that, let's pray.

"Father, lay obstacles in our path and help us meet them ... and Father, remind us that sometimes coaches can change their minds."

But McClure -- the guy who once swam across the Ohio River -- isn't about to welsh. Only there's a problem. The door leading from the locker room to the pool is locked. A key is found, and it slides smoothly into the lock, but won't turn. There will be no swimming tonight -- and just as well for McClure. It's sub-zero outside.

The doors to the yellow school bus swing open after pulling up to Northfield at 10:21 in the cold silence of a country night. McClure has proven Thomas Wolfe wrong. You can go home again, especially for a short time, and find the visit most rewarding.

The wind-chill factor -- wind and temperature combined -- is 34 degrees below zero as the Norsemen hit the road again at 4:50 on December 15.

Bob Slee, who McClure prefers to drive the team bus, has it warmed up as the players take their seats for the 45-minute drive to Tippecanoe Valley High School.

It is deceiving outside -- crystal clear and sunny. But the bus windows are frosted, blocking any view and creating a cocoon-like feeling.

The kids are loose. They've won their opening three and gotten the monkey partly off their collective back. And the Rosses' performance at Oak Hill has earned them the "21 Alive Players of the Week" honor from Fort Wayne television station WPTA.

Tippecanoe Valley, which has about 500 students, is one of those places in the middle of nowhere, five miles from Mentone and five miles from Akron, small communities with about 1,000 people each. But the gym seats 2,700.

Valley goes into the contest at 3-1, having lost only to Whitko on the road in a game which saw Whitko Coach Bill Patrick whistled for two technical fouls in the first half and manage to avoid banishment in the second.

As in the previous two road contests, the Northfield bleacher area is filled before the junior varsity game tipoff. And Bill Ruppel, a Wabash County Councilman, is in the Tippecanoe Valley section. Although he lives in North Manchester, in the northernmost part of the county, he's taught at Tippecanoe Valley for 17 years, and this is one night he'll root against a Wabash team.

The blackboard message tonight reads:

Play with your
Heart

Like Oak Hill, there is a pronounced quiet as the players begin to dress midway through the third quarter of the junior varsity game. Peck Chay has a new pair of $48 Nikes to get him through the season.

McClure walks in just as the players have pulled on their sweats and exclaims, "You look like a bunch of farm boys, stinkin'!" Only his smile gives him away. Then he pulls out a big cardboard box and dumps new warm-up attire on the floor.

"All right! Let's kick some butts," Brad Hampton responds. As the players start fishing for tops and bottoms -- there are two especially large outfits for the Rosses -- Hampton says, "He's smart. We weren't pumped up enough."

In his pre-game talk, McClure uses baseball to make a key point.

"Hank Aaron said he always got his cuts in, guys. He never got cheated at the plate. He rarely ever took a called third strike because he was always a competitor, he was always at his best when it meant the most. And that's what we need to develop. Don't let yourselves get cheated.

"You know, we had a great game last Friday, but that's history. Now continue to move forward. Just lead the way with your mind. Your body will follow."

Before getting dressed, Joe Ross posted on a window a page entitled "What It Takes to be No. 1," words from the late Vince Lombardi.

"That's neat," McClure says, pointing to the message. "I like that, whoever put it up there."

He turns from the window. "Both teams are gonna play extremely hard out there. We're the better team. We're diversified -- fast, slow, we can handle anything they throw at us .... I see great things comin'."

So does Tippecanoe Valley. The Vikings give Northfield a taste of its own medicine, opening with a 9-0 spurt in less than two minutes, causing McClure to call a timeout.

Almost three minutes elapse before Hampton's short jumper breaks the ice, and Northfield edges back, despite several turnovers, to 15-10 at 2:49. Tippecanoe Valley Coach Bob DuBois, no relation to his 6-9 center, Chris, waves his green towel to signal his own timeout.

Despite being called for traveling five times in the first eight minutes, Northfield manages to get within one, 17-16, on two free throws by Jon Ross. "You played like crap, you're down one," McClure tells his troops at the break.

Northfield finally gets even at 20 on Noi Chay's two free throws with 6:13 left. And less than a minute later, Scott Johnson, the Vikings' best outside shooter, gets his third foul, causing DuBois to twist his unbuttoned sweater in agony.

The Norsemen, though, cannot get on top. Their foes' press has rattled them into numerous turnovers, allowing Tippecanoe Valley to cling to a 33-29 lead.

Just inside three minutes, though, Noi hits a three-pointer, Hampton gets a free throw, and Miller follows with a lay-up to give Northfield its first advantage, 35-33.

Despite committing 16 turnovers, the Norse end the half on top, 39-38. McClure is calm as he says, "You're screwin' up monumentally, but you've played with heart except for the first two minutes. You're one point ahead. What can you do when you start playin' basketball?"

He wants more ball rotation. "Cut!" he yells at the top of his lungs. "And Joe and Jon, you need to be more active at the 10-second line to help out on the press."

Then, shouting again, he asks, "How bad will we beat 'em when we stop givin' up the baseline? If you don't match their intensity, it's gonna be 9-0 again."

Instead, it's a 7-0 run -- for Northfield. Noi hits a trey, goes coast-to-coast for a lay-up and Jon flips in a short jumper. Valley gets a hoop to make it 46-40, but Joe comes back with a huge stuff, only to be called for a technical for hanging on the rim. It's a questionable call, at best. But the normally steady Steve Dunnock misses both technicals.

At 4:17, Peck's drives gives Northfield a 50-40 lead, and the home team calls time out. "Suck it up higher!" McClure shouts in the huddle. "You know they're goin' to keep comin'. Ain't this fun?"

McClure is right about one thing, wrong about another. Tippecanoe Valley keeps coming, and it's not fun for the Norsemen.

At 56-46, McClure's club starts to crumble. Still, after three quarters, it's 58-53. But not for long, as Johnson's three-pointer forges a 58 draw at 6:36 left in the game.

Thirty seconds later, Joe is called for his fifth foul. But Northfield contends that it should be on Jon, and after a brief discussion, he's assessed the personal. DuBois, shackled by the twins the first half, comes alive, starting with two free throws for a 60-58 Tippecanoe Valley lead.

The statistics sheet tells the story. Northfield has scored one basket in its last 16 possessions. The Norse have turned the ball over nine times. And they've allowed the Tippecanoe Valley crowd -- not much bigger than Northfield's -- to get into the game.

At 4:50, the picture turns even darker as Joe fouls out for the third time in four games. And at 3:57, McClure calls his last timeout with Valley ahead, 66-60. The Viking strategy from this point on is basic: Sit on the ball.

Noi's lay-up off a steal makes it 68-64 at 1:59, but it is too little very late. Northfield is forced to foul in the final minute -- to no avail. Tippecanoe Valley hits freebie after freebie to seal the upset, 78-64.

Deathly silence shrouds the Northfield locker room. McClure has left the players to themselves for a few minutes before coming inside and gathering them in close.

"You aren't on top of the world, guys," he says calmly. "You aren't in Ohio yet."

The last comment is in reference to tomorrow night's game at Ohio University in Athens, where the Norsemen will play Wellston, Ohio, in the McDonald's-Day's Inn Classic.

" 'It's gonna be a pretty plane ride, isn't it?' That's all I heard. Plane ride. This kind of stuff.

"The bare fact of it is, we choked. We don't have guts. When we came out strong and the crowd was goin', you enjoyed that. But when they came, you didn't enjoy that."

He turns to the Lombardi message, which concludes:

"I believe in God, and I believe in human decency. But I firmly believe that any man's finest hour – his greatest fulfillment to all he holds dear – is that moment when he has worked his heart out in a good cause and lies exhausted on the field of battle – victorious."

McClure points to the window, says softly, "You didn't do it this way, and they did." A pause, then, "See, you can do all that kind of stuff. You can put neat little slogans up, have all these great ideas. But unless you are willing to talk - on - the - floor, forget it.

"We're not competitors at this point. We want it easy. We want it to look pretty. And ... I don't know. We obviously didn't want to win that game, because it was there to win.

"Are we together as a team, or do we have some selfish teammates? I don't know, I'm just kinda graspin' for straws here.

"Let's pray."

Outside the locker room, McClure says to freshman coach Harold Christie, "We panicked, we choked."

A bystander asks him to elaborate.

"We practiced beating the press against eight guys during the week, and then when it came time to do it, we choked. We managed to beat Caston's press a couple of weeks ago, but Valley's quickness panicked us."

How much of a factor was tomorrow's Ohio trip?

"You'll never know. But we have no excuses. Valley has to get most of the credit here. They did what they had to do to win the ballgame. I mean, it's one thing to be distracted (by the Ohio trip), if we indeed were, but it's another thing to have your team prepared to take advantage of that. And they were certainly ready. Whatever we did or didn't do, we really won't know. We just have to come back and see what happens."

It's mentioned that, like Oak Hill the week before, the quietness in the locker room seemed to signal good things.

"Welcome to the world of teenagers," McClure sighs.

On the bus, the Kunkel family's sandwiches are fine. But some appetites don't seem to be as the bus rumbles home in near silence, a moving cocoon in the cold on top of cold.

•••••••••

In the final analysis, two key factors -- Tippecanoe Valley's quickness and Northfield's panic -- sent the Norse reeling to its first defeat, as McClure noted. The first essentially led to the second.

Quickness is an ingredient that can cover a lot of sins and shortcomings, and Tippecanoe Valley proved that both offensively and defensively as the game moved into the fourth quarter. The Viking press caused problems all night, forcing the Norsemen into 33 turnovers. And once Valley got a small lead, quickness allowed the Vikings to run the clock.

Extreme panic then set in for the first time in the season.

What Desper had feared in the thrilling season opener against Whitko took place at Tippecanoe Valley.

After the Whitko victory, Desper had commented, "I was afraid they were going to run the clock when they got up on us. When the other team runs the clock on us, that's like a kiss of death."

Playing the clock worked perfectly for Tippecanoe Valley, forcing Northfield to foul in a desperate effort to get the ball and score quickly. By this point, panic was thorough.

Sitting in the bleachers, waiting for the players to shower and dress, Desper explained it in clinical succinctness: "When you're playing well and a team plays much more aggressively at you, your mind must stay calm or slow down a little bit. If it speeds up, panic will set in, and then you lose all sense of what's going on around you. And that's pretty much what happened tonight."

Indeed. Northfield was playing well, forging into a 10-point lead after starting in a 9-0 hole. Then Tippecanoe Valley got much more aggressive, and Northfield couldn't maintain its composure.

There's a lesson there -- one that McClure will surely use some day as the season marches on.

Chapter 6: The Laotian Connection

Two departures -- one complicated and daring, the other simple and gutsy -- play particularly important roles in determining Northfield's basketball success for the 1989-90 season.

Unhappiness with communism led to the escapes of Edward and Vanh Chay.

Unhappiness with a coach led to the exit of their oldest son, Pick, from the Wabash High team.

The Chay odyssey takes root in 1953, when the family's native country, Laos, gains full sovereignty from the French. Free from direct foreign control, Laos becomes a battleground for power among three factions: pro-West, pro-communist, and the neutralists led by Premier Souvanna Phouma.

As the struggle for domination continues through the years, Edward Chay grows up in the countryside while his future wife, Vanh, matures in the city.

By the spring of 1970, the Vietnam War spreads deeply into Laos, where the heart of the Ho Chi Minh trail lies. North Vietnam begins using the so-called trail to make insurgencies into South Vietnam. In April 1975, Laos, a landlocked nation of 3,500,000 people, falls to communist Pathet Lao forces.

Edward and Vanh Chay, now with six children, soon feel freedom slipping away from them. They begin planning an escape from their homeland. It will not be easy.

Edward has arranged for a boatman to take them across the Mekong River, which forms the border with Thailand to the west.

Other Laotians had hired boatmen, paid their money and been left stranded -- double-crossed -- and so Edward is not sure what will happen.

The children know nothing of a plan calling for two boats, one carrying Edward and the three boys, the other Vanh and the three girls, to simultaneously take them across the Mekong to Thailand. The parents do not tell the children for fear that their planned escape will leak to the communists and they will be arrested.

Still, the plan goes awry. Only Edward and Noi manage to get on one boat and make the river crossing. Vanh and the other children must retreat to a relative's home.

A happy-go-lucky teenager today, Noi is a four-year-old tot when he and his father begin the family's flight in June 1977. They make it safely across the river, but once in Thailand are jailed, charged with illegal entry. They stay imprisoned for almost five weeks, unable to pay $200 in fines for their release.

Two days after Edward's escape, a friend who is an officer in the communist Pathet Lao army visits the Chay house and asks about him. A fearful Vanh tells the officer, "He go see his father. His father, he real, real sick."

A week after Edward and Noi's escape, Vanh takes the other five children, ranging from two-year-old NuNu to nine-year-old Pally, for a boat ride of their own, uncertain of their fate. She has bought a huge box of candy to keep the youngsters quiet while they cross the river.

For the the children, leaving is an adventure. For Edward and Vanh, leaving is a matter of life and death. One wrong move, and they face death.

Vanh and the youngsters make the right moves, and soon, the Chays are reunited in a refugee camp in Thailand. They have the clothes on their backs and little else. But Edward and Vanh Chay know that the future can hold much, starting with freedom.

Escaping *to* Thailand is one thing, getting *out* of Thailand is another.

The Chays' first choice is the United States, their second, Australia. After completing his application, Edward undergoes tests and interviews dealing with his background and education. The Chays are put into the third, and lowest, priority category of immigrants seeking freedom in the United States. The key factor is Edward's background. He had left the farm, served in the Laotian army in 1960 and become an electrical engineer. For various reasons, others with different personal and occupational histories ranked higher.

Freedom does not come for more than two years. The Chays are held in a United Nations-sponsored camp until a foreign sponsor can be found and not before Edward takes several tests and undergoes several interviews.

Finally, however, the First United Methodist Church of Wabash, Indiana, agrees to sponsor the Chays, and on November 11, 1979, they arrive in a strange new city, population 13,000.

The Chays move into a house on West Sinclair Street, about a block from the basketball court at St. Bernard's Catholic church and school, where the young Ross twins play, too.

When the Chays arrive, they know only Laotian, except for Vanh, who can speak broken French. Kathy Geible, the French teacher at Wabash High School and a member of the church, spends much of the next six weeks helping the family learn some basic English.

Edward is hired as a janitor at Markhon Industries, a major local company specializing in products related to the computer industry. Later, after taking tests, he becomes a welder with the firm. And Vanh eventually gains employment, too, as an assembler at another major company, DiversiTech, formerly known as General Tire.

A smallish man with smooth tan skin, Edward speaks in broken English today, but the message is clear: "I stay with them (the communists) two year. I thought everything real, real bad. Like, politic or economy is wore out -- like bad and bad. I decide to escape to Thailand."

Vanh adds: "I love the freedom, I love the liberty. Then we decide to escape, because we don't like communist regime."

Pick Chay has a real "Hogan Hero."

He is Fred Hogan, a former teacher at West Ward Elementary School in Wabash who gave Pick and his siblings their first basketball for their first Christmas in 1979.

The youngsters thought the ball was for soccer, a major sport in Laos, and they kicked it around. That's blasphemy in Indiana, but forgivable under the circumstances.

Hogan came to the Chay house on Sinclair Street and began teaching Pick, the oldest of the three boys, the game of basketball. A hoop was needed, so the Chays fashioned one out of a bicycle wheel. They cut the spokes out and nailed the tire rim to a pear tree -- reminiscent of what basketball's inventor, Dr. James Naismith, did in 1891, using two peach baskets and a soccer ball, of all things.

"Fred Hogan was more than a teacher for me," Pick says. "He was like my second father, my guardian. Like on basketball applications and stuff, he would be like my dad."

Hogan was a member of the Methodist church that sponsored the Chays. Like Miss Geible, he volunteered to help them adjust to American life and wound up becoming an unofficial representative for the congregation.

A soft-spoken man, he says, "Pick and his family were a joy to be with. They became friends, and they were a very interesting family. I enjoyed being around them."

Hogan does not have much contact with them these days and rarely sees Peck and Noi play. He left teaching in 1986 to become a meatcutter -- a job that put him through college -- in Fort Wayne, about 40 miles from his Wabash County home.

Pick played for Hogan's sixth grade team, which won the city elementary school championship. The teacher recognized the youngster's talent and sent him to basketball camps at Purdue and Indiana universities.

Fundamentals learned in those camps were refined by Harry Frick, an enthusiastic young coach at Wabash High School for two seasons. "Basically, it was Frick who taught me ballhandling," Pick says.

As Pick developed his skills, he passed them on to Peck and Noi, and now the three -- all about 5-10 and 155 pounds -- essentially mirror each other. They possess excellent touch from outside, solid ballhandling skills and quick hands that produce steals.

The rapport Pick had with Hogan and Frick never materialized with Frick's successor at Wabash, Ron Slaton. Pick's unhappiness as a sophomore reserve player grew. He wanted out badly.

He saw an opportunity with Carl and Peggy Sundheimer, who knew the Chay family through their daughter. She had married a Laotian who was sponsored by the Wabash Rotary Club and had arrived about the same time as the Chays.

Then as now, the Sundheimers lived in a three-bedroom home in the tiny community of Urbana, just north of Wabash, in the Metropolitan school district.

Not shy, Pick asked Mrs. Sundheimer if he could live with them to establish residence in the Metropolitan district.

Fine, she told him, if his parents approved. In fact, all three Chay boys could move into the Sundheimer home if they wished. "Pick was so determined to play ball," Mrs. Sundheimer remembers.

The Sundheimers met with Wabash attorney Steve Downs "to make sure everything was aboveboard." She and husband Carl, who had retired from a local trucking firm, were prepared to become the Chay boys' guardians. But getting approval would be difficult, Downs told them, because the family lived so nearby in Wabash.

Guardianship, however, wasn't needed. And because Pick was 18, there would be no transfer tuition fee if he paid rent at the Sundheimers. They charged him a small weekly sum to ensure legal status. The substantial transfer fee would apply to Peck and Noi, however, so they remained at home.

For Pick, it was a bold, gutsy move into a new school and strange surroundings, let alone leaving the comforts of home.

"I didn't think he was getting a fair shake in Wabash," Mrs. Sundheimer says. "My son was killed when he was in a car-truck accident two years before that. I felt I could help somebody. He is a very nice boy and they are a very nice family."

Northfield officials called the Sundheimer home periodically, making sure he actually lived there, she recalls. "He would go home on weekends. I was willing to do his laundry, but he insisted on taking it home."

Pick lived with the Sundheimers his junior year, but was not eligible while establishing residency. He practiced with the team, and it was tough on him, not being able to play, but the year was "worth it in the end."

By then, rumors were circulating through Wabash County that Pick moved in with the Sundheimers because he didn't feel Slaton treated him fairly.

The Chays said nothing publicly. They didn't want to cause any trouble.

By the time his senior year began, Pick's parents had rented a home in the country, where Edward yearned to live again. The location, north of the City of Wabash, was in the Metropolitan district.

Even today, Pick, who received a basketball scholarship to nearby Taylor University, is not comfortable talking about the situation. But when asked, he is straightforward.

"Yes, the rumors were correct," he says. "I guess I thought I was good enough -- a lot of people thought I was good enough -- to play, and I didn't get the fair shake at Wabash. I thought at Northfield I would."

He pauses for a moment, then opens up candidly:

"When Slaton came he asked who was good coming back, and a lot of teachers mentioned Pick Chay. And from then on, he got on me. He had his personal reasons, I guess.

"Basketball wasn't fun anymore. It was work -- worse than work. I mean, you didn't enjoy it at all.

"Northfield was the best move I ever made in my whole life. It changed my life around, about me viewing people and things."

The move caused one negative, he says. Brother Peck caught heat from the Wabash coaches, forcing him to quit playing for the junior varsity as a tenth grader. Noi, an eighth grader, was not affected.

Under McClure, Pick says, basketball went from being "worse than a job" to something he loved, something that taught him more than just athletic skills. "It was learning what you had as a person. I became a better person; I matured. Coach McClure taught us that basketball is not just a team, it's a family. Everything we learn on court, hopefully we can use in life later on. We glorified God and prayed, which is great. He is a great coach."

Slaton, who left Wabash to coach in South Carolina, flatly denies the charges.

Whatever the case, Pick went on to have a solid senior year as a Northfield starter. By the time it began, he had moved back with his parents in their rented Northfield-district home.

When he left the Sundheimers, he presented them with a bouquet of flowers and a card "that touched me," Peggy Sundheimer recalls with joy. Clearly, a close bond had grown between the gentle woman from the Hoosier countryside and the appreciative youngster not long from Laos. Peggy Sundheimer stayed close to Pick by chronicling his senior year in a scrapbook and presenting it to him as a graduation present.

At Taylor he's majoring in international business, which will open doors to different people and different places -- such as Laos.

"I miss Laos, I really do," Pick says. "I'm a U.S. citizen -- everyone in the family is -- but my parents won't let us forget where we came from, what our backgrounds are, which is good. My mom and dad always talk in Laotian at home so we don't forget how to speak our first language, our native tongue."

Pick hopes to visit Laos some day and relive memories. Vanh, too, would like to return to visit relatives. But Edward says he has no desire to go back.

All Edward Chay wants is "peace of mind," he says.

Moving to the country has helped. "I like the peace and quiet," he says. "I don't like bother anybody. I know my boys and teenagers make lots of fun and lots of noise. Some people don't like that; some people work at night, sleep at day. My boys bounce the ball all the time."

Edward does not have complete peace of mind yet. As the 1989-90 season opened, he still was not sure what occurred between his oldest son and Ron Slaton. Everything Edward heard was second-hand; he and Slaton never talked about the situation, he says. All he heard from other people, he adds, was, "My boy had problem with coach."

When the subject comes up, he asks, "What scandal say?"

And Vanh Chay adds, "What the rumor say?"

But while he is not sure what happened, Edward has used the situation as a teaching tool.

"When people blame them (the boys) for things, I tell them they have to learn from them," he says. "The boys have to ask themselves *why* other people blame them for something. They have to learn from bad things and make something good from them."

Which sounds a little like Steve McClure, who on more than one occasion, has told his team in practice: "Think about what we did wrong and what we need to do to make it right."

•••••••••

Laotians have a family name and a "play" name, which is like a nickname.

Pick's family name in Laotian was Palisack. His play name was Pick. Among friends and family members, he was called Pick.

Chay (rhymes with "hi" in Laotian but is pronounced like "hay" locally) was the play name for Pick's father.

When the family came to the United States, they needed two names. So Pick's father adopted his play name, Chay, for the family name and took a solid Anglo-Saxon name, Edward, for his first name.

Thus, the children became Pally Palixay Chay, Bey Palisay Chay, Pick Palisack Chay, Peck Palacsith Chay, Noi Lipaseuth Chay and NuNu Palida Chay.

Pally and Bey, the two oldest daughters, possess an Oriental beauty. After being graduated from Wabash High School they went to modeling school and now take jobs while attending classes at Indiana-Purdue Fort Wayne.

The youngest girl, NuNu, is a freshman at Northfield and has her older sisters' beauty. She played basketball for a while, but found she didn't enjoy it that much. Instead, she's a junior varsity cheerleader.

66

And like the Rosses, the Chays are known by almost everyone.

Chapter 7: Buckeye Bound and Beyond

The first gut-check of the season will take place on the banks of the Hocking River, which rims Ohio University at Athens to the south.

Steve McClure had hoped that his team could go into the McDonald's-Days Inn Classic unbeaten before facing an unusually tough step up the ladder against Jim Derrow's Wellston, Ohio, Golden Rockets

A step up the ladder normally means playing well and winning. Now, though, McClure feels another rung can be achieved even in defeat if Northfield plays much better than in its upset loss the night before at Tippecanoe Valley.

One thing's for sure: winning won't be easy. Derrow's team is 4-0, coming off a 70-58 victory four days earlier at Alexander High School, just up the road at Albany, Ohio. After the game, Alexander Coach Jay Rees told Kenneth Smailes of the Athens *Messenger*: "People thought Wellston would fold without (last year's District Player of the Year) Scott Bragg, but they haven't folded. They are just as good if not better."

Derrow launched the "Classic" in the 1988-89 season after having been invited to a similar event in previous years. Twelve teams participated the first year.

This year, he and five others formed a committee that narrowed a list of 150 teams to 25 before selecting the final 14, adding two teams and one game to the tournament.

The committee invited defending Indiana State Champion Lawrence North, which would be a particularly strong draw because of Eric Montross. But scheduling forced Lawrence North to decline.

Derrow had read about Joe and Jon Ross in the *Street and Smith* basketball magazine, and he liked "the idea of having All-American twins." So he called McClure in December 1988, asking about the Rosses and Northfield's program.

Once the 14 teams were set, the tournament committee worked out the best potential matchups. "We didn't put my team against Northfield for any other reason," Derrow said. "The way the teams stacked up, it worked out that way."

When the Ohio coach extended the invitation in February 1989, McClure wasted no time accepting. It would mean canceling one game to stay within IHSAA rules of 20 regular-season contests, and it could mean a long bus ride on top of another bus ride -- from Tippecanoe Valley -- the night before. But McClure knew the game would benefit Northfield's program.

McClure asked Athletic Director Jim Kaltenmark to reschedule the Tippecanoe Valley game, perhaps for right after Thanksgiving instead of December 15, but the matter fell through the cracks.

However, as game day dawns on a bitterly cold Saturday, a long morning/afternoon bus ride will be avoided. The Shirt Shed, a local firm specializing in printed T-shirts, has donated the use of its two company airplanes.

The planes seat six and eight, allowing Northfield to get 12 players and McClure and Steve Desper aboard. It is the first flight for some -- including Desper.

There are a few ashen faces, including Desper's, at one o'clock as the two planes take off from Wabash Municipal Airport. Nervous or not, Desper has a sense of humor. He made out a will in his classroom Friday afternoon, bequeathing his golf clubs to various students.

A very nervous Brad Hampton slept fitfully, dreaming that the planes went down en route to Ohio. It was a vivid nightmare -- flames, mangled bodies, "the whole thing," he admits. "You always hear about small planes crashing in weird planes with weird people on them."

But the pilot puts his passengers at ease quickly. Hampton and Nathan Winegardner occupy the pilot seats for a brief time, learning about radar and various controls.

Hampton's fears evaporate, and by the time the plane lands, he's thrilled with "a really neat trip."

Like Hampton, Desper relaxes once the plane gets airborne, prompting McClure to joke later, "Steve's talkin' about buyin' an airplane."

Fifty-three minutes later they are in Athens -- full of excitement and flashing wide smiles. It will be another five hours before the Norsemen take the floor, so they head for the Days Inn. The motel chain has provided the teams staying overnight with five rooms. Sunday-morning breakfast will be courtesy of McDonald's.

After a short rest, McClure gathers his troops at 3:30 for a pre-game meal at a local restaurant.

Two hours later, the Norse leave for Ohio University to watch part of the game that precedes their encounter against Wellston.

Northfield's contest is the sixth of the seven games, the opener pitting Ceredo-Kenova High School in Kenova, West Virginia, against Jay Rees' Alexander team. The final game has Cooley High in Detroit against Colonel White High in Dayton.

The Rosses will be the two tallest players during the day. And when they take the floor, there's murmuring in the crowd. "*Look* at those two guys," people are heard saying.

But the Rosses, like their teammates, are awed, too. There are only 1,000 people in the 13,000-seat Ohio University Convocation Center, but the facility's size has McClure's players wide-eyed.

Wellston's top player is Rob Hardee, a 6-5 senior who was an all-district and all-conference selection the year before for a team that went 20-4. He comes into the game as one of Wellston's four double-figure scorers, collecting 13.5 a game while pulling down nine rebounds. His scoring average can be deceiving. In this same event last year, he scored 28 points, while getting 19 rebounds, as Wellston lost to Columbus' Bishop Wehrle High School, 71-59.

But while McClure has to worry about Hardee and guard Chris Graham, Derrow has to fret about the Rosses. Three days before the game, he told Phil Beebe, sports editor of the *Wabash Plain Dealer*, "Their size really concerns us. You can't practice playing against size like that. We're concerned with playing them on the glass. We can't afford to let them get it and put it back up every time down the court."

Derrow, who scouted the Norsemen in their opener against Whitko, says he will try to counter Northfield's size with quickness. "We'll try to push the tempo every chance we get."

In the locker room, McClure, who is still bothered about his team's lack of focus in Friday night's game against Tippecanoe Valley, tells his people they have to "come back tonight and show that we learned from it, and that we're ready to move on."

He tells them to "chew up anything they throw at you. You didn't come down here to play in this arena just so you can say, 'Look at those pretty green seats.' You came down here to cross the line onto the court, and it's your opportunity to make the best of it."

Northfield fan buses were canceled because not enough people signed up -- not because of the distance or sudden disinterest after one defeat, but because people have chosen to drive on their own. Later, Derrow reports that Northfield's pregame ticket sales far exceeded the other schools. So some 200 Norse rooters, most of them decked out in blue and white, are on hand.

It is a game they will never forget.

Like the previous night against Tippecanoe Valley, Northfield finds itself down early, as Wellston races to an 11-3 advantage. But the Norse put together an eight-point run, topped off by Joe Ross' thunderous, back-to-back dunks -- one off a feed from brother Jon. A Wellston basket closes the quarter, giving the Rockets a 13-11 lead, and it's clear that this one will be a nail-biter.

The scoring streaks continue. Wellston rattles off five straight points to open the second quarter, for a run of seven. The Norse answer with a 12-2 blast, giving them their first lead, 23-20. And they cling to a 27-25 advantage at the half.

Northfield builds its margin to 38-33 in the third quarter. But Graham goes to work outside, Hardee inside, propelling the Rockets into a four-point advantage early in the fourth quarter. The margin could be eight, but Wellston has missed front-end free throws twice.

Northfield rallies, forcing two turnovers. And when Jon Ross scores, the Norse lead again, 48-47, with 2 minutes and 58 seconds left in the game.

The lead is short-lived as Graham hits a three. But Jon ties it at 50, putting back Nathan Winegardner's miss.

Mike Potts responds with two free throws at 1:24, putting Wellston on top, 52-50.

Sixty-one seconds remain when Hampton knots things at 52 with a 10-foot jumper.

As the seconds dwindle away in the final minute, Wellston holds the ball for the last shot.

Graham, who has hit four three-pointers, is open along the baseline -- his favorite spot -- and he lets fly. It bounds off the rim, no good. Winegardner gathers the rebound.

Time out, Northfield, with one second left. In the huddle, McClure tells his team to "go long to Joe." The pass is thrown and Joe makes the catch. He puts up a 10-footer. No good. Overtime -- 52-52.

Twenty-one seconds into the three-minute overtime, Joe hits two free throws to give Northfield a 54-52 lead.

The margin shrinks to one at 1:28 when Potts hits a front-end free throw, for 54-53, but misses the second, and Jon clears.

Joe is fouled again with 41 seconds left, but he can't get the free throw down this time, and the ball goes out of bounds to Wellston.

The Rockets miss a shot and Jon grabs the rebound with 20 seconds left. The Norse crowd is going wild, seeing victory in their team's grasp.

But Scott Lackey makes a steal and converts it into a basket. It's 55-54, Wellston, with nine seconds left. Timeout, Northfield.

Winegardner inbounds to Hampton, who brings the ball up. Hampton feeds to Troy Miller. McClure has designed an offensive scheme that will produce a lay-up for Joe or Jon. But Miller sees it won't work. He dribbles to the top left of the lane, puts up a three.

Swish. Northfield, 57-55. There's no time on the clock.

But wait, Jim Derrow says, the horn didn't sound. He wants more time on the clock. McClure tends to agree.

"The clock showed zero, and the officials really didn't know what to do," he explains after the game. "Well, I had seen a situation like this before where you turn the clock on and if there is no horn, the game is over. But if you put it on and there is a horn, then there's still a second left."

After much discussion, the game resumes with one second, but Northfield doesn't allow Wellston to get a shot off. Northfield wins, 57-55.

"If we make our free throws we win the game," Derrow says afterward. "It's that simple."

And about the last second? "We thought they would go to Joe or Jon, and I think they probably would have if we hadn't sucked in so far. We knew after scouting them that Miller was an excellent three-point shooter. But you're going to take a chance. He hadn't hit any all night. If we're going to lose, we don't want to lose to the big kids."

And about the big kids? "They're just so doggone big, and we knew they would give us problems. They're better shooters than I thought they would be. Their shots were falling from 13, 14 feet. They handle the ball very well against pressure, and they make good decisions. I think when they gain some weight they'll be very nice collegiate players. They're very polite and hard-playing basketball players. You can't say enough about them."

And, as usual, they have led the way. Joe turns out to be the fourth highest scorer of the day with 23 and the top rebounder with 14. Jon has contributed 13 points and nine boards.

Asked to vote shortly before the game ended, the media gave the Most Valuable Player award to Graham when it looked like Wellston would win. But after the presentation, Derrow told his younger brother and top assistant, John, he thought someone on the winning team deserved the award and suggested Joe Ross. John Derrow agreed, and they approached Graham.

"I didn't force Graham to give up the award," Derrow said later. "I just told him our reasoning, and he agreed without hesitating."

So Derrow and Graham went into the Northfield locker room and presented the plaque to Joe. After Derrow and Graham's outstanding display of sportsmanship, McClure told his happy warriors, "That's a class act."

Then: "As soon as we left the (Northfield) gym last night I think Jon said something to the effect that we were going to come down here and have a good day. And as soon as I saw you guys at Ponderosa (for the pregame meal), you had your sweaters on and you came out with smiles on your faces. The sun was definitely up the next day and you had your heads high.

"You had to really block out some things to get it done. We didn't get the total weekend out of it. I really felt like we could handle Friday and Saturday. But we got on that plane this morning, our managers and everybody met us down here, we got to the hotel and there were Northfield people swarming the place.

"I just kind of thought, man, the day's been a success. Then you come down to overtime and I think, still, it's been a success. And there's nothing wrong with putting a little icing on top of it."

Miller is asked if he knew his shot was good when it left his hand. "Yes," he says. "I could feel it immediately."

Before the team showers and dresses, looking forward to watching the last game of the day, McClure tells them, "We're going to have a little devotional period tomorrow morning, since we'll be missing church."

Asked to reflect on the day, McClure says, "It was a good experience for us. We felt like it would be at the time we signed the contract, that it was something we could benefit from regardless.

"Wellston's a team that you definitely have to beat, because they are well disciplined, they play great defense and offense. They can play at any pace. Really, they're the type of team that we want to be or become. We had to beat 'em. They surely didn't beat themselves. I think they had somethin' like only 10 turnovers, and our defense had to force those. So we really feel good about what we accomplished.

"We needed a game like this ... with nothing riding on it. Well, I can't say nothing. But we just needed a chance to get out and have some fun ... and we did. We made progress, and that's the key."

And passed their first gut-check with flying colors.

After four straight on the road, the Norsemen are home for a rare mid-week contest, a conference game the following Wednesday, December 21, against North Miami.

The Warriors are 2-4. This one should be easy.

Outside, the wind chill is 51 degrees below zero. Inside, there's a warmth and coziness as another capacity crowd settles in.

The mood in the locker room is noticeably different as the players dress. The eerie silence of the last three games is missing -- not replaced by boisterous behavior, but by a positive feeling of looseness. Perhaps the loss at Tippecanoe Valley and the win at Wellston have removed some early-season pressure.

There's less tension in the room as McClure delivers a brief pregame talk that's balanced between tactics and psychology.

"They're not a bad ballclub, guys," he says flatly. "They're capable of a great game -- you just play a great game. We came back with a great effort Saturday. Let's not have the Caston syndrome. Let's not look for the 40-point win. Let's just play better. We've got to start feeling it like we did Saturday night against Wellston."

Joe Ross sinks two free throws after 16 seconds, and Jon follows with a field goal from in close 24 seconds later.

North Miami's top player, an outstanding guard named Brandon Fites, responds with a field goal. But Troy Miller comes back with three baskets, and at 4:47 it's 12-2. Tenacious defense is responsible for the quick lead.

It's 18-2 at 2:15 in the quarter when McClure goes to his bench, bringing in Winegardner and Noi at guard. The quarter ends at 24-8.

It's an old expression in sports, but it fits tonight: Northfield has too many horses. By the half, it's 40-14, and McClure has already substituted freely. He waits outside the locker room for a few minutes, "so they can talk among themselves. It's good for them."

"Keep it up, guys," Jon says. "Don't let up."

"No need to rush it; we're in control, " Hampton adds.

"Just like Oak Hill," Joe says. "We've got to get stronger."

McClure enters. "Everything works when you play with your bodies," he begins. "And you did a great job. You had good ball movement, exactly like the way you practiced this week. I love it! I love it! You've got a great evening of basketball goin'. We're playin' at our own standards tonight and they can't keep up. That's their problem."

But Northfield will not run up the score, McClure says. "We're not goin' to be pressin' as long as we're 20 ahead. They don't get any closer. We just build on the lead."

As the players warm up for the second half, Santa tosses candy to the kids in the crowd and the Northfield band plays White Christmas, seemingly in slow motion. It's a festive occasion for the home folks.

Peck Chay starts the second half with a short jumper off the glass from the middle of the lane, Joe follows with a semi-dunk and free throw, and Troy Miller pitches in with a jumper. It's 47-14 and the building process that McClure talked about at the half has begun.

The lead reaches 41, 58-17, on Hampton's two free throws at 2:09 in the quarter. North Miami's only score has been a three-pointer by Fites. A pretty reverse lay-up by Jon sends the crowd into a tizzy just before the quarter ends. It's 62-19.

At 6:19 of the final quarter McClure begins substituting, pulling the twins first. Scott Kunkel and David Pefley come in, and Kunkel, playing with his usual seriousness, goes two-for-two and grabs three rebounds.

But the other subs are a bit sloppy, allowing North Miami to score more points in the fourth quarter -- 21 -- than it had in the previous three.

It doesn't matter, of course. Besides, the crowd is getting a big kick out of Pefley, an excellent football player but average basketball player. A young man who doesn't take himself too seriously, Pefley was cut in his ninth-, tenth- and eleventh-grade years before making the team this year.

Now, in the final seconds, he scores from in close, bringing a huge cheer from the crowd. But he's not finished. As the clock dwindles down to five seconds, he gets a long rebound, dribbles behind the three-second line and lofts a trey. It's good. The announcer can hardly be heard.

The final is 80-41. In slightly more than three quarters, the Rosses have led the way again, getting 40 points between them, 23 by

Jon. Joe has also picked up 13 rebounds. And young Noi Chay has played well again, collecting 12 points on four of nine shooting.

In his locker-room prayer, McClure says, "Father, don't let us mess up our priorities. We'll never be No. 1 because you're No. 1."

Then he tells his team he didn't like the last four minutes. "We had no leadership on the floor."

He wants them to have fun, he says -- "Sure, it was a kill all the way" -- but he doesn't want them to play well for only three and a half quarters.

Enough said.

The team presents him with a Christmas gift -- a pen-holder for his desk, featuring a nameplate and a small basketball pole and hoop.

As his youngsters head for the showers, McClure walks outside to greet reporters. "We're startin' to put things together," he tells them. "What we're seein' in practice we're startin' to see in the games."

When defense is mentioned, he says, "Our defense has been steady all year, and we're goin' to keep improvin' it."

The Norse will need to. The two-day Wabash County Tournament starts in eight days, and while Northfield will be the favorite, winning the championship won't be easy. Two years ago, Wabash, which wound up winning four games all year, scored two stunning upsets to nab the title. And last year, with Northfield playing host, Manchester topped the Norsemen in a one-point overtime thriller.

But for now, McClure just wants to think about celebrating Christmas with his family and savor a nice rebound from the humiliating loss at Tippecanoe Valley.

Chapter 8: Brad, Troy and Nathan

When Brad Hampton was nine years old, his father took him out to the backyard for a game of catch. Only it wasn't a game. It was a lesson.

Susie Hampton remembers it well: "Brad wanted to play Little League baseball, and he didn't like sitting on the bench. Bob was the coach, and he told him, the only way you're gonna be able to play every game is that we need a catcher. I remember Bob puttin' him out in the yard with a piece of plywood behind him and just throwin' at that little kid as hard as he could."

Mrs. Hampton thought her husband was going to throw the ball right through her son. "Brad got to the point where he'd dodge the ball and get out of the way or either catch it. And I guess he just learned the hard way."

What he learned, she says, was toughness -- at least, in her eyes.

But not in Bob Hampton's eyes. Brad, he maintains, is too nice a kid, and therefore allows himself to be pushed around in athletics.

At 6-4 and 230 pounds, Bob Hampton is a bear of a man, thick of beard, who knows how to talk only one way: honestly and frankly.

"I grew up at a big-city school, Fort Wayne Central, and we were always taught nice guys kind of finish last," he says. "Brad is a nice boy.

"Don't misunderstand what I'm sayin' on that. It's just that I think you have to be physical and you've got to be mean. You don't give an inch; you don't let anybody push you around. I just don't believe in that. I believe in standing up for what's right. I don't believe that if a guy pushes you, you don't push back. If you get intimidated, you're walked on, and I don't believe in being walked on."

Hampton is right about one thing. His carrot-top son is a nice boy who probably doesn't have a mean bone in his body.

What he does have is an abundance of heart and basketball brains. And a propensity for getting hurt. His shoulder injury before the season opened was not unusual. He has had accidents on a mini bike, in a car, on the baseball diamond, and, frequently, on the basketball court.

But Susie Hampton doesn't worry much about her oldest son. "He's never been severely hurt," she says. "If maybe he was sometime, I would have been. But everything's always healed, and he has a positive attitude."

One time that she did worry was the Oak Hill game, the Norse's third of the year, when Brad smashed his face into the floor while diving for the ball. She experienced angst as he lay on the hardwood before learning he was okay.

And then there was the automobile mishap after last season's county tournament.

Northfield had just suffered what would be its only regular-season loss in the championship game, 68-67, to Manchester. Dejected, Brad sought solace at his girlfriend's house. His mother had told him to be home by midnight, but by the time he left LeeAnn Ford's house, he knew he was running late.

Driving too fast for the weather conditions, he hit an ice spot and spun into a ditch on a country road in the cold, black, loneliness of the night.

When midnight passed, Mrs. Hampton called Steve McClure, thinking that maybe the team had assembled at the coach's house. But no.

McClure suggested he drive one search route, Bob Hampton another, and Randy Keaffaber, Brad's good friend and then-teammate, a third.

By two o'clock in the morning, they were back at the Hamptons, empty, when a short time later, Brad appeared -- almost frostbitten. He had managed to rock his little car back and forth and dig away some snow with his feet and bare hands, freeing the vehicle.

Bob Hampton was not mad. He and his wife were relieved. Brad was shook up.

And then there was the combine accident, when he almost lost a thumb. It happened just before his sophomore year began, on a farm owned by his grandfather Eugene Wilson and great-grandfather Ira Wilson. Brad was standing on top of the combine when Eugene got into the cab and accidentally kicked the machine into gear. Brad tried to regain his balance, but fell into the combine's bin. While falling, his left thumb scraped the sharp auger that levels the corn.

Brad sees farming in his future.

"He loves to be outside and he loves to be his own boss," his mother says while working in the office of the Scottish Inn motel. "He's a very personable person, but he's very private."

Well aware that the successful farmer is a businessman, Brad is studying his college options after graduation. He's an average student who struggles, Susie says, adding, "I think he could do better with more effort."

This would be his senior year if the Hamptons had not delayed enrolling him until he was six years old. "When he was little, he had a lot of pneumonia -- three or four times before he was six," Susie explains. "He was kind of a frail kid, and our doctor advised us to hold him back."

Now, though, he's a basketball talent who wants to play at the college level.

By his senior season, he says flatly, he will be two inches taller -- 6-7 -- and at least 200 pounds.

He'll grow a little more, his mother agrees, but notes that while he puts away lots of food, his metabolism burns it up rapidly. "He's never still -- like his father."

His father and Susie Wilson, a beautician at the time, met on an unplanned blind date, leading to marriage.

He works for John Wendt and Sons, a Wabash firm that operates cranes and other heavy equipment. At times, he is assigned jobs that require him to leave home for several dasys or weeks.

His absences have meant more child-rearing responsibilities for his wife. He lavishes praise on her. "She's raised the kids; she's got to," he says, which gets him talking about his in-laws, the Wilsons, and why he thinks Brad's a bit timid.

"The Wilsons are great people, and he's got a lot of Wilson in him," Hampton says sincerely. "That's why I say he's a good boy, 'cause they're just basically that way. I mean, if I got something to say, I say it. But Brad won't. He's always been that way."

When his dad's on the road working, Brad turns to Grandfather Wilson or Steve McClure for advice.

"I really think Steve has more or less matured him," Susie Hampton says. "They've become real close as coach and player; also as friends. If Brad has a problem, a lot of times he'll go to Steve if Bob's not home. And I really think Steve's Christian life has been an influence on Brad."

Bob Hampton says of McClure: "Steve's got his ducks in a row. He's a good, God-fearing person."

Like the other players, Brad considers the basketball team a family and keeps those matters to himself.

"Sometimes," Susie Hampton smiles, "I'll say, 'Boy, I'll bet you really got a chewin' at halftime, didn't ya?' And he'll say, 'Well, yeah, we got chewed out pretty good.' But you know, that's another thing about Brad. He never complains about his teachers, his coaches, ever. He would rather do as the coach said than not. Even if it's wrong. He'll say, 'I don't care, the coach told me to do that and that's what I'm gonna do'."

While Brad looks up to his father, grandfathers and McClure, his little brother, eight-year-old Aaron, looks up to him. They have an amazing resemblance. "They do look exactly alike," their mother says with a nod. "Brad has freckles. Aaron has freckles. And the red hair. Bob's grandfather had red hair, and it's just evidently worked its way out."

Despite their different personalities, Brad and his father have similarities.

They both love sports. They both are fiercely independent, preferring to work things out themselves. And they're *both* nice people. Never mind the tough talk, there's a streak of kindness that burly Bob Hampton can't hide, especially when it comes to kids.

And when it comes to kids, they flock to Brad before games, some asking for autographs, some wanting to sit on his knee. He smiles and accommodates. Watching him, it's easy to forget that he's just a wiry kid, himself, who plays high school basketball with joy and abandon.

TM is the symbol for trademark. TM + A could be the symbol for the Charles and Judy Miller family.

The TM stands for the Millers' three sons -- Todd, Tim and Troy -- and the A stands for athletics.

Troy, the youngest, has begun the season playing a vital role as an outside threat in Northfield's quest for basketball prominence.

At 6-0 and 160 pounds, he's a lean senior who has followed in the athletic footsteps of big brother Todd and middle brother Tim.

And naturally so. Charles Miller has been associated with athletics all of his life.

If ever a family had the right to bleed "Norse Blue," it's this Miller family. Now a guidance counselor and the assistant baseball coach, Miller has been at Northfield since the 1976-77 school year. His wife has worked in the administration office for 13 years.

Todd Miller is the sports information director and an assistant basketball coach at Manchester College, just up the road. After winning 13 Northfield letters in baseball, football, basketball and track, he earned a bachelor's degree at Anderson College in Indiana and a master's at Pembroke State University in North Carolina.

Tim Miller was a 6-3 quarterback for the Norse, and by the time he was graduated, was the fifth-leading all-time passer in Indiana high school history. He earned all-conference honors not only in football, but also baseball and basketball, and he owns more than 30 school records in the three sports.

Like Todd and Tim, Troy is multi-talented athletically. He, too, played quarterback, and before suffering his only sports injury, a stress fracture to his left foot, ran cross country. After basketball, he'll wrap up his Northfield career as a starting outfielder for the baseball team.

But all Troy has on his mind now is Steve McClure's basketball team, especially after his disappointment as a junior when he excelled for the JayVee but didn't make the varsity roster for the Sectional tournament. As a freshman, he led his team in scoring. Now, having worked hard during the summer, he is on a mission: to prove that he is an outstanding basketball player.

An exceptional outside shooter -- he brings the ball up from his hip when firing from deep -- Troy hopes to play in college and is looking at smaller schools in Indiana.

But as a mature youngster, he knows that in choosing a college, academics take precedence over athletics.

"I never try to tell him what he should do," says Charles Miller, a guidance counselor. "I try to help him look at all the options and give him guidance. The main thing that he has to do is decide on something that he's going to be happy doing. If he wants to go to college just to play basketball, and gets a degree in something that he doesn't enjoy doing for the rest of his life, I think he's making a mistake."

Judy Miller says of her youngest son: "He's a fun kid, always up. He's a clown at home ... always got something funny to say. Our older two boys were awfully quiet, kept everything to themselves. Troy doesn't. He comes home and talks."

But the conversation seldom involves the inner workings of the basketball team, Charles says. "I think he kinda goes along with that family notion that a lot of things that are said there and done there

81

are left there. But once in a while he'll mention something that maybe took place in practice -- more in practice than games."

When McClure is particularly upset and unloads on the team -- perhaps kicks a waste can or pounds a blackboard -- does Miller get upset?

"Troy doesn't talk about those things," he responds. And if his son did, no, he wouldn't be bothered, Miller adds.

"You gotta remember, I was a football coach for 25 years, and I've probably done some things very similar to that in my days. Things like that were commonplace 15, 20, 25 years ago. And probably parents are a little more sensitive today. But it doesn't upset me as long as he doesn't do physical harm to any kid.

"I think kids can be motivated in different ways. And some kids respond to that type of thing, some don't. The key is, some kids need praise, some need motivation like kicking the water bottles or kicking a door or something. It takes all kinds of different things to motivate a kid."

Knowing kids and knowing coaching, he's asked, how much has McClure influenced Troy?

"I think the biggest thing that's helped Troy is Steve has developed a family concept in basketball ... all the guys working together for the same goals. The kids are very, very close. I think Steve's helped Troy mature by being honest with him, giving him the opportunity to play and giving him praise when he deserves it."

Judy Miller says Troy looks up to McClure. "He's somebody you'd want your kids to look up to. He sets good examples, high goals -- even outside school."

It's easy to spot Nathan Winegardner. He's the kid who is a reminder of the '50s with his flattop haircut.

If it weren't for Nathan's porcupine top, an outsider could mistake him for Troy Miller's brother. The similarities between the two guards are striking.

Both of their fathers are educators and coaches at Northfield, Craig Winegardner being assistant principal and varsity baseball coach. Both have older athletic brothers, Nathan's being a former Norse second-baseman named Jason. Both are multi-sport athletes themselves, Nathan playing infield for his dad's team. Both stand six feet. Both are heady, mature seniors with a curious nature.

And like Troy, Nathan suffered a foot injury that slowed his athletic progress.

The break to his right foot occurred just before the start of his junior year, essentially wiping out the basketball season.

"At the beginning of his junior year," Craig Winegardner says in a voice soft in tone, "we felt he had a chance to play some behind Pick Chay and Randy Keaffaber. But it threw him back. He never really got full use of his foot, I don't think, until baseball season. It really bothered him with his shot, which may be affecting his feelings about this year. He doesn't shoot a whole lot."

When he mentions Nathan not shooting much, Winegardner is not making a negative judgement, only observing his son's play compared to his freshman and sophomore years.

Another observation his parents have made is Nathan's maturing as the basketball season has progressed.

"As a person," Winegardner says, "Nathan enjoys being with this basketball team ... the other fellas. He's happy, whatever role he's given. And I really have grown to like that, because he's helped me in that case. I'm a very competitive coach, and I want the best for my son. Now I understand that he's probably doing the best he can, and he's happy and that's important."

Like the Millers and Hamptons, the Winegardners credit Steve McClure in part for their son's growth as a person.

"I think Steve's association with the Fellowship of Christian Athletes has been real good for all of us, because we're committed Christians. He's kind of stabilized the group here at Northfield, along with John Diener. Nathan has willingly gone to religious retreats."

McClure and the FCA have helped Nathan understand priorities in life and realize "that not everybody can be the hero, not everybody can be the starter, that other jobs are important," Winegardner says. "And he's probably helped his father accept that, too. He's made me understand that he can be happy not being a starter and that he is fulfilled. That's all anybody can ask."

Like his teammates, Nathan does not mention McClure's tough talk and actions at times.

"Being a coach myself, we've kind of agreed that what happens in the locker room stays in the locker room, what happens at home stays at home. Yeah, I can relate to what happens in the locker room. I've lost my head at times, too. Sometimes there's a good purpose, sometimes you're just frustrated, and we don't take anything personally.

Carolyn Winegardner says Nathan is "not easily rumbled.. He's a religious boy, has a deep faith. He's intelligent. He's more laid back than his brother Jason, who was more like his father ... a little more quick tempered. It's very hard to get Nathan upset."

Winegardner's view of Nathan is an extension of his wife's. "He's not as aggressive as I'd like for him to be in a lot of cases. He's an easy-going boy with a good sense of humor, looks for good in other people, listens to his parents, understands what our priorities are, and he seems to want to to please us. I believe that's real important to him.

"I believe he's very good with all types of people. He does not see boundaries or barriers. He accepts everybody. And I like that in him."

Then, perhaps, some of the coach in Craig Winegardner comes out as he continues to size-up his youngest son: "Now, as for work ethic -- this is the other part -- I don't believe he understands that he hasn't tapped himself fully. And I guess that's frustrating to me in comparison to Jason -- a very aggressive, goal-setting individual. But you've got to understand that Jason is a smaller individual who has had to battle to be recognized. He's 5-6."

Winegardner smiles when asked about Nathan's flat-top. "He went through a lot of haircuts, and I don't know who or what inspired him, but he likes it. I think possibly because he doesn't have to worry about it."

Carolyn Winegardner adds: "Nathan went through permanents, too; curly permanents."

And the girls like it, Winegardner smiles. "He gets a lot of attention and a lot of head rubs because of it. He's a teddy bear. He really is."

•••••••••

Six people who score points that never appear in the box score are the student managers. Their points come from the players and coaches, who know that without the managers, the team would have difficulty functioning on and off the court.

Northfield's group is headed by Jeremy Bever, a senior who, like other managers, tried out for the Norse squad but didn't make it. But because they wanted to be part of boys basketball, they took on the unglamorous, but rewarding, role of manager.

Bever is joined by Scott Sweeney, Tony Holmes, Scott Ross, Ryan Stout and Flo Huber, all of whom -- except for seniors Sweeney and Huber -- expect to try out for the team next season.

Bever is McClure's main man, directing and coordinating an assortment of duties, including the videotaping of every game. He's proud of what he and his "team" does.

"Without us," he points out, "there would be no stats, no films to look at, no water containers, no towels, etcetera. The managers do the things that the coach doesn't have to worry about so he can concentrate on the game. He has confidence that things will be done without him telling us."

Bever also acts as the team's "Traveling Secretary/Director of Publicity." On road games, he takes charge of the locker room key, making sure the room is locked and unlocked on time. It's an important duty, ensuring valuables are safe and that sweaty bodies don't wait in cool corridors at the end of the half and the game. After games Bever calls media that haven't staffed the contest, including wire services and broadcasters.

Huber brings an international flavor to the manager corps this year. A foreign exchange student who's staying with David Pefley's family, Huber is a solid 6-3 West German easily recognizable with a thick shock of curly, blond hair. An excellent outside shooter, he tried out for the team and nearly made it. His lack of court presence and experience were factors. When he finishes his year-long stay, he plans to study law or sports medicine in either Munich or Berlin.

One of Scott Ross' main functions is to film the game from high in the bleachers. And while he's not related to Joe and Jon, he takes personal charge of their warmup attire. When the twins get to Notre Dame, however, Scott will be rooting against them on one day a year - - when the Irish battle Indiana University. Scott Ross is a huge IU fan, and the controversial Bob Knight is his hero. "He may be mean," Scott says, "but look at what kind of teams he has. One of my wishes in life is to go fishing with him (Knight's an avid angler) and go to a home game at IU."

The other camera person is Tony Holmes, a stocky, 5-5 youngster who can whoop it up with the best of them after a Northfield victory. His older brother, Rod, was a manager, too, concentrating on statistics.

Scott Sweeney, who helps Bever with organization, is planning on college, majoring in business management. His hero, he says, is Larry Bird, "because he was poor when he was young but with hard work he made something of himself."

Ryan Stout's interests parallel Brad Hampton's. Ryan plans to attend Purdue, major in agribusiness and then work on the family farm. One of his primary responsibilities with the team is taking care of minor injuries. He makes sure medical supplies, including a generous share of athletic tape, are available at all times.

Asked who his hero is, he replies, "Myself. I feel you cannot accomplish your dreams through someone else; you have to do it yourself."

Chapter 9: Ending a Drought

A thin layer of frozen snow covers the main parking lot, vacant now on a bleak Tuesday, December 26, because of the week-long Christmas break. But in a smaller parking area off the gymnasiums, some 15 vehicles sit in the cold, evidence that the players have arrived for a four o'clock practice after having two days off.

In three days, Northfield will face conference foe Manchester to open the Wabash County Tourney. It will be a crucial test for Steve McClure's team.

Before practice begins, the squad sits in a circle at midcourt to hear briefly from senior Bob Bratch.

A solidly built, 6-2 senior, Bratch had reconstructive knee surgery in July, knocking him out of the football season and at least half the basketball campaign. Now he's been cleared to play again by Dr. Steve Ahlfeld, a former Northfield star who played for an NCAA championship team at Indiana University and then became a specialist in orthopedic medicine.

Bratch has not been around the team much since the season began, but now he asks to be part of it. McClure wants to know how the team feels. The team agrees Bratch should return as a manager who will practice with the squad and later, perhaps, be added to the roster.

"Bob was away from the team physically," McClure says during partner drills, "and probably the biggest mistake he made was he got away from the team mentally. He mentioned something to the fact that he sees one of the best basketball programs right at his back door and he's wantin' to be a part of it. So he was lookin' to kind of feel us out as to how we would feel about him comin' back to the team. He did not attend practice, which, you know, is somethin' he should have been doin', and Bob's the first one to admit that."

Among a half-dozen visitors today are Pick Chay and Kevin Leming, who played guard and forward his senior year under McClure.

Pick is red-shirting his freshman year at Taylor University, because his grades weren't up to NAIA standards, which are tougher than the NCAA's. Leming and his wife are back in Wabash County for the Christmas break from Indiana State University, where he's concentrating on track as a pole vaulter.

"The big difference between Steve McClure and Gary Baker (who preceded McClure)," Leming says, "is McClure put fun back in the game of basketball. Baker had this thing that you had to pass the ball at least five times before you could shoot, even if you had practically a lay-up. McClure came in and said basically, 'The object of the game is to put the ball through the hoop.' We played a looser game."

Sitting in a bleacher section under a basket, Leming says off-handedly, "I've heard there are people saying that McClure's trying to play too much half-court offense instead of pushing the ball up the floor more. I couldn't believe some of the stuff I heard."

He's told there will always be critics, whether the coach is Knight, Wooden or Bill Green, Marion's former great mentor, no matter how good his record is.

"Yeah, I guess so," Leming says, keeping his eyes on the floor.

The scrimmage, as usual, is not designed specifically with the next opponent in mind. Instead, McClure works on strengthening various phases of the game -- proven defensive principles, patience on offense, taking better care of the basketball.

Still, McClure does not ignore Manchester completely. He has seen the Squires enough to know some of their players' characteristics. "Like a (Andy) Holderman or a (Tony) Friedan," he says, "they're good enough kids that you can't stop 'em, just limit 'em. And I just tell the kids, imagine his man averaging 30 points and do the job on 'em."

Manchester has had outstanding teams the past few seasons, winning the Columbia City Sectional in the 1987-88 season. The Squires' victory over the Norsemen for last year's county title was Northfield's only regular-season defeat. It was the third straight year Manchester handled Northfield in the tournament.

On Wednesday and Thursday, McClure varies practice little, pounding home the principles he has preached all year on defensive pressure and offensive opportunity. And when Thursday's session concludes, he's happy with what he's seen the last three days, particularly the maturing of Noi Chay.

It is a 10-minute bus ride Friday from Northfield to Wabash High School, this year's tournament host. By the time the Norse arrive at 5:45 for their 6:30 opener against Manchester, the stands are filling fast.

Now, as his team dresses, McClure is asked if there is a revenge factor.

88

"Not really," he replies evenly. "We beat them last time when we played them for the conference title. We've talked about this. I told them it's a big game only because it's the next game, not because it's the Wabash County tournament."

McClure, wearing a white, crew-neck sweater over a dark, plaid dress shirt, is clearly upbeat about his team.

"Earlier in the year," he twangs, "we were practicin' one way Monday through Thursday and then playin', you know, a different game on Friday. But we feel like we're startin' to come together now.

"But who knows, they (Manchester) come out and hit three-pointers like they did last week against Southwood we'll have our hands full. But then again, if we defend that shot and block out, we'll be in great shape, because inside, they don't physically match-up with us."

Thirty minutes to game time, and now McClure has a few final words:

"We're gonna start in 44 (full court man-to-man). Peck, you have Holderman, and *just* guard 'em. And if he hits a *shot*, it won't be the first, won't be the last. He'll try to lull you asleep. He'll try to get you to think, 'Aw, I' m not gonna attack.' Well, you jock-style 'em anyway. And I'd rather see him penetrate than stand out there and line up at three-point range, you understand that. 'Kay?"

He points to Troy Miller. "You have (Doug) Fahrnow, and again, we want him pressured comin' up the floor. Because if he's gonna be their ballhandler, we want his legs nothin' but rubber by the fourth quarter.

"Be the aggressor. You hear this stuff all the time. And you win and you play well when you do that. You just go out there and you play hard, and you play smart, and you don't let the little minor things bother you. You major on majors, not minors."

He turns to Hampton. "Brad, you got Friedan. How does he like to get started offensively?"

"Rebounds," Hampton says softly.

"Rebounds," McClure echoes. "Block 'em off. Get out on 'em tight. He's not real tough when he goes to the hoop with it."

He tells the Rosses to think about Manchester's front-line players as being as good as Eric Montross and Alan Henderson, an outstanding junior at Indianapolis Brebeuf.

"I take it by the tone I see here that you're ready to play some basketball," he says. "I noticed it when we came in on Tuesday. A lot of times, when you're the coach, you're on vacation, you think, Well, I've got to think of a way to make it exciting and stuff. And I knew the moment you guys stepped on the floor you're only takin' a vacation from school, not from basketball."

Then, as he often does, McClure switches suddenly from the mind to mechanics. He mentions the press, a defensive maneuver Northfield's foes have exploited all year. "When they press, what're you gonna do?"

"Attack it," Jon Ross says.

"Attack it," McClure echoes. "We're goin' to our basket. We're not throwin' cross court or behind. We're goin' forward. And then they're gonna have to run their guts down tryin' to stop you. We're goin' to make good decisions, aren't we, Noi? 'kay?"

Noi nods, a smile on his dark baby face.

"We're gonna to put down that landin' gear in the three-pointer, aren't we, Noi?"

Another nod/smile.

"I don't know why I'm thinkin' about Noi, but ... we're gonna to do nothin' but take great shots."

He leads them in prayer: "Father, the biggest victory has been won. We just celebrated that Monday. We need to continuously give you the credit ... "

He reminds them of this year's slogan, "Forward, March!", says, "We *are* marchin' forward." And so, enthusiasm flowing, they pour out of the dressing room and through the opening that leads to the court. But can they stop Holderman?

The Wabash gym can squeeze 3,200 people in, and now about 2,700 whoop it up as the teams take the floor.

Manchester, the home team, gets to choose its bench. McClure gets to select the basket he wants to start with offensively or defensively. Normally, he likes his offense in front of him for the second half. Tonight, though, he wants his defense before him for the last 16 minutes "to see really what's goin' on."

Joe Ross easily controls the tip, a bad pass results in the first Northfield turnover, and Manchester misses two shots from in close. The teams are tight. Then Troy Miller's jump shot at 7:25 and Jon Ross' follow at 6:28 give the Norse an early 4-0 lead.

Holderman, a 6-1 senior guard, is a brilliant shooter, probably the best Northfield will face all year. He draws Peck's first foul as he starts a drive and then soars for a jumper. McClure screams at the official, "He's leanin' in on that!" Holderman, almost perfect from the line, calmly drops in a pair.

Miller, as in some past games, is off to a quick start, getting another hoop for 6-2. Seconds later, Joe blocks Holderman's drive, and the Northfield crowd goes crazy, while the Manchester people yell for a foul call.

With almost six minutes gone, Manchester takes the lead, 11-10, thanks to two steals off the press and Frieden's three-pointer. Northfield calls time out, and McClure is hot: "If you don't attack! ... I want some basketball playin'!"

But Doug Fahrnow gets a "three" and Holderman a field goal, making it 16-10 -- a run of 12 straight points.

It's 18-12, Manchester, as the first quarter ends in a game reminiscent of earlier contests in which the Norse started fast, only to let the opposition catch up and forge ahead.

Two baskets by Northfield to start the second quarter make it a four-point game. But Holderman, as usual, is sizzling. In an eight-second span he bombs a three-pointer and a deuce for a 23-16 Manchester lead with six minutes left.

McClure looks for help outside, shuffling his guards. He's forced into playing zone to protect Jon with two fouls. The result is a struggling defensive effort eased only by some rag-tag play by Manchester.

McClure calls time out again, trying desperately to right his team. He swings his left hand to make a point to Joe Ross. But he makes a rare mistake in identity and unintentionally catches Jon Ross on his sweaty right knee with a stinging slap that leaves an imprint. Jon acts like nothing happened, and it's obvious McClure is not aware of what's occurred as his team leaves the huddle.

As the second quarter dwindles down, Manchester clings to the lead -- five to eights points -- until the brothers Ross get back-to-back baskets in close to make it 29-28 with two minutes to go. Holderman, though, answers with another three from 25 feet out.

Jon gets a free throw at 1:18 to make it 34-31, Manchester, and then the Squires turn it over. McClure calls for one shot. "Goin' 4 with 10 seconds left," he yells to his team in front of him. He wants to set up Hampton along the baseline. But a bad pass snuffs out the opportunity.

McClure is raging mad, by far the angriest he has been all season, as his team piles onto the locker-room benches. He kicks a waste basket, putting a deep dent into it. Then he turns his back on the tense troops and smashes his left hand against a row of lockers.

The man is genuinely incensed.

"What did we practice all week!?" he bellows, and then smashes his right foot into the waste can again, sending it spinning.

"Give me some reasons why you do that?" he screams, referring to basic mistakes.

No answers.

"*Why!?*"

Hearts are thumping.

The coach's voice, now raw, lowers slightly. "You're supposed to win. You have fondled and farted around and you're in the ballgame."

The volume soars again: "How long are you goin' to practice as the great team that you can be and go out here and screw it up on Friday night?"

Silence.

"How long!? I'm gettin' tired of it! How many times has Holderman gone back-door?"

No answer.

Then, almost frantically, "When you gonna guard 'im?" A pause. "I don't hear any answers. Which probably tells me you're a bunch of wieners. God, guys, sickening."

McClure questions their guts: "That's hard on me, that you come out and see somethin' on their shirts and you just lay down and die."

He is talking very rapidly now, as he is wont to do, his mind ahead of his mouth: "That press is a piece of crap. The whole floor is wide open, and not once have you guys broke up and got it. And then you hand it (the ball) to each other, and then you get it, and you say, 'Whoa, slow down, that's Manchester, we're not goin' to throw anything at them.' "

He has not singled out anyone in particular by pointing; "you" is collective.

But then he turns to the Rosses: "You guys aren't goin' to the middle," and they both nod in unison.

He turns to Hampton: "How many rebounds you got, Brad?"

Hampton's mumble is unintelligible.

"Your toe hurtin'?"

"No."

"By God, start playin' some basketball," he responds, looking directly at Hampton now. "You got Holderman the second half."

Hampton nods shyly, like a wounded puppy.

"How many's he got?"

"Twenty-two," Steve Desper replies.

"Yeah," McClure says, mockingly. "Gonna let 'im have 40 or 50? Get on his butt. He's gonna lean into you. Let 'im shoot one of those things where he's fallin' down. How many times have you guys come up to help when Andy drives? No, you just stand back there and don't contest. Whew! It just makes me sick."

He pounds the wall. "*God!*" he exclaims, almost under his breath.

Then: "When - are - you- ever - *gonnagetmentallytough*!?"

There are teams that want to win the county tournament, "but not you," he says. "Oh, yeah, you say, 'We want to.' I looked at you on the floor in practice and believed that you want to do. But then you left a yellow streak out on the floor. You let J. P. Pitts, (Chad) Lauer, and those guys literally kick your butts. You let one guy get two-thirds of their points. ..."

"We're goin' man ... and we're goin' 32" -- a 2-1-2 zone three-quarters of the court on a score.

McClure asks Jeremy Bever how much time is left, is told five minutes.

"When you get back on defense, you go 2 (a 2-1-2 match-up zone) until Brad gets Holderman," he resumes, voice even. Then, that raw shout: "Just like we practiced! And then you do it in the game!"

He pauses briefly, wipes his brow. It has been his longest halftime talk, but he hasn't lost anyone's attention one whit.

"It's *time* we started doin' things in a game the way we do in practice. You guys are forcin' it in there when you got people draped all over you. We go to the point, we go to the other side. How many times have you done that? We did it against North Miami. That's a game. But, see, it says North Miami, doesn't say Manchester, so you figure you can't do it."

The frenzy enters his voice again: "You can do anything you want to these guys. You can name the score."

Another pause, then: "I'm not goin' to watch very long this sickening bull crap out there. You don't get the job done, you're goin' down." He points to Scott Kunkel and David Pefley, says, "You got a quarter and you got a quarter and you watch, buddy, you're in if we don't get people to get with it, because I'm not goin' to sit here and watch our ballclub play half as good as you are."

There is little time to loosen up for the second half as the team files out of the locker room. It probably doesn't matter.

The third quarter opens with Joe getting a free throw 17 seconds in. And the Norse get even again at 36 with 5:54 remaining on Joe's bunny.

Peck gets four quick points on a steal and short jumper, giving Northfield its first lead since early in the opening quarter. But Holderman breaks the string of seven straight points with a trey.

Northfield surges to 46-39 on Hampton's rebound basket and Jon's follow. And now, at 3:14, the Norse are playing tough man-to-man defense in front of their bench -- as McClure had planned and hoped.

But Manchester won't fold. John Bazzoni hits from underneath and draws Jon's third foul. It's 48-46, Northfield, as he goes to the line for a possible three-point play, but he misses.

Jon is fouled clearing a defensive rebound and calmly drops in both free throws, but Holderman comes right back with another trey at 1:24. It's 50-49, Northfield, and as they like to say in Indiana, this one's a real barn-burner.

Noi immediately answers Holderman with a drive, and seconds later, he's off again, beating the third-quarter buzzer with another drive off a steal. So at the end of three it's 54-49.

"Make them work," McClure tells his team. "Run Boiler (offensive entries into the corners)."

Noi starts the fourth quarter where he left off, getting a short jumper. Then it's Hampton's turn to make a steal and drive for the hoop. He's hammered as he goes up, hits the deck hard -- as he has done so many times this still-early season. He hits one free throw for a 57-46 Northfield lead.

Holderman responds with a "three."

But Northfield's lead goes to double-digits again at 59-49 on Joe's tip at 6:15.

With just under six minutes remaining, Manchester Coach Pete Smith pulls Holderman, who has three fouls, and brings in Kent Kerschner. The youngster responds almost immediately with an uncontested three-pointer. 59-52, Northfield.

McClure calls time. "That's three stupid errors in a row," he says. "What are you tryin' to do, just give it to 'em?"

At 4:46, Jon gets his fourth foul on a charging call, negating a basket. McClure is livid at the call. Manchester can't convert, though, and Joe clears. But his outlet pass sails out of bounds when Hampton fails to look up as he lopes along the left sideline, across from the Northfield bench.

Holderman's back for the final 4 minutes and 21 seconds -- and everybody in the place is thinking the same thing: Northfield's seven-point margin is far from safe with Andy around.

Peck gives Northfield some momentum with two free throws at 3:46 for a 61-52 advantage, and Holderman finally misses one of his bombs.

Inside of three minutes now, and Joe scores in close for an 11-point Norse lead. Still, there's Holderman.

Northfield maintains the margin, and with 2:18 left, Holderman picks up his fourth foul. Pecks hits the front-end, misses the second.

It is Jon who fouls out, though, at 1:38 on another questionable blocking call. But by now, the issue is settled.

Hampton's drive at 1:07 makes it 70-57, and 30 seconds later, McClure clears his bench.

The final is 70-60, and Northfield has finally beaten Manchester in the Wabash County Holiday Tournament.

As he leaves the floor, Smith is asked what the difference was in the second half.

"I thought the officiating was terrible," he says without hesitation.

Both ways?

"No."

Against you?

"Yeah."

Later, in the locker room, he elaborates: "The officials were pathetic. They didn't beat us, but it sure didn't help us. We couldn't get the body fouls called against them. For us to beat Northfield, the body fouls have to be called."

Smith is partially right. It has been the worst officiated game Northfield's been in all year -- but one-sided, no.

More accurately, the big difference in the second half was McClure going man-to-man, reducing Holderman's effectiveness, which is considerable against a zone.

And, too, the Rosses had another big night, Jon getting 30 points on 13 of 21 shooting and collecting 17 rebounds. Joe contributed

12 points on six of seven shots while adding six rebounds. Their effort offset Holderman's game-high 34 on nine of 22 field goal attempts and 11 free throws in 12 tries.

In the locker room, a much calmer McClure tells his team that while Manchester played close to its potential, Northfield didn't. His voice is almost gone, and someone asks, "What happened to your voice?" He responds with a hint of sarcasm, "You gotta keep screwin' up is what happened to it."

Head down, he says, "I can't do this stuff, I can't lose religion like that. I got to go sit by Ryan (Dubois) in the church on Sunday. He knows some of the things I'm sayin', and I'm definitely human, so guys ... from now on, jack it up a little bit."

He tells them that they need to get their level of thinking up before their level of play will go up. In essence, they need to think about competing against the top teams in the state -- Bedford North Lawrence, Pike, Concord, Lawrence North, Marion, Gary Roosevelt -- not the Manchesters, as good as the Manchesters are.

"You know," he says, "you can screw up and beat good teams like Manchester, Whitko, Wellston. You can do that, but guys, why don't we just turn it loose?"

Jon asks to speak. "I think coach is right when he says we're nervous. We need to use that nervousness, that excitement, that gosh kind of stuff in positive ways. I can think of one example -- the press. I think when we get the ball we pass it three feet when we could pass it half-court."

McClure interjects, saying: "You need a little Oklahoma in you," referring to the race-horse brand of basketball played at Oklahoma University. "Right? Really. Guys, I appreciate very dearly what you're tryin' to do, the way we teach it, move here, move there. But you got to try some unusual things."

In his prayer, McClure says, "Father, control my language and my actions. ... I love you, Father, and I love these guys."

Managers Sweeney and Huber have brought the food for this "away" game, and as the players finish dressing, they dig into the goodies.

They will go out to see the night's second game, Southwood against Wabash, and find out who their opponent will be in tomorrow night's championship.

The Wabash Apaches have been down for several years, but already in 1989 they have won more games -- three -- than they did all last season. The team's new coach is Ray Sims, who has come over from Marion after coaching there as an assistant for six years, including five with Bill Green. Sims is getting high marks for creating a team concept.

The Southwood Knights' program has been only slightly better than Wabash's in recent years. Southwood has always been a football school, as indicated by the Knights' success again this year in advancing to the state semi-finals. Basketball has not received the school-community support football has, long-time observers agree.

Monte Moffett, who, ironically, was Steve Desper's assistant when Northfield last won the county tournament in '79, took over the Southwood program two seasons back. Moffett, who also teaches history, government and related subjects, went 9-12 his first year and 8-14 his second.

And so Southwood is a slight favorite to face Northfield for the championship. But Wabash ekes out a 66-64 victory that doesn't overjoy Sims. "To be honest," he says, "I'm very upset with the way we played tonight, very ragged at times. We stunk up the gym."

Now, 24 hours later, Sims must contend with the Rosses, but he notes that they have a fine supporting cast. He says he'll try different things and stick with whatever works -- if anything. One thing is for sure: the ball will be in Donny Blair's hands a lot. A senior guard who stands 6-3, Blair is an excellent perimeter shooter and can be tough on the boards.

McClure begins his pregame remarks at the blackboard, diagraming offensive maneuvers. He wants his team to look for the "11-Man Drill," which means push the fast break.

"And let's go for as long as we can without turning the ball over," he adds. "Doesn't that sound familiar? Have we practiced for this at any time this year?" And he answers himself: "*All the time.*"

He wants to push the ball -- get the rebound, make the outlet pass and go. And if that's not there, "Let me diagram Boiler. Seems to me you forgot it overnight." Patterned after Purdue's offense, Boiler is designed to spring people for good outside shots.

McClure has been low-key on the mental aspects until now. But then: "They're gonna come out, they're gonna get all over you, they're gonna be excited, they're gonna be emotional, they're gonna really be gettin' after us. Just be prepared."

He points out that "there's a championship for takin' tonight. It's yours to take or to give. But there's no question about it, you'll have to give it to 'em."

Hampton will guard Blair. "Blair gets over here," McClure says, pointing to the corner, "keep 'im there. Don't put 'im at the free throw line; good free throw shooter."

He concludes: "You make 'em shoot long field goals. You make 'em play some defense. You make 'em run the floor. You make 'em do what you are capable of doing. They *can't* do it. They don't have the God-given ability to do what you can do."

It's another near-capacity crowd -- more adults than students -- as the players warm-up. Sims, at 6-3, towers over McClure as they make "coach talk" in front of the Northfield bench. Lisa McClure walks by, and she and Steve exchange "Fives," say nothing.

In the huddle before the tipoff, McClure says, "We're goin' 44" -- man-to-man pressure early.

Troy Miller pops a three-pointer and Brad Hampton follows with a jumper of his own, so it's 5-0 in 35 seconds. Another fast Northfield start.

A basket by Gary Cooper gets Wabash on the board, but Northfield responds with a run of eight points for a 13-2 margin after four minutes.

Wabash claws back to 17-9, and McClure goes to Nathan Winegardner and Noi in the back court at 2:18.

Then that old bugaboo -- fouling -- catches up with Joe Ross; he gets his third with a minute and 29 seconds left in the quarter. But McClure stays with him, and 28 seconds later Joe gets loose for a monstrous dunk and is fouled by Nils Dekau. It is Dekau's third, which puts a crimp in Wabash's rebounding and defense.

Jon Ross closes the first quarter with a drive from the left side to make it 28-16.

Following McClure's pregame instructions -- "Just build minute to minute, quarter to quarter" -- Northfield increases its lead to 38-22 at 3:24 of the second quarter. Hampton, still playing with a small sore on the right foot, is the key man tonight.

At 2:29, Miller hits a short jumper to make it 42-25, but Jon is called for his third foul. Blair offsets Miller's bucket with two free throws, cutting Northfield's lead to 15. And there's a feeling in the air that Wabash is far from dead.

McClure stays with the twins. His thinking: since they got themselves in foul trouble, they have to learn to play in foul trouble.

The 15-point margin holds until the half, 44-29, but the Wabash fans feel that the Apaches are in the game. The two big guys have three each, and the officials seem to be calling them close tonight.

In stark contrast to the previous night, McClure is all chalk talk at the half. No harangue is needed; waste baskets are safe.

"Wherever Blair is, you three guys on the perimeter, you get on him, man to man. He likes that left side, so whoever's wing is over here, step in that passing lane. He goes back-door, you go with him. (J. D.) Hamilton can shoot the three. (Chad) Daugherty has done what? 'Kay, he hit one. You gotta stop Cooper, you gotta keep Dekau off the boards. You're givin' up too many points."

Offensively, he wants better shots, which, he says, will come with more patience. "Step out, rotate, get some movement, and they cannot guard you. Be patient, guys!"

Only 10 seconds tick off the clock in the third quarter before Joe is called for his fourth foul. McClure sits tight.

The 15-point halftime advantage bulges to 22, 51-29, as Miller hits a trey and Hampton follows with a dunk at 6:27. It's beginning to look like Northfield will finally win another county tourney.

At 4:01, Northfield holds a 58-37 lead when trouble occurs off court. A Northfield fan in a row of seats reserved for the media and tournament organizers has heckled Sims and the officials all night. Now Sims wants him removed, and as play continues, a cluster of police officers gathers at the scorer's table. Finally, an official calls for a timeout.

The officers and school officials want to eject the fan, but he won't budge, insisting he is not the guilty party. Sims persists. "Play ball, play ball, play ball," the Northfield cheering section chants. Wabash Principal Steve Eikenberry, accompanied by five law enforcement officers, asks the fan to come with him. Twice he starts to obey, but each time, Northfield rooters urge him to stay. Nine minutes later, a compromise of sorts is reached: the fan will change seats.

Play resumes, and 31 seconds later, Joe is gone, to the great joy of the Wabash cheering section. Northfield fans simultaneously boo the officials and give Joe a thunderous ovation.

Joe's departure seems to give Wabash a lift. The Apaches cling to life at 59-41. But Dekau picks up his fourth foul, rapping Jon underneath, and draws a technical when he complains. Hampton misses both technicals, and Jon gets only one of two on the personal, so it's 61-43 with just under two minutes remaining in the third.

Wabash won't quit. At 1:34, Jon gets his fourth foul, and Cooper converts to make it 63-46. More than a quarter remains; McClure sits tight.

As the clock winds down, McClure calls for working the ball inside, but Peck unloads from three-point range and misses. He's pulled immediately and gets an earful from McClure. But he goes right back in, replacing Jon, as McClure figures the "lesson" on fouling has taken hold by now.

Strong outside shooting by Wabash cuts the margin to 14, 63-49, at the end of three quarters. In the huddle, McClure says, "We do not shoot anything but uncontested lay-ups."

Northfield hasn't "sat" on the ball all year, but now, with a quarter to go, McClure spreads the floor.

Wabash, desperate for the ball, fouls Peck at 7:03, and he calmly hits both free throws. Seconds later, Peck makes a steal, races for the basket and feeds brother Noi with a clever pass. The youngster scores. The house goes wild. It's 67-53.

The Apaches won't die, as Blair hits from the outside and Cooper scores in close. It's down to 67-57 with 5 minutes and 22 seconds remaining.

The Norse have been following McClure's instructions perfectly, looking only for lay-ups and making foul shots.

At 4:30, McClure sends Jon back in as Blair picks up his third foul. Peck's two free throws make it 69-57. And a minute later, Jon's slam increases the margin to 14 again, 73-59.

Blair counters with a trey for 73-62. But Peck hits two more free throws and Hampton scores from underneath to make it 77-62.

Blair responds immediately with another "three" from 30 feet out for 77-65. It's Wabash's last gasp.

With 43 seconds left, Sims and McClure stroll toward each other. They hug at half court; a friendship seems to have been initiated.

The final is 88-67, Northfield hitting free throw after free throw down the stretch. The first concrete goal of the season -- winning the Wabash County Tournament -- has been reached.

The Rosses have played about five and a half quarters between them. Despite limited action, Joe gets 11 points and 10 rebounds, while Jon pitches in with 14 points and six rebounds. Hampton has been the big gun, getting 22 points on 10 of 14 shooting. Wabash's Blair and Cooper have also scored 22 each.

As Sims starts to leave the court, the parent of a Wabash alumnus says, "That's the first time I've seen a Wabash team not quit in a long time."

Sims flashes a smile, says: "It's a credit to our team that they held the ball on us with about five minutes to go, and we were playing well at the time. Northfield's a good team. It's very hard with two 6-10 guys. One you can handle, but two, it's kind of difficult. But I'm very proud of our guys. I've always told our guys, win or lose, I just want to be proud of our guys. They played their guts out and I'm very satisfied."

As the Northfield players start to cut down the nets, McClure watches from midcourt. "We had a lot of foul trouble -- again -- and I'm gettin' tired of it," he says. "But we learned some things. And Joe went out in the third quarter, and that's kinda embarrassing. So with Jon with his four late in the third quarter, we decided that being up about 12, 15 points -- and as long as we were 10 ahead -- we were going to make them come out and play some defense, 'cause they packed it all night. And we were able to buy four or five minutes with Jon on the bench, which I think was a big key. And, see, we had four guards with Brad Hampton, who can be a guard, so I think that strategy really worked well."

On the radio, Bill Rogge reminds McClure of all he's accomplished in a little more than three years, including two Sectionals and now a county tourney, and asks, "What's next for Steve McClure?"

"Plenty, but right now, we got Rochester comin' up next."

A guy who likes to talk, McClure goes beyond the question: "We're like a big, souped up race car -- in gear and the throttle half-way down -- but the clutch is slippin'. I'm just tryin' to encourage them to hold that throttle to the floor and pop that clutch and let that baby squeal tires, and let's gun this machine down the stretch."

In the locker room, Hampton is asked about his toe. "It was better tonight," he says, flashing his usual happy grin from underneath his goggles. "Must have been Mr. Christie's special salve." Harold Christie, standing nearby, flashes a grin of his own.

As Hampton peels his uniform off, he says, "They were sayin' some things out there."

Four-letter words?

"Yeah, one that starts with 'Mother'. They tried to taunt us. They said, 'You guys are ranked number 17 and you're runnin' away from us (with the spread).' " Hampton smiles. "I just said, 'Look at the scoreboard.' "

As the players chow down on food brought by Jeremy Bever, McClure finally enters the room.

There will be no post-game talk tonight, only a few details.

Practice will resume four days hence, January 2, with a renewal of the quest to reach the top of the ladder.

Chapter 10: Little Loyal Lisa

Lisa McClure stands all of 5-2 and weighs 110 pounds. But it's best not to mess with her.

When she hears negative comments about her husband, her eyes narrow behind her glasses and her scowl hits you in the face like a chest pass in from three feet.

She had not heard the creeping criticism of Steve until the Saturday morning after Northfield won the county tournament. A friend referred to the "heat," assuming she knew about it.

"I had not heard a thing, and that gets me, that upsets me," she says. "How can people be so nearsighted that they can't see everything he's done for this team, not only in basketball but ...?"

She sits in the wing chair in the McClure living room on a gray afternoon three days before Northfield will start the second half of the season at 9-1. Her words spew out when describing the year thus far.

Yes, she admits, the season's been different because of the high expectations. But no, she's not feeling extra pressure.

She takes note of something more personal: the difference this season is that it's the last one for Steve's first group of players.

"You get to know these kids really well," she points out with a hint of sadness. "And it gets harder to see them go the longer you know them. Randy Keaffaber was the first boy Steve had for three years, through all of varsity."

Lisa has known some of the players longer than Steve. As a substitute teacher for more than 10 years, she had them in junior high classes, including Joe and Jon Ross. "They probably don't remember me," she smiles. "But I remember them. One of them belched in class one day and I let him know that we didn't do that sort of thing."

Then, too, for the last three years, the kids have spent much time at the McClure home, drinking Cokes and eating snacks while watching film and talking basketball.

So when Lisa says, "They're just like my own kids," her ire at the team's detractors is not only in defense of Steve, but also her extended family.

She leans back in the chair, as if relaxed, but anger is boiling in her.

"They wait 'til you're a winner, and then, by golly, they're gonna jump on you," she says of the "knockers."

103

Loyalty carries great importance with her. "I don't care if he did a crummy job, I'd still be mad" about attacks on Steve and the team, she seethes.

Perhaps she really is responding to more pressure this year, it's suggested.

"No, I don't feel any more pressure," she reiterates, calming a bit. "But I just get a little ticked off when I hear someone that says, 'Boy, so and so wasn't very happy about taking out so and so.' And I think, Well, what does he (so and so) know about it anyway?

"Let Steve do the job, you know. Why does someone have to second-guess everything Steve does? How many jobs has *he* had? How many teams has he had? Does he have the record like Steve?

"I shouldn't even let it bother me, but that's my make-up."

She has a temper?

"Yes, I do, and it's getting worse," she says without hesitation.

She admits that she was a small, fiery little girl while growing up.

And there was a Midwest, farm toughness about her, propelled by a strong sense of the work ethic. Shoveling manure at an early age was -- still is -- no big deal.

"We just worked a lot," she says of her early years. "And I don't want to get into the old syndrome here, poor little girl. But we didn't take any vacations, except I remember once during elementary school we went up to Ford's museum (in Greenfield, Michigan). And then, when I was a freshman in high school, we went out to Colorado to see my sister. That was it. Never went swimming, never did anything like that. I was just on the farm. But I like the farm."

She says she inherited her temper, in part, from her father, Merle, who still farms 300 acres.

Even with her fiery nature, however, she behaved herself better in previous seasons. "In the last four years," she says with a touch of a smile, "I've noticed that I've gotten a lot more outspoken; lots more. I feel like sometimes I make a fool of myself during a game. And I can't stop myself."

Yelling at officials?

"Yeah. Yeah."

Isn't that natural for many coaches' wives?

"Yeah, but, you know, when your parents say, 'Oh, would you shut up' ..."

It's gotten to the point where Merle and Bette Ann Custer don't want to sit with the youngest of their three daughters.

"That's why I'm always sittin' on the front row, so I don't yell in anyone's ear," Lisa says with a grin. "Because I try as hard as I can, but it just slips out. I really do try."

After the game she is disappointed in herself. "I think, Why couldn't I hold some of that in?"

She and a friend, Becky Mast (husband John coaches the Northfield seventh graders) perhaps egg each other on, she confides. "I hope not. I hope I'm more of an adult. But I just kind of revert to childishness during the game. You know, Steve wants to yell at appropriate times and he can't. So I feel like, nah, I'll do it for ya, Steve."

She's always upset when she feels the officiating hurts Northfield. "If I can see something so apparent, why can't those refs down there?" she asks. "And I feel like, Oh, gosh, Lisa, you're always on the refs. But I really feel like I have a reason to be."

And yet, she notices the disrespect that other fans and players show to the officials, which reminds her to catch herself "before I embarrass not only myself, my husband, the team and the school. I feel a great loyalty to Northfield, because I went there. I only want to be a class act. And I want others from other schools to do the same."

Meanwhile, her father has mellowed, she says.

"He's really enjoying this," she says of the current season. "What's funny, though, he doesn't show much emotion during the game. He does not yell or anything. Very seldom do I hear him, which I think is kind of ironic."

But while she's noticed a change in her father, she hasn't noticed anything different about Steve. He is the same guy this season, she says. His demeanor, philosophy, goals, thinking -- they're consistent with what they have been in the past. "He's always wanted to win, but he's always been able to keep things in perspective."

One thing she misses this season is the contact with colleges interested in Joe and Jon Ross. "We don't have the coaches going after the twins and getting all the calls all the time," she says. "We miss the recruiting.

"I mean, it was just crazy here. But you kinda liked the craziness, 'cause all these men that you've heard about and seen on TV, they call you, and you've got meatloaf on and the peas are cooking, and the guy says, 'Hi, I'm Lou Henson,' and I want to say, 'Yeah, sure, Lou, whaddaya want?' And at that time I can't even think of who Lou Henson (the Illinois coach) is, and then it dawns on you that, you know, gosh, this happens really once in a lifetime.

"It was fun. That's a lot of attention you're getting. Anybody likes attention."

Including Steve McClure, and he's getting it.

"You know, a lot of things could open because of this, the further we can go," she says. "He's more marketable."

Moving would be hard for her, but not for him, she says.

The McClures' future, however, doesn't revolve around just Steve. She's a bigger part of the equation now that the three children are in school.

Whereas once she wasn't overly enthusiastic about teaching, now she's excited to do what she's trained for. She has her resume out at more than one school corporation in the area. Although it seems natural for her to become part of the Metropolitan system -- and she'd like to -- she doesn't feel a powerful need to be a part of it.

Would she accept an offer to teach at Northfield's main basketball rival, Manchester?

"You bet," she says without hesitation and a nod.

Her earlier coolness toward teaching was caused by too many things going on in her life, she says -- her mother's illness, her marriage's bumpy start, Brady's birth.

"I know I'm a good teacher," she says. "I want a full-time position. I'm ready to go somewhere and do the job."

One gets the feeling that her husband's success has inspired her, has rekindled the desire she had many years ago as a Purdue student.

••••••••••

Lisa McClure hopes that some day her husband will coach their three children.

Brady, 12, and Cody, nine, are look-alikes with their burr haircuts. Understandably, they eat and sleep basketball.

Talk about "gym rats." The Northfield gymnasiums are like second homes to the youngsters. "Our family kind of lives here during the winter," Steve McClure says. "While I'm working with the team, the boys are shootin' around and Lisa jogs on the track with Katy."

Lisa wants Steve to be the only coach the youngsters have, including Katy, who is seven years old.

Lisa knows, of course, that he can't coach the girls team at the same time he's coaching the boys.

"He's talked about quitting and then coaching Katy," Lisa says. "Yes, he really has."

That's a few years down the road, she acknowledges, but will be here " 'fore you know it."

Katy's interest in the game isn't as great as the boys', Lisa says, but she likes it along with other things. "She plays ball with the boys all the time. She likes anything that's active."

Steve, of course, is already coaching his sons on shooting and passing techniques.

When the youngsters get home from Sharp Creek Elementary, which is just a few basketball courts away from the McClure residence, they hop in the car and Lisa drops them off at the gyms.

"We're a basketball family," Lisa says matter-of-factly. "It's as simple as that."

It wasn't always that simple, though. In the mid to late '70s the McClures were far from being a basketball family. They were a family struggling for an identity. Lisa had farming in mind; Steve had coaching in mind.

After the early marital trouble, Steve decided he could be content as a track coach and/or assistant junior high football coach, just so he could keep working with young people.

But as the McClure youngsters grew, and grew fond of gyms, Lisa realized that the entire family could support Steve. She became the catalyst that got him thinking again about seeking out one of the most coveted sports roles in the Hoosier state: Boys Varsity Basketball Coach.

She smiles when reminded about watching a Northfield-Wabash game she and Steve saw while he was still at Oak Hill and looking for a change.

It was a sloppy contest, and Steve was coaching in his mind: what would work for this team, for that team, what he'd say to the players, how he might use the atmosphere psychologically. He could visualize himself on one of the benches.

Lisa was thinking too -- *knew* that Steve *belonged* on one of the benches. And so she gave him a sharp elbow to the ribs, causing such pain that he thought for a moment she had broken three.

"You know you could do wonders for those kids and help them become better

people and better players," she said almost as a dare.

So McClure applied for the North Miami and Wabash jobs when they came open. Although he lost out both times, at least now he knew something vitally important: his wife was ready, willing and able to support him as a head basketball coach.

When the Northfield job opened a year later, there was little, loyal Lisa, telling her husband, "Go for it!"

In maturing, Lisa realized that where Steve belonged -- in coaching -- is where their family would truly take root.

Chapter 11: Happy New Year

It is a "thawing" Wednesday, January 3, 1990, and Steve McClure's troops have returned to basketball practice "brain dead" after the Christmas break.

"Physically," he says with a smile, "they're here, but mentally, that's another story. You can tell they've been back in classes after a break."

The team actually returned on Tuesday for a two-hour practice that began with McClure doing what he excels in: communicating.

They need to set their sights on where they want to go, not where they've been, he told them. And, he pointed out, they've truly been someplace. They have already played four conference games and won three, which means they can aim for another Three Rivers Conference crown.

"We've been through all the hype now," he noted. "Now it's time to understand that success is when opportunity and preparedness come together. The successful tournament team will turn it on now, not wait until right before the tournament."

He reminded them that they have a unique opportunity: for the first time in the school's history, Northfield has a chance to be "a big winner in the tourney" -- meaning the Norse can go beyond not only the Sectional, but the Regional and who knows where.

Now, on this soggy Wednesday, McClure continues to work on basics, and despite the team being lethargic mentally, he's not unhappy. "They've just won the county tournament and had Christmas break and now they're back in class, so you've got to consider all of these things," he says during a "rinse."

On Thursday, their minds are more in tune with basketball as they stroll into the gym to the music from *Top Gun*, McClure's all-time favorite movie. For the last few weeks, he has played music during warm-up drills the day before a game.

"I feel it loosens 'em up," he says over the din of bouncing balls and blasting brass. "And it has. They enjoy it."

Shortly before the warm-up drills, McClure got good news from Joe Ross, who gave him, literally, "thumb's up" after visiting Dr. Ahlfeld in Indianapolis. Joe has been experiencing arch problems in both feet, particularly the right one. Dr. Ahlfeld has told him he will feel some soreness, but he can play. He's been fitted with temporary insoles for additional arch support while permanent ones, made from molds of his feet, are constructed.

"I think Joe may still be growin'," McClure says of the 6-10 twin. "His legs don't have the muscle definition yet of a mature young man."

In his scrimmage today, McClure stresses patience. He wants them to take an extra 10 seconds to find the good shot. "What it also means, guys, is you have to play less defense. And the almighty zebras have less chance to call a foul on you."

Zebras refer to referees, of course, not Friday night's opponent, the visiting Rochester High School Zebras.

But while McClure pushes patience, he wants the fast break first. After putting the squad through a running drill, he mutters, "Now, if they'll do that in a game, we're dangerous."

In recent games, he has stressed "run early," which does not mean looking for the fast break from the outset. It means moving into an offensive scheme quickly before the opponent's defense gets set. "If our offense can be organized before their defense," he explains, "this reduces the chances of gimmick defenses against Joe and Jon getting set up. By now, after eight games, we should be executin' this pretty well."

By now, too, McClure's squad should have a clear idea of what he's after offensively: 1) Look for the fast break first, with Joe and Jon clearing the boards and making the quick outlet pass; 2) If the fast break doesn't work, run early; 3) If the defense has organized quickly and "early" won't work, take an extra 10 seconds, have patience and look for the good shot.

"Good rebound, Bob," McClure shouts out at Bratch, now practicing with the team, although still considered a manager. Under IHSAA rules, Bratch must get in 10 practice days before he's eligible.

McClure concludes practice with a defensive drill that stresses moving quickly in a match-up zone. He becomes the sixth offensive player, stationing himself in a corner, creating an arc of four players outside and two players inside against his starting five.

McClure is shouting instructions almost non-stop as the ball moves -- and he's shooting from the corner. He hits two of five long jumpers and then moves to the point in the six-man formation. Bratch and Allen Strait are the inside players, and they get a taste -- unpleasant -- of what it's like for an opponent to face Joe and Jon.

"Ten-Sixty," McClure yells.

He has told them that if they hold the ball an extra 10 seconds and look for the high percentage shot, they will shoot 60 percent.

Shortly before five o'clock, he gathers them under the hoop for a few words. He ends by saying, "We need to come out tomorrow and play as a great team."

They have heard that before, more than once. But the look in their eyes indicates that's it's something new. And one wonders if their looks say one thing, their minds another: namely that they don't need to play as a great team tomorrow at home against Rochester. The Zebras have lost seven straight after opening the season with two wins. If Northfield plays well, it should win with little trouble.

The music of Aerosmith fills the locker room as the Norse dress for Rochester.

"Those rockers still around?," Nathan Winegardner is asked.

"They've made a comeback," he says with a smile while lacing up his right shoe.

Comebacks. The pattern much of this season has seen Northfield jumping to an early lead, frittering it away and then coming back to win.

On the blackboard McClure has written:

Play Like
A
Champion Today

His brief pregame remarks begin with a reminder about 10-60 on offense. Defensively, he says simply, "Make everything work."

They pray, and then McClure says, "I'm not sayin' another thing 'cause I know you guys are ready to go."

It's another near-capacity crowd as Northfield band director Ross Trump puts his kids through "Sweet Georgia Brown." Never mind that the Globetrotters aren't around, Indiana high school basketball will do just fine.

As usual, the Norse start quickly, Brad Hampton and Troy Miller hitting jumpers in less than a minute for a 4-0 lead. Rochester counters, though, with five straight points, and in the first 2 minutes and 31 seconds, Northfield makes four turnovers.

"Early," McClure yells.

111

Rochester's top player, 6-7 Tim Corn, has been stationed at guard by Coach Bill Titus. He figures his big kid, who can hit from outside, will fare better there instead of having to duel the Rosses. But that strategy goes awry when Corn picks up his second foul at 1:59 of the quarter.

The first eight minutes end with the Norse holding a 20-16 lead. They are playing well, despite the early turnovers, running the fast break better and moving into defensive schemes quickly. But something's missing.

Still, Winegardner's free throw at 5:35 of the second quarter gives Northfield its first double-digit lead, 30-20, and one senses that while there's lots of basketball to play, Northfield has this one in hand.

At the half, it's 44-29, Peck Chay closing out the first 16 minutes with two free throws.

Walking to the locker room, McClure says, "There's not much intensity on defense, but we're doin' better on offense. We're runnin' better."

There's a distinct calmness in the locker room, a lack of the frenzy that has permeated the atmosphere of earlier games. Low-keyed, relaxed, McClure tells his team, "Let's go ahead and play an up-tempo game. Jack up the defensive intensity."

Northfield, which has played a decent first half and is ahead comfortably as expected, plays better -- almost great -- to start the second half.

By 4:46 of the third, the margin has ballooned to 20 points on Winegardner's Sam Jones-type jumper off the glass.

McClure is still coaching with fervor, though, telling his players that they are allowing too much penetration on defense. And, "Early! Early! Move!"

Jon Ross is playing his usual all-around game. At one point, he demonstrates his outside ability, hitting two straight 12-foot jump shots from the side in less than 20 seconds. Brother Joe is a horse on the boards, as usual; if his feet are hurting him, nobody can tell. And the two big kids are staying out of foul trouble.

After three quarters, Northfield has its biggest lead at 70-41. The final highlight of the evening occurs at 6:35 in the fourth quarter: Jon Ross scores his 1,000th career point.

The public address announcer informs the crowd, which applauds wildly but is probably surprised, because even the most rabid boosters don't keep track of such things. The most surprised guy in the gym, though, appears to be Jon.

The final is 86-60. Jon finishes with 27 points and 11 rebounds, while Joe is good for 14 and nine boards. Hampton and Troy Miller have contributed 15 and 13 in a balanced Norse attack.

As Bill Titus heads for Rochester's locker room, he's asked who's the best ballplayer he's seen in his team's first ten games.

"The two Rosses. There's no question about it," he responds immediately. "They play great at both ends of the floor. Steve McClure can't ask anything more out of those two kids."

Are they better than last year?

"They're much improved. You can tell they put in a great deal of time this summer playing the game. That's what I tell my kids -- that's where they improve their skills, playing in the summer."

Before going into the locker room, McClure says, "We got a little fatigued tonight. Right at the end of the half. Our conditioning showed. But, you know, it's a long season, and we gave 'em some time off during Christmas."

In the locker room, he tells his squad: "Get used to poundin' people like that. We need to have a bunch (of games like that). We should be steamrollin' some people."

Then, before sending them to the showers: "Bring on them Squires; we're gonna kick their butts." He's referring to the Three Rivers Conference clash in eight days at Manchester, where Andy Holderman and Co. are anxious for the return match.

Normally, the schedule calls for games on Friday and Saturday, or just Friday. Next weekend will be different. Northfield will be idle on Friday and travel to Manchester on Saturday.

Will the slight schedule change be a factor?, McClure is asked as his team showers.

"Yeah, it's a little unusual, practicin' on Friday and playin' on Saturday," he says matter-of-factly. "But, you know, if we get to the Regional, that's the way it's scheduled (Saturday games only), so you just have to look at the positive side. I tell the kids to take an unusual situation and make somethin' unusually good out of it."

On Monday, January 8, McClure has a surprise before practice for Ryan Dubois, Troy Baer and Scott Kunkel, the three junior varsity players listed on the varsity roster.

He's wants their varsity uniforms.

They have not commited a major wrong on or off the court. McClure simply wants to send a message: he's not that pleased with them and he might use three other junior varsity players as reserves against Manchester.

Kunkel, self-effacing kid that he is, goes to McClure with uniform in hand and says politely, "What do you want me to do with this, Coach?"

"Earn it," McClure replies.

When practice ends on Monday, Steve Desper tells McClure, "Kunkel had one of his best practices of the year."

It's surprising that Kunkel has been relieved -- at least temporarily -- of his varsity jersey. Is this part of McClure's mind games?

"No, not really, and, really, I'll tell you, Kunkel's been playin' good all season. But, see, Baer and Dubois have been a little disappointin', and I wanted to let them know that we can always bring up other kids. And I felt that Kunkel needed to get that message, too."

What about Bratch, who has now gotten his 10 practices in?

"He doesn't know it yet, but he's gonna get Kunkel's number 34."

Does that mean Kunkel definitely won't be on the bench against Manchester?

"Not necessarily. See, we can shuffle kids around until the Sectional. Then we have to send in a roster of 12 kids to the IHSAA. All I'm sayin' is, look, if somebody earns a varsity spot, they come up. (Jason) Wesco and (George) Samons have been playin' well for the junior varsity. So I might bring them up or just give Kunkel 10 (Dubois' number) or 11 (Baer's)."

What McClure has not said, but seems obvious, is that he's looking for strength and size for the second half of the season to back up the Rosses and Hampton. Wesco is a solid 6-4 and Bratch is a muscular 6-2.

In this Monday's edition of the North Manchester *News-Journal* -- published twice a week -- an intriguing classified ad appears under the "Wanted" category:

Hometown Referee
for Manchester-Northfield game.
Must be loyal -- Call 982-BLUE.

Blue, of course, is Northfield's color. A woman teacher at Manchester has placed the ad to show her unhappiness with what she felt was unfair officiating in the holiday tournament game between the two teams. The ad is the talk of the town, drawing guffaws everywhere in the community of some 6,000 people.

A call to the number brings no answer, because it belongs to an elderly woman who -- fortunately for her sanity -- has gone to Florida for the winter.

Later, Pete Smith plays mind games, at least in McClure's eyes, although there's legitimacy in what the Manchester coach says about his team's injuries.

In Thursday's *Plain Dealer* under the headline "Crippled Squires to host Norse," Smith elaborates on the wounded for Phil Beebe.

Starting forward John Bazzoni, who earlier suffered a hairline fracture in his right hand, severely sprained his ankle in practice Monday and is out for three to four weeks. The ankle is "the size of a bowling ball," Smith says.

Before hurting his ankle, Smith continues, Bazzoni blocked one of Chad Lauer's shots and in the process scratched one of Lauer's eyes just below the pupil. And while Tony Friedan is back after missing 10 days with torn ligaments in his right ankle, he's moving gingerly.

Switching tack, Smith tells Beebe, "The whole town and school is buzzing" about the rematch.

On Friday, after Smith's comments have appeared in the *Plain Dealer*, McClure says sure, revenge is a motive for the Squires in the wake of Northfield's 70-60 victory in the county tournament. "Yeah, we'll be goin' into a real hornets' nest."

But he tells his team that Smith's comments about the injuries are "just coach talk."

In practice, he stresses offense, including out-of-bounds plays that will spring his best outside shooters, Miller, Winegardner and the Chay brothers, for 12- to 15-footers from the side behind a Joe Ross screen.

After practice, McClure is clearly ebullient. He gathers the squad under a basket.

"Let's go up and turn it loose, guys," he begins.

"It's a big game for them; no question about it. They'll have a pep rally and be all charged up and have the home crowd. But, you know, we don't depend on the home crowd down here when we play.

Remember, the biggest opponent we're playin' against is ourselves. You know what we can do when we let it rip.

"It's just like any other road game, but expect more hurdles. Take your game to the court. A court is a court. You know, when I was in junior high, we played on a cement court and I've played on mud courts.

"Guys, if you give 'em 12 mental points in the first quarter like you did last game, I'm gonna cry. No baseline, guys. And Holderman, Frieden, we gotta play 'em tough."

Sure, he says, they'll be nervous in front of a packed, roaring crowd. "He'll be on the pot," he says, pointing to Winegardner, whose stomach is more active before a game than a washing machine.

"We go tomorrow, we take no prisoners," he concludes.

While McClure sits in the bleacher section under the basket, the players sprawl in a circle just off the lane and josh among themselves.

Why is he so upbeat?, he's asked.

"Because we're gettin' our success principles through to them. We're an improvin' team and we've had good practices all week. We're ready to kick some butt. But somethin' else is that we've got team maturity. We got togetherness and a family atmosphere -- see, look at 'em over there havin' fun with each other -- and people are adaptin' to roles."

Then, in the cliche-ridden talk that works for him, he says: "We've got a foundation, now let's build a house. We've weathered a lot of storms already. Steel is best when tempered."

And: "We're in such a good mental state ... it's a pleasure to come to practice."

Most of the team drifts to the showers, but Joe Ross sticks around. He lifts Cody McClure up to the front of the basket rim to see what life looks like up there. Then Joe goes to work at the free throw line. At the other end of the court, brother Jon is occupying the line.

What about the officiating tomorrow tonight? McClure's asked. And he's reminded that Smith complained after the last game about not getting body fouls called on the big guys.

"You should see the film," McClure responds. "If anybody had some complainin', it was us."

Joe, within hearing distance, looks over, smiles and takes another free throw. The ball hits the front of the rim, bounding away harmlessly.

In North Manchester, like so many small towns in Indiana, basketball has a unique aura. And the Manchester-Northfield matchup has become the fiercest rivalry in Wabash County in recent years.

The host Squires go into the rematch off a 92-73 road victory Friday night over North Miami, boosting their conference record to 4-1, identical to Northfield's. As the sportswriters say, each team controls its own destiny.

By halftime of the junior varsity game, there are few seats available in the gym, which accommodates 2,900 in mostly theater-type seats. During the break, the public address announcer says he's aware that people are taping the Indiana-Purdue game at Bloomington. So he asks for a vote: Should he announce the score periodically or not? The crowd votes for hearing the score. It won't matter later, because the noise will reach such a crescendo during the varsity game, the announcer will barely be heard at times.

On the blackboard in the locker room, McClure has written:

Good or Great???

Bratch has been assigned jersey number 10, normally worn by Ryan Dubois. Shortly before the junior varsity games ends, Kunkel hustles in, peels off his sweaty JayVee 34 and dons his varsity 34; he's earned his spot thus far.

McClure comes in a few minutes later and points to the blackboard. "You're in control. You can choose to be great. If you choose, they'll fall like bowling balls."

How much psyching is needed?, one wonders while listening to McClure.

"When you come out, they're gonna call you names and do all kinds of things with the lights, but when the smoke clears, it's 0-0, and then we separate the men from the boys." The Rosses lead the clapping.

Don't worry about what people in the Northfield community are saying, he says, alluding to the recent jibes that the Norse aren't playing as well as they should. "Somebody chews butt, it's mine they chew. I get paid for that."

He tells them they have a chance to do something that has not been done for so long, few people can remember when it last occurred: beat Manchester at Manchester.

117

"Guys, they gave up 95 points to Whitko and more than 70 to North Miami. Let's see if they've been savin' their defense for Northfield. Try to run; look deep."

Then, as in the past, he turns to another sport for analogy: "Steady jabs, guys, then the knockout punch. Instead of tryin' to throw the haymaker right off the bat, jab, jab, jab, and then wham," and his right arm swings up in a huge arc.

"He's yours, Bradley, and you know who I'm talkin' about. And that's not with a capital 'h'."

Holderman, of course. On Friday night against North Miami he was his usual self, getting 30, including five treys. He's not just a shooter, but a fine all-around player.

And he doesn't get rattled, which is no surprise, because "Holdy" has been driving street stock cars at small local tracks since he was 16 and says he'd love to be a professional driver. Coincidentally, Bob Hampton once drove race cars and knows Andy and his dad, Jerry, well. In fact, during the junior varsity game, Hampton interrupted a conversation with a friend to chat cars with Andy. After the youngster left, Bob commented, "He's good. He's got guts."

McClure's pregame comments are brief, and as the team files out, David Peffley reminds his mates, "Remember what Mr. Desper says: The body's got to go fast, but your mind's got to go slow."

Now it appears that more than 3,000 fans -- easily Manchester's biggest crowd of the year -- are on hand for this one. In the gathering is Pat Aikman, game director for the Indiana-Kentucky all-star game sponsored each summer by the *Indianapolis Star*. He's here to look at the Rosses and Holderman.

As the teams warm-up, McClure sits alone on the bench, next to the scorer's table. There's a tenseness about him reminiscent of the season-opener against Whitko. McClure wants this one badly.

It's hard not to be tense. The game's 20 minutes away, but already the crowd is cheering and trading mild insults. The bleacher noise, arena heat and Manchester band create an electricity unlike any of the first nine games, including Whitko at Northfield. One wonders whether Pete Smith will get the calls tonight.

The ball goes up for the opening tap and Holderman, facing Joe Ross in a concessionary move, bats it out of bounds before it reaches its apex. The violation gives Northfield the ball and there's bedlam after only one second's off the clock.

Forty-four seconds later, Jon Ross opens the scoring with a dunk, and then there's momentary trouble. J.P. Pitts, Manchester's 6-4 center, and Joe Ross get into a brief shoving match, bringing play to halt. The officials cool things and play resumes with Peck Chay hitting a jumper seconds later for an early 4-0 Norse lead.

Doug Fahrnow hits a "three" for 4-3.

Then Northfield goes wild. Miller's jump shot makes it 12-3 at 3:52. Noi's jumper with 50 seconds left gets it to 18-5. Northfield scores six more points for a 24-5 lead after one.

It is easily the best quarter the Norse have played all year, good enough to deal with anyone in the state.

Holderman, cold initially, finally gets his first basket at 6:23 in the second quarter with a short jumper. But Jon answers with a dunk and converts a free throw, for a 33-12 advantage -- which will prove to be the biggest of the night -- at 5:19.

Then, as it is wont to do, Northfield sours and Holderman sizzles. With a minute and 16 seconds left, his trey has the hosts back to 37-26.

Eight seconds later, a big play occurs. Trying to go early, Jon drives in for a dunk and is undercut slightly by a moving Holderman. Jon is called for charging. Instead of Northfield slowing Manchester's momentum, getting the lead back to 13 or 14 and having Holderman charged with his third foul, the Squires have the ball and Jon has a seat. It is an egregious call, and McClure is as incensed at an official as he's been all year, but not close to getting a technical.

One thing is for sure now: this one is far from over. And as things get unruly in the stands, the public address announcer intones, "Sit back, relax and enjoy the game."

Northfield manages to get the margin back to 15 at the half, 41-26, on Miller's jumper, but McClure is piqued with his team in the locker room.

"Why do you feel sorry for 'em. Why?" he asks. "You couldn't believe you were beating the great Manchester at Manchester."

It is his way of asking why the Norse backed off in the second quarter.

"They pressed, we panicked," he says evenly, and then the volume goes to maximum: "We're goin' for the basket! Baseball pass!"

He looks at Hampton. "Holderman drives to the elbow (where the lane boundary meets the free throw line) and Brad gets no help. Brad's working his butt off."

It is extremely important how well they play the first five minutes of the second half, he tells them before they head back to bedlam.

Joe's tip at 7:42 of the third gets the lead back to 17. But Manchester is far from dead, and at 3:16, a Holderman bomb shaves the margin to less than double-digits -- 47-38 -- for the first time since the opening quarter.

It's not a matter of Northfield folding. McClure's team is not playing the way it did against Tippecanoe Valley, when it blew a 10-point lead and had that disastrous period of 16 possessions resulting in nine turnovers and one basket. It's just that Manchester is playing inspired ball and getting every charge/block call.

With 53 seconds left, Holderman's trey narrows the gap to 51-46, and at the buzzer, he sends up up another bomb that can even the game for all intents and purposes. No good.

Fifty seconds into the fourth quarter, Holderman is called for his fourth foul and has to come out. The dangerous guy now is Frieden, who has played tough and not shown any signs of his foot injury.

At 5:03 and Northfield up 55-50, Holderman returns and immediately is fouled. He gets the front-end to fall to make it a four-point game. Northfield is hanging on tenaciously, but its grip is slipping. When Holderman gets another "three" at 3:46, it's 57-54.

Seconds later, Joe is fouled, and one wonders if his practice on Friday will pay off. It does. He sinks both; 59-54, Northfield.

The roar, the heat, the band, the whistles, the competition, the emotion, the coaching -- it's all rolled together into hysteria, Hoosier style.

Chad Lauer converts both free throws of a one-and-one situation at 2:29, and so it's down to one, 59-58.

Twenty-four seconds later, Jon is called for his fourth foul -- a charge. McClure leaps from his kneeling position in disbelief. It is a player-control foul; Manchester's ball. The Squires move into the forecourt. A minute and 53 seconds remain. Holderman drives underneath from the left side, puts it up. Good. Manchester 60, Northfield 59. The noise can't get any louder.

Nine seconds later, Joe is fouled in close. He drops in two more free throws. Northfield 61, Manchester 60. Time out, Squires.

A turnover gives Northfield the ball, and Manchester fouls early. Hampton sinks two free throws for 63-60.

Fifty five seconds to go. Frieden, whose treys played a major role in bringing Manchester back earlier, is fouled as he maneuvers for another jumper. He calmly drops in both tosses for 63-62, Northfield.

Twenty seconds to go. Joe is whistled for charging in another call that seems obviously wrong to everyone, except diehard Manchester fans. The press table agrees that the defensive man did not give Joe any room to land in after going up for a shot underneath the hoop. Again, it's player-control, so Manchester comes down on offense, looking for the lead.

The ball is in Holderman's hands almost exclusively as the Squires look for the last shot.

Now, with seven seconds left, he tries to duplicate the drive he made earlier. But he's forced to go up off balance and misses badly. Joe snares the rebound -- and Northfield finally gets a call. An intentional foul is called with four seconds left.

Joe drops the first one in, misses the second; 64-62, Northfield. The intentional foul gives Northfield the ball at its defensive end. The pass goes in to Joe and Frieden fouls him at 0:02. Joe hits both free throws.

It's over -- Northfield 66, Manchester 62.

Joe has turned in a magnificent performance under great pressure, scoring 27 and grabbing 14 rebounds. Brother Jon has contributed 13 points and 11 rebounds, while Hampton has added 14 points. Holderman has been his usual self, getting 25 points, although hitting only eight of 24 shots. Frieden pitched in 17, including three big treys in the second half.

As the players congratulate each other, Smith is approached for questions. But before they can be asked, the Manchester coach growls, "No comment" and heads for his locker room.

Later, though, he tells the *Plain Dealer*'s Beebe, Northfield is "the best in Wabash County. If there was ever any doubt in my mind, it was cleared tonight."

In the Northfield locker room, the players flop on the floor, and McClure greets them with a shout, "Relax, you bunch of gutty champions!"

Standing before them, he lowers his voice and delivers a post-game speech that's mostly a rehash of what he's said before, yet has a spellbinding quality to it.

"Why?.. Why?-Why?-Why? Why? Why when we find somethin' that kicks their butts do we go away from it? You're too nice. I'll tell you what, you aren't goin' to be too nice to our enemies; I'm gonna to see to that. You will have the fire to put it to 'em.

"Hey, look what we've been through, guys. You usually start off with Southwood. They're a foe right away in the TRC. So, instead we go with Whitko, the hottest team in northeast Indiana -- 3-0. We don't get to play a game. Our guards never played a varsity game, other than Peck a little bit, and he played like he never played in a varsity game before. And we got the job done.

"Caston. We learned a bunch there. You gotta play the whole time. We learned that nobody is goin' to physically beat our butts without gettin' it back.

"You go to Oak Hill, another team that's on the rise. Two big guys and quick guys who we destroy. We destroy them.

"You go to (Tippecanoe) Valley -- first time your mind is not on things, or the right things, for a total game. And this is still not bein' a good team. We were five points ahead at the first quarter and playin' like crap.

"You go to the *unknown*. Wellston, Ohio. Fly in an airplane. Stayin' all night with each other. Huge arena.

"You come back to North Miami, just blitz 'em in your next home game. You won the county tournament. You beat these guys twice.

"Hey, there's people been pretty critical of this team; I'm gettin' tired of that crap real quick, 'cause how many of those suckers have ever walked out here and won? *You ask* that question, baby."

Until now, the room has been deathly quiet, but now there's clapping, and McClure rolls on: "There ain't a one of 'em. There hasn't been a one of 'em living since you've been born walked out of here a winner and you're gonna do that tonight. You're walkin' outta here a winner tonight, baby. Man, I got tired of that losin', that bull crap they blow at us.

"Winners! 'Cause you could have given it away. It really looked like you were suckin' the gas out there. You were extremely exhausted. I had that experience in football one time. Our team came out and played a great quarter and a half and then emotionally ran out.

That's what'll happen to ya. Your emotion left ya, and yet, the concentration was still high enough to still execute the way we can

"If you don't realize now that you can beat anybody, you never will. 'Cause these guys are 25 points better on this court. Especially when they (the officials) call them stinkin' charges like the way they do. And you know what a sweet thing this is: We beat all that bull crap, didn't we?

"You're the winners. You did it on the floor where it counted. You came up with the defensive play and ... this man (pointing to Joe) stuck in the free throws."

Suddenly, there's a loud bang at the door, and McClure looks back, yells, "Go away, I'll bust your head," and his smile is wide and his kids laugh.

"Hey, I love it; I love it. Like I've said, I'm still not satisfied at all, but I guess what I really enjoy are a couple of things. Number one, you guys are a joy and pleasure to have together. And you're goin' to have to continue to do that, 'cause the crap gets deeper the farther you go.

"But remember, you're on the ladder, and you just keep climbin' and you sooner or later get out of that stuff. I'm talkin' mentally right now. Mentally, you have elevated yourselves above the challenges. *Now* you got to combine that mental with physical so we can take off.

"This was a game that I saw that we had to come in and win. Mentally, we had to come in and do it, and you've never been more ready mentally. That was super. And now we got to learn how to come out like that every time mentally and sustain and stick with our game plan.

"But this was the game, mentally, that you had to win, to beat the sludge down, to beat the monkey off your backs. Now, guys, we're takin' off, 'cause you guys can do it, 'cause you got ahold of a gold mine. Don't let it get away."

They pray, and then the unexpected occurs: the Manchester team comes into the locker room to offer congratulations.

As they leave, a Manchester player says, "Don't let up, win the TRC."

Sitting against the wall, checking his feet, Joe is asked if he's surprised by the visit.

"Yeah, some of those guys," he says. "Not Holderman. He's a good guy."

What happened in the opening minutes with the pushing and shoving?

"I just said to them, 'You guys are above this'," meaning the blatant physical play.

Outside the dressing room, McClure meets with reporters. "We still got to win six for the TRC," he says. "We've only got five."

He's asked about the fast break that was so effective tonight. "Early in the year, Joe and Jon were ready, because they could run last year. Our guards weren't ready. Now, we're gettin' confidence."

As the team piles onto the bus, the Rosses pass out the post-game snack, and a radio blares the Indiana-Purdue game, which has gone into overtime. The kids yell out their allegiances, having fun.

The McClures' alma mater comes back from a 13 deficit to win by two in overtime. It's been a big night.

Next Saturday will be another one -- the longest bus trip of the year at Eastbrook. Unless, of course, Northfield earns a trip to Fort Wayne for the semistate. At the halfway point in the season, at 10-1, the Norse have quieted some of the early doubters.

Three days after his team's defeat, Pete Smith praises the Rosses in Phil Beebe's column: "The Ross twins have improved 100 percent, no matter what people say. It's tough on them the way people are sagging on them and putting two or three people on them.

"It's a crying shame if they don't make the all-star team (for the Indiana-Kentucky series). Besides (Eric) Montross, there's nobody in the state 6-9 or taller as good as them. I've heard talk about maybe one of them making it, but they both deserve it."

As expected, Pat Aikman wasn't talking as he departed. "If I say I liked what I saw," he says, "then everyone will expect them to make the team. And if I say I didn't then I upset everybody." He's right, of course.

••••••••••

The huge Manchester triumph was the cake. The icing arrived earlier in the week.

On Monday, Garry Donna, editor and publisher of *Hoosier Basketball Magazine*, called Steve McClure with a question: Would he ask Joe and Jon Ross to play in the East-West Indiana All-Star Classic in Richmond on April 7?

Like other promoters, Donna needs to line up commitments early, because high school players are allowed only two all-star games while school is in session. Thus, "classics" must scramble for top talent.

In last year's East-West game -- the first -- 18 of the 26 boy and girl players who participated went on to play in the Indiana-Kentucky series, which takes place in the summer.

Sure, McClure told Donna, he'll talk to the twins, who saw last year's contest with their parents and came away feeling good about the event.

Donna had one more request: he'd like McClure to be one of the two east coaches.

"I got the big lump in my throat," McClure admits in retracing the conversation. "I didn't know what to think. And, of course, I coach track at White's and I thought, Do we have a meet that day? How's it gonna work out on the schedule?"

A bit stunned, McClure said nothing.

"I think my silence made him a little uneasy," McClure continues, " 'cause he said, 'Well, Jack Keefer'll be one of the coaches.' "

That did it.

"Yeah, I'd be interested," McClure finally replied, and the irony couldn't escape him. He recalled how he was supposed to coach with Keefer at Oak Hill until the new Lawrence North beckoned Jack.

"And, of course," McClure says with glee, "as soon as I mentioned it to Lisa, she was makin' plans. So I sent in the form sayin' I'm committed."

Before sending in the form, though, he approached the twins at practice that Monday. He had warned them earlier not to jump at the first chance they got to play in an all-star game.

In extending the invitation on Donna's behalf, McClure decided he would have some fun. After giving them the good news, he told them they need to look at who the coaches will be before making a decision. "You want to go absolutely with the best available," he said, "and therefore, I recommend that you play on the east all-star team."

The twins gave him a funny look, which was a cue for McClure. He stepped back and held out his hands, as if to say, "Here I am," and the two big kids jumped up and began hugging him.

"I'm gonna be Keefer's assistant, just like we were supposed to do 15 years ago," McClure notes, seemingly still a little awed by the turn of events.

Chapter 12: Four Games, Eight Days

The second half of the season will open with four games in eight days against teams Northfield should handle. But Steve McClure knows the unpredictability of high school basketball players, and occasionally he sighs, "Welcome to the world of teenagers."

What's more, two of the three games are against county rivals -- Wabash, which hung tough against the Norse in the holiday tournament, and Southwood, which has shown promise.

But first Northfield must travel to Eastbrook, and never mind that the Panthers are 1-11, they've given McClure's clubs fits every year.

"I don't know why," he says while the players shoot around in street clothes before boarding the bus. "We beat 'em only six last year here, and two years ago down there, we had trouble."

Still, McClure's much more relaxed this Saturday than a week ago before the Manchester biggie.

"I'm not satisfied at all after ten games," he volunteers over the sounds of Alice Cooper, "but we've done a lot better than the NIOPs think."

NIOPs?

"Yeah. Negative Influence Other People. Scott Kunkel ran into some at the barber shop the other day, and they started givin' him crap about why we don't do this and why we don't do that and gettin' on Joe and Jon and me."

Kunkel, shy youngster that he is, was uncomfortable with some of the questions, McClure says. "But Scott defended Northfield well and with honor."

Among the questions was why certain kids had been cut, including one who played as a freshman and a sophomore. That's a question for the coach, Kunkel responded.

Some Northfield followers still think Tom Miller should be at the helm. He was the last successful coach before McClure, but he became controversial -- which is not unusual in Indiana -- and eventually was forced out. When one barber-shop antagonist mentioned Miller, Kunkel pointed out that McClure's record is the best in the school's history.

And for the Northfield faithful, now is what counts.

It is Saturday, January 13, and the days are beginning to lengthen, so as Bob Slee wheels his bus out of the Northfield lot at

4:30, plenty of daylight shines for the hour drive south into Grant County.

Ensconced in his usual front-row-aisle seat opposite Slee, McClure is asked what the biggest surprise has been thus far.

"Good question," he chuckles and then searches for an answer. Finally, he says he's not surprised by some things the team has accomplished -- handling the early pressure, getting in position to at least share another conference crown, winning in Ohio, beating Manchester on the road.

"The biggest disappointment?," he repeats the question. "I can't be disappointed in any way. They give me a 100 percent and there's nothing else to give. I feel good about what they've done, but what they've done is what they're capable of doing. That's all I can ask."

Still, of course, he wants improvement the second half of the campaign. "Our schedule's not, as I see it now, gonna be near as tough as what we've experienced up to now," he points out honestly and correctly. "So hopefully we're just gonna see our level of play continue to increase each week."

The toughest of the final ten games figures to be Maconaquah on the road or Fort Wayne Harding at home, he says as Slee wheels the bus past LaFontaine, a small town in southern Wabash County. "You gotta figure our county rivals playin' well, too. It'll be interesting to see how we handle them mentally."

Are the Rosses playing better, worse or about as expected?

"I think they're doin' about the way we expected, but I expect them, before the year is over, to give more. It's a situation of where they've become comfortable playing with their supporting cast, and I think they can feel more aggressive 'cause we've shown we can do some things without 'em. But we haven't seen the true Joe and Jon yet."

An objective observer would likely say that the twins have carried the team, as expected. And McClure would agree, but he's not satisfied with them. "Because they've had the foul trouble," he says quickly, " and they've made some poor decisions on both ends of the floor. No, they're not near their potential yet."

He pauses, scratches his dome. "I'm waitin' on 'em to be great players, and that means moldin' everything they do in with the team."

He's told that Nathan Winegardner, one of the team's headiest players, feels the twins are handling the pressure quite well.

"They are right now," McClure agrees. "But earlier in the season, during the tryouts and early practices, that wasn't the case at all."

He admits he felt pressure before the season. "The summer was so hot and heavy with recruiting. And then I found myself havin' to make the transition from focusin' on Joe and Jon to gettin' our team ready to go for the year."

He thinks the Rosses felt the pressure about the same time and it continued a while for them after he began to calm down.

"They're the ones that actually have to play with the kids," he points out as the bus hits a bump in the road and bounces past the stark, flat countryside. "I think at times they were tryin' so hard to prove to the other kids that they wanted to be part of the Northfield team more than they cared about their college at this time. I think they really struggled with that early. But I think after a few games and a lot of practice under our belt, they're on top of it now."

They've been the target of opposing players, coaches and officials their entire careers at Northfield, he asserts without apology. He has used this point to try to keep Joe from foul trouble. Success has been limited.

"One of the things that we've been workin' with Joe on lately is tryin' to impress on him that he enters the game with three fouls. The officials are gonna get 'em. He and Jon perform right in front of the official under the basket the entire game. They're targets and they're gonna get nailed three times on cheapies.

"So we've tried to impress on 'em that they've got two fouls left they can control. If they're aggressive and movin' their feet and playin' good defense, they'll probably be in good shape. But if they're out there not concentratin', they'll give up a free foul, and instead of that bein' their first, it's their fourth."

McClure doesn't want the Rosses backing off. "There's no need to pull in your horns even if you do get in foul trouble, because I've always contended that the more aggressive you are, the more you're goin' to be in position and the more breaks you'll create for yourself. I would rather try to pull back their aggression than try to build it into 'em, 'cause you can take an aggressive kid and make aggression constructive. But if it's not there to start with, you're fightin' a losin' cause."

Early in the season, when foul trouble started immediately, McClure was concerned more about Joe and Jon backing off than losing them early in the game. "I don't think Joe realized he wasn't doin' a very good job with the two or three fouls he had control of," McClure says as the bus passes through Marion, a basketball-batty town of 36,000. "And he saw that in the film. Sometimes I saw it and we talked about it, and he's smart, willin' to learn. And I think lately you've seen Joe makin' better decisions with his defense."

Speaking of defense, will McClure try the "run and jump" he's worked on in practice the past week?

"We should. It's a press, or it's a defense where you line up man-to-man and you encourage the person with the ball to dribble. And as he dribbles at ya, at a time when you think would be most effective, you just rush him and you double-team the ballhandler. Then the other three people rotate through the area vacated."

Offensively, McClure has spent the week working on new entries calling for more motion. He noticed from the Manchester film that his players tended to stand around when they felt good defensive pressure. "We've put in entries to get certain people the ball that need to have it at certain times," he says as the bus reaches Eastbrook on Marion's southeastern edge.

By the time the junior varsity game starts, a scattering of people are in the stands, which seat 3,600, although the Northfield section is full, as usual.

While Steve Desper's kids are working toward their fifth victory against as many losses, McClure prints on the blackboard:

Goodness

Or

Greatness

Thirty minutes later, as the varsity dresses, Brad Hampton says, "Just another day at the office." His comment illustrates the looseness in the locker room, an indication that the Eastbrook Panthers are being taken lightly.

The looseness fades a bit and the trips to the toilet begin, but there's a feeling that the team is still a little "high" after Manchester a week ago. McClure seems unconcerned, though, as he talks briefly, going over X's and O's on the blackboard. He reminds them to look for the motion offense if the lob to Joe or Jon isn't available. On defense, he warns, "Watch (Mike) Bragg, the little red-headed kid who's a good shooter."

In the warm-ups, Joe moves well, still wearing his temporary insoles. And his right knee is okay. He stretched ligaments while jumping in practice early in the week, necessitating a trip to Dr. Ahlfeld. Nothing serious.

McClure has made roster changes, elevating Jason Wesco from the junior varsity in place of Troy Baer and suiting up Bob Bratch in place of Ryan Dubois. And McClure will open with Winegardner and Noi Chay at guard.

"We're always lookin' for different combinations," he says of the back-court change. "If they never get a chance to start, we'll never know whether our team can get a good start. And, I just thought, maybe we need to give them an opportunity to see how they respond. Peck, he's the kind of kid that sometimes lacks confidence, and I want to see how he plays comin' off the bench."

McClure will have to see about Peck and Troy Miller quickly, because Northfield in the first quarter is a totally different team than a week ago against Manchester. Never mind that the Norse take a 17-7 lead after one stop, they show little intensity.

But there's no lack of intensity from Eastbrook Coach Moe Smedley as he yells to his players and pleads for three seconds against the Rosses.

Eastbrook hangs tough, scoring three quick hoops before the half, reminiscent of the Caston game, when Northfield let a double-digit lead get away before intermission. This time, it's 29-23, and the Eastbrook crowd, which has finally arrived, is feeling good.

McClure walks into the locker room and says nothing for a minute or two before unloading with a tone of resignation: "This is the only team in the history of Northfield to do somethin' but doesn't have the mental toughness. We got four guards in the game and can't beat the press (just before the half)." Suddenly, his voice spurts to full volume: "You bunch of wimps!"

He mentions fouls. The Norse put the Panthers into the bonus with three minutes left in the first quarter.

"You don't have the mind to do it," he says softly. "I don't think you have the guts to be great. You had 'em bellyin' up and you turned your butts up."

He looks up at the blackboard with the pregame tactics. "There isn't a thing I can tell you. It all works (pointing to the blackboard). We had no X's, no cuts, no reverses."

McClure has kept his anger in check, seemingly more frustrated than teed-off -- and probably drained, as are his players, after Manchester.

He opens the second half with his regular starting lineup. Two quick baskets by Peck and one by Joe double the lead to 12 points.

With a little more than two minutes left in the third quarter, Hampton -- Mr. Injury -- gets hit in the right eye underneath the defensive end and comes out with blurred vision.

Meanwhile, Smedley works the sideline and his team works the court, so it's only 45-34, Northfield, after three.

Hampton is okay, and he's back for the start of the fourth quarter, giving his teammates a momentary lift. Joe's dunk gets it to 53-38, but the Norse can't pull away. And it's not until 1:02 that McClure goes to his bench.

The final is 65-50, but this one has been ugly.

They file into the locker room and sit silently on the long bench in front of the lockers, looking like losers instead of 15-point winners. They know they've played rotten, and they anticipate McClure entering shortly and doing some "chewin'."

By the time he finally arrives, almost 10 minutes have passed; they seem like an eternity. He strolls past the entire team, between them and the wall that holds the blackboard and bulletin board. He says nothing. He turns and walks back toward the locker-room door, out of sight.

Seconds later, he's back. They wait for an explosion. They love the man -- it's quite obvious -- but they fear him, too, as they fear their parents. And so they sit in sweat and dead silence, wondering, wondering, and looking as if they've been beaten convincingly.

McClure's roiling, but somehow keeps his cool, talks softly. "Talent-wise, we win a lot of games, but mentally, we're not doin' it.

"My stomach hurts, my head hurts. I had to endure this tonight. But I hope you did, too. I hope it was as humiliating for you as it was for me. I don't know what it was, I really don't. Maybe you decided you needed a week off from the Manchester game.

"But I'll tell ya, I saw a team last night (Marion) that'll beat you half to death, if not totally to death."

His mind begins to race, spewing out thoughts and betraying the calmness in his voice. "There's teams down the road that's gonna beat you completely to death before you ever have to worry about comin' back to this town again." (Translation: If you keep playing like you did tonight, you won't have to worry about returning to Marion for the Regional.)

Was it starting different guards? he asks. It shouldn't make any difference, because, "When we put five people on the floor this time of the season, they oughta be able to play together ... function as a great unit. And we gave 'em, gift-wrapped, eight points in the last 40 seconds or so (of the first half). I need some guards to emerge who will play a full game."

Eastbrook has been "the low point of the season, without a doubt. The only place we've won tonight was the scoreboard. That is all we got out of this sucker, a W. And we should be jumpin' and runnin', right?"

Maybe some selfishness has set in, he mutters. "You're just kinda hung up on certain areas of your game, and you're feelin' sorry for yourself and thinkin' about yourself, and, 'Oh, I can't hit' and doin' this and makin' mistakes. If you don't know by now that you're on a team that'll pick each other up, I don't know where you've been."

The juxtaposition of his thoughts takes over, as it does frequently: "Don't be afraid of enthusiasm. It does work. We need to get it to be fun. We need to get it exciting. We need to get it goin'. And I can't do it. I'm not gonna lose my enthusiasm. I don't give a crap if you guys play worse the next games, I'm not gonna lose it. It's somethin' God put in my heart, and I'm gonna let it shine through.

"Does anyone have a suggestion?"

"I got one," Steve Desper says. There's fire in the assistant coach's eyes and voice. "When you guys make an error, don't look over at the bench like, huh? What the heck is he (McClure) gonna do? What're you lookin' for, sympathy? Cut that crap out! I hate it. I can't stand it when someone makes an error and looks over at the bench like, huh? I'm sorry, but I don't like that. When you look at the bench, it's a sign of mental weakness. You're looking for somebody to help you. And that's bad. You gotta do it yourself."

McClure reminds them that they play for the conference championship Tuesday night at home against Southwood. It's the postponed season opener.

Finally, they head for the showers, and as they do, McClure finds one bright spot: "I saw some things from Peck I liked tonight with him comin' off the bench. He finally got determined out there. He at times seemed much more relaxed. Foul trouble limited him, but see, I think we discovered something."

Outside the locker room, in a small entry way, McClure greets his wife. There's a look of concern on Lisa's face when she says, "I don't want you to be upset." He smiles back an okay.

"A stinkpot job," he says to her, taking her right arm gently. "We can't be any worse than that."

Brady appears. He wants to go back with the team on the bus and eat with the players, but Dad says no, he's to go with Mom. The 12-year-old complains mildly.

Mike Wainscott of the Marion *Chronicle-Tribune* approaches. McClure repeats what he told the team: Tonight was the low-point of the season. But then, "Maybe we should give Eastbrook credit, because we haven't played well in four years against 'em. The area we succeeded in was the scoreboard, and that's not the most important thing."

The team stops at Wendy's on Marion's north side for the post-game meal. For the last five years an anonymous donor whose son graduated from Northfield has given the team money for food after one road game. The donation this year is $100.

They file into the empty restaurant shortly before closing time, Joe and Jon deliberately waiting to bring up the rear with the coaches. The bill comes to $103.07.

Brady has been dropped off by Lisa at the restaurant. He sits with Joe and David Pefley.

"It's frustrating," Joe says between bites of his burger, "that a big man can't do anything to get things going outside. We really can't take charge and start something offensively."

But the big guys can rebound, as evidenced by Joe's 16 for the night.

Nearby, brother Jon, whose 26 points on 12 of 19 shooting led the way, is quiet while the Chays chatter. Before the game, Jon told his teammates, "One of our goals at the beginning of the season was to develop a killer instinct. Let's do it."

The killer instinct will have to come another night, though. Perhaps in three days against Southwood.

Nathan Winegardner sees the Southwood games as two of the toughest remaining.

"We usually don't play very good as a whole against Southwood," the senior guard says. "It takes a lot to get up for them.

We know everybody on that team. We're pretty good friends with everybody, so it's hard for us to do the job."

A lot of "pretty good friends" will be getting together tonight, Tuesday, January 23. The opening-season postponement has given Northfield athletic director Jim Kaltenmark an opportunity to put together four games for three dollars. The girls were scheduled to play this night at Southwood, but Kaltenmark has arranged for the varsity girls to play in the main gym at 6 p.m. while the junior varsity boys play in the smaller facility. The boys varsity and girls junior varsity contests will follow. The chance to see at least parts of four games for a few bucks is the best entertainment buy in town, and people throughout the county know it; they start arriving -- some right from work -- by 5:30.

While the crowd moves back and forth between the gyms, separated by locker rooms, McClure is in his team's dressing quarters, working over the blackboard. For tonight he writes:

Do the Common Things
Uncommonly
Well

His troops file in a short time later and listen to Salt-N-Pepa rap as they dress.

Hampton's eye has recovered from the poke at Eastbrook. It was swollen shut until noon Sunday, when he put ice on it.

The girls varsity game runs long, so some players sack out on a bench or the floor, lying flat on their backs and holding a basketball to their tummies. As game-time nears, though, they begin jumping and shouting, bouncing the balls hard on the floor. They are wound-up youngsters tonight.

McClure is brief, going over X's and O's, but his main message is simply this: "They can't guard ya, guys. They can't *guard* ya! You put yourself here, in a championship position. Now finish the job."

The job might be a little easier than first thought. Tim Mohr, a talented, 6-3 starting forward, is out for Southwood with a hairline fracture of his right wrist. It will mean an even heavier burden on guard Joe Duncan, whose 18-point average is fifth best in the county.

At the tip-off, a near-capacity crowd is on hand, including Wabash Coach Sims, who will face Northfield in four days for the second time this season.

135

Nothing goes right for either team in the opening minutes, but Northfield plays with more purpose, more desire than it showed in its sad effort at Eastbrook.

Southwood has an opportunity, but Rick Mahan misses two free throws and Brad Weaver, the Knights' beefy, 6-3 center, a short turnaround. What's more, Joe Ross has picked up three fouls in 5 minutes and 54 seconds.

McClure replaces Joe with Bob Bratch, and he provides spark, immediately plucking a rebound. He is the only bright spot as Northfield commits nine turnovers in the first quarter but still manages a 13-6 lead.

In the huddle, McClure's voice is raw with rage: "I'm sick and tired of this! Get your heads in the game!"

Jon Ross, steady all year, hits while his brother sits; and Jon is playing tough defense inside.

Bratch, still not in shape, must come out, and as he does, McClure yells at his troops, "We got one guy playin' hard."

More guys start playing hard. Northfield reduces its turnovers to five in the second quarter for a comfortable 25-8 advantage at the half. The Norse defense has been solid, not great, but Southwood's shots simply won't fall.

In the hallway outside the locker room, McClure admits, "I feel a stompin' comin' on." Then he walks in and proceeds to ream his players.

"Terrible," he begins. "We can't have that. We cannot have turnovers that are stupid."

Yes, he tells Winegardner, he had to play out of his normal position, but that's no excuse for not knowing where to be on a 3X (on the side of the ball). "I don't care if you go sit on your girlfriend's lap, get out of the way (of the opposite guard)!"

It's not all brickbats. He compliments them on the last 90 seconds of defensive play.

And then, softly, "You can name it, guys. Name the score. But more importantly than that, I want execution. This is the same floor you practice on. And when you practice, you don't make 14 turnovers all week."

Then he turns mean again, lashing out at his team's tentativeness. "I can't stand that bull crap, bein' afraid to beat good ol' Southwood. They're hustlin'. That's the reason they're in the game."

He heads for the door. "You come out when you're ready. We'll go with the starters," which tonight have been Peck Chay and Troy Miller in place of Noi and Nathan.

McClure's comment about Southwood being in the game was not true, of course. In one stretch of the first half, Southwood went scoreless for 9 minutes and 10 seconds, resulting in two points in the second quarter. The Norse registered 18 unanswered points. Mind games are always on McClure's mind.

He does not need mind games in the second half.

Hampton hits a short jumper off the glass in the first 14 seconds, and Jon slams one home 21 seconds later. The stompin' has begun.

After Hampton scores from in close -- off a "Boiler" offensive entry -- McClure stands, turns to the bench and, with arms outstretched, says, "Tell me it won't work."

Meanwhile, Southwood's offense still hasn't arrived. Duncan goes until 4:28 in the third quarter before getting his first points. They finally get the Knights to double digits.

It's 43-16 after three quarters. The final will be 69-23, David Pefley doing his thing by beating the horn with a trey and sending the Northfield folks into spasms of delight.

Another goal -- at least a share of the conference championship -- has been achieved.

Jon Ross has led the way again with 24 points and seven rebounds. Hampton, who had just one rebound against Eastbrook, has picked off a game-high nine and scored 17 points.

Southwood Coach Monte Moffett points to the opening minutes as the key -- the missed free throws and Weaver's missed field goal.

Asked about his counterpart's analysis, McClure smiles. "He had to say somethin' to make his team feel better."

McClure is certainly feeling better. His team's turnovers fell sharply to just six in the second half, "and two were sympathy calls here and there."

How can his team play so well in the second half after so-so the first? Was it the brief but harsh halftime speech?

"If it was, they're in trouble," he responds. " 'Cause I just simply will not do that every night. And we're gonna go from this point on to challenge them to motivate themselves as individuals and don't count on anyone else."

They played better because they were convinced that they could, he continues -- and maybe his screaming did some good, and maybe they knew his patience had run out, and maybe they realized what they needed to do.

"They've been under a lot of pressure this year," he says, sounding like the love-fear parent rising to defend his children. "And now I think we're startin' to merge above that pressure and concentratin' on what we can do."

Will the final score mean anything, psychologically, to his team?

"I tell them not to be scoreboard scouts. The score doesn't matter, 'cause you know the Apaches (Wabash) are gonna be ready. What matters is playin' solid for 32 minutes."

Two days before the return match with Wabash, the Apaches suffer a psychological blow. A story in the Marion *Chronicle-Tribune* reports that James Barnes, president of Indiana Wesleyan University in Marion, has discussed his school's head coaching job with Ray Sims. The school's current coach, Mike Fratzke, tendered his resignation January 16.

Sims tells the *Chronicle-Tribune* and the Wabash *Plain Dealer* he's happy where he is and isn't job-hunting.

Coincidentally, a day earlier Sims was featured on WISH-TV, Indianapolis, in a story on the rebuilding of the Apache program. Sims' team has won five of its first 13 games, compared to last season's 2-19 record.

Sims, who is black, told veteran sportscaster Jim Barbar of WISH he was "accepted with open arms here in Wabash." After Bill Green left for the college ranks, Sims continued, he felt he didn't get the Marion job because, in part, of being black.

Despite Sims' denial and despite a team meeting to reassure his players, a mini tempest has come to the fore.

As practice at Northfield concludes on Thursday, McClure is asked if the Sims story will affect the Apaches.

"Some, probably," McClure says. "Kids are kids."

What does he make of the story?

"I think Ray is runnin' out of ways to get press, and he wants press, because it helps keep some excitement in his program. The Wabash program is comin' back and needs excitement. So ..."

Are the Norse showing any fatigue as they approach their third game in seven days?

"A little yesterday and today," he says, but, as usual, he finds something good in something bad. "It's good to practice under these conditions, when you're a little tired. It's a blessing for later on in games, when you're tired late."

Has he heard anything about running up the score on Southwood?

He turns his head away from the court, looks his questioner right in the face: "You know, I'm down at White's with a lot of Southwood people, and they were givin' me a hard time, sayin' it was a blowout and stuff. How can you run up the score when you take two less shots than the opponent?"

Forget the blowouts, "Give me 32 minutes of good basketball," he says.

In that evening's *Plain Dealer*, Sims sounds the same theme: "We have to be able to play 32 minutes of almost error-free ball," he tells Phil Beebe.

Sims says he saw some things Tuesday night at the Southwood game that Wabash will look to exploit against the Norse. And, of course, there's the three-point shooting of Donny Blair, who is third in the county scoring race behind Andy Holderman and Jon Ross.

It's an early-arriving crowd at Wabash -- a crowd that will swell to the largest of the season, packing Coolman Gym.

Downstairs in the locker room, McClure puts on the blackboard:

Play at Your
Level

Offensively, to start, he doesn't want anything fancy -- just move the ball around, try to spring people and look for the twins in the post. Defensively, they must control the boards, especially Gary Cooper.

"We need a great start, primarily ballhandling," he says with a touch of pain in his voice.

"Live team," he switches sharply in approach. "You can screw up, 'cause you love each other. But we know that when we hit on all cylinders, we can beat any of 'em."

139

His voice raises to a roar: "They can't guard ya! They don't have the ability. They got the mouth to guard you, but you don't guard with your mouth."

For the first time, McClure starts both Chays at guard, as if to say to the Wabash crowd, "Look what we have." But what appears to be "mind games" is really much more.

"He's earned it," McClure says simply when asked about Noi teaming with his brother. "He's a sophomore, and earlier in the year he wasn't respondin' fully to the things we were wantin', primarily on the turnovers. And then we saw the improvement come. Athletically, I just think he's better than the other kids, and, you know, there's no substitute for quickness. With our size underneath, the more quickness we can put around it, I think the more effective a defensive club we can have. Going into the tournament, I'll be lookin' for ballhandling and defense. Those are two of Noi's strengths."

Defensively, McClure continues, Noi is able to put more pressure on the perimeter, "which is not a knock on the other kids. He's just got more of a total package at guard than either Nathan or Troy have."

Noi makes McClure's move look brilliant by hitting four field goals -- three jumpers and a layup -- for eight first-quarter points as Northfield gets off to a blazing start.

The fast getaway McClure wanted comes, in part, from Blair being cold from three-point range, where he takes most of his shots. Hampton has played him tough. So it's 24-9 after eight minutes.

But Joe collects three fouls and must sit, so Wabash plays Northfield even in the next eight minutes as Blair warms to the task. Two late treys give him 18 points at the half, making it 44-29 -- not a commanding margin with an outstanding three-point shooter around.

Despite a decent lead, McClure is frustrated as he, Desper and Christie huddle at the top of the stairway leading to the locker room. "We worked against the 1-3-1 trap in practice, but when Joe comes out, we don't know what to do," McClure sighs.

Frustration turns to anger by the time he descends the stairs. For the first time in the season his language becomes profane.

"Blair's got four three-pointers. Is he a new kid? You're not playin' like you've won a championship. You're shit! Every one of you."

He steps toward the seated Joe Ross and bends only slightly to look him eyeball to eyeball. "And you're too stupid to adjust to what's goin' on," he yells, referring to Joe's three fouls. Joe doesn't flinch; his flat, serious expression stays intact. He takes the heat stoically, respectfully.

McClure steps back and suddenly kicks a plastic water container across the floor. "Second quarter, you got back down in the muck with 'em and wallowed with 'em. What defense did they run in the second quarter? You act like ya don't even know."

The anger reaches its acme. He slams his left hand flat against the backboard, causing the metal side framing to fall off and bending his pinkie into pain.

"Peck, what're you doin' when they're in a trap? Tell me." Peck is semi frozen. McClure points to the blackboard, talks in pronouns: "What're you other guys doin' runnin' clear out here when they're gettin' pressure back here (on the press)? Why the hell didn't you run a hook back and help 'em? I don't hear any answers, guys."

He pauses for air, takes off his glasses, puts a towel to his soppy scalp.

"You play like that this half, and I'm takin' every one of your practice jerseys and burnin' 'em. You see if I'm lyin'. You play that crappy ..."

He sucks in air momentarily. Then, slowly, softly, deliberately: "You're the best team I've ever had -- at breaking your own momentum. You're the best team I've ever had at stopping yourself. You guys sit on the bench and you pee in your pants when it counts."

He turns to the blackboard, focuses on the lack of offensive movement. "Christsakes, guys, they outsmarted you." The chalk moves quickly. "This is us. We got a man here, we got a man here, Jon is in the middle. You gotta be active in there. Brad and Joe are on the sides. Guards, you got people on you. If you're gonna do somethin', pass it here (to a side), or take it through the hole; look for this guy or look for him and that guy."

It's easy, he tells them, but they must *make* it easy, not expect to have it come to them easy.

"Guys," he sighs, "you keep playin' like this, I'll never make it to my 37th birthday (four days away)."

He turns toward the stairs, says, "I'm not sayin' 'Forward march!' 'cause you guys aren't marchin'."

They huddle on their own, and as the coaches climb the stairs, words of encouragement for each other filter up the well.

In the opening two minutes of the second half, the teams play evenly. But with 4:49 remaining, 6-3 Nils Dekau, who has the unenviable task of dueling Joe Ross, picks up his fourth foul. And by now, a bloodletting that was not foreseen has begun to unfold.

Northfield will score 25 points in four minutes and eight seconds, many coming off a rapidly improving fast break. After Joe rebounds and tosses a long pass to Hampton, who scores and is fouled, McClure yells: "There you go, Joe, now you're playin' like a man."

Seconds later, Hampton is loose again on a fast break, and as he goes up, he's hit by Blair, causing him to fly into Northfield fans sitting in a small bleacher section. There's a hush. Seconds later, Hampton is up, shaking his head, trying to clear the cobwebs.

Any thought of Wabash coming back is gone now. Northfield has outscored the hosts 34-8 in the third quarter. McClure will play his subs for almost the entire fourth quarter. The second half has been a mirror of the final 16 minutes against Southwood.

The final is 98-48, Northfield's highest offensive output of the year by far. The century mark looked certain when the Norse had 90 at 4:11, but the reserves couldn't get it done.

Hampton has played his second straight strong game, leading the way with 27 points and nine rebounds. Jon has scored 23 and pulled down 13 boards, while Joe has picked off 12 despite limited play. Blair has matched Hampton's 27, but only nine came in the second half.

As Sims, a friendly guy, leaves the floor, he's asked if there was a difference tonight compared to the first game, when Wabash forced Northfield to hold the ball to preserve a victory.

"Yeah," he smiles wide, "the score ... the big difference."

Why?

"Well, basically, Northfield played an excellent basketball game. They were clickin' on all cylinders. We have to play a perfect game. We don't have two 6-10's. Too much size. Too much size. In a couple of years, next year, they'll come back to the field with everyone else, and then everyone will be able to compete."

Was he upset by the Northfield fans chanting for a 100 points?

"It's always nice to score a 100 points," he says. "I don't consider it pouring it on by the other team. You don't substitute and tell your bench not to score. I've seen coaches substitute too early and lose."

He's told his kids didn't play that badly.

"Well, in the first half we were okay, but, at the same time, this is one of our worst ball games." He smiles wide. "The one good thing about this is that we made some money tonight. This is our biggest crowd of the season. We had a big crowd for the holiday tourney, but (tonight) it was a big crowd for us."

Downstairs, McClure tells his people, "If you didn't like poundin' these guys tonight, I don't know what's happenin'. I don't care who plays against you, the way you played the third quarter, there isn't anything they can do about it. Not a thing. You gotta believe that, and you gotta believe it every single minute of every single day."

He steps back for a moment. "I read before where men think about one particular subject 90 percent of the time. What do you think it is?"

"Basketball," Allen Strait says, drawing laughs.

"Sex," Joe says, and McClure responds, "That's right."

His point: They need to think about basketball. Yes, he adds quickly, other things are important -- "I'm not tryin' to change any priority list" -- but the team must constantly think about its goal, "which is the crown you want to wear this year."

Despite being pleased, McClure says, he won't sleep well at night until he sees 32 minutes of the kind of ball he saw in the third quarter.

Desper is called on. "What I saw in the third quarter was no hesitation on offense. I saw it in the first half. You'd look -- Where am I supposed to go? Who do I pass to? Where do I move? The first thing you do in basketball is look to shoot. You did that in the third quarter. I thought the second quarter we looked first to pass."

McClure is not through. "Let me ask you something. Anything magical happen that made us play well? No. There was no magic. Just go out and do it the way you've been trained."

He has pounded them hard lately, but now he ends with a pat. "You have done an incredible job of gettin' where you are, but there's so much more ahead of ya. Move forward. I'm not gonna burn your jerseys. Wear 'em proudly."

He looks at the blackboard momentarily. "I'll break every blackboard if it takes it. I don't care."

It is time for prayer. "Forgive me, Father," McClure begins. "And thank you for bringing us around. ... "

While the team showers, managers Bever, Ross and Stout repair the blackboard, putting the frame back in place, like new.

McClure grabs a ham sandwich and a Coke, heads for a radio interview.

Joe Ross is still in uniform, peeling tape and paraphernalia from his sore feet.

Why has his team played just average the first half, so astoundingly the second in the last two games?

Joe searches for an answer. "I think we just won't open the valves wide the first half and go into it."

Does the coach's "speech" at halftime have any effect?

"Yeah, it does," he says in a flat, you-better-believe-it-does tone.

When the coach was eyeball to eyeball with him at the half, was he bothered?

"It didn't bother me," he says evenly, "but it -- I understand. I'm afraid coach doesn't think I think out there. I think. It's just sometimes maybe I'm over aggressive. Sometimes I don't even notice people underneath me. I don't feel them until I go up. And I don't want to lose my aggressiveness.

"But I think that after coach does something like that (talk tough at halftime), we just open it up and we just pull out all the stops and say, 'We're goin' for it.' And that's what this team can do. This team can run. If we run, we don't make as many turnovers. If we don't hesitate to pass, we're getting the ball inside or wherever it needs to go. And that's what we have to do."

At the broadcast table in the now-empty gym, Bill Rogge asks McClure why he didn't take Joe out after his fourth foul early.

"Well, you know, I kinda agree with Al McGuire, who says a person with four fouls is worthless on the bench, he might as well be on the floor and play 'til he gets it. And it becomes a mental game ... and I just left Joe in to give him some experience while in foul trouble. If he fouls out, his night's done, and if he keeps foulin' out, maybe he'll get the message."

In the hallway leading to the gym, Bob and Andris Ross are with Fran McCaffery, a Notre Dame assistant coach who has come to watch the twins.

He's asked for his view, but begs off, saying he's not sure whether NCAA rules allow him to comment.

Even though the twins have already signed?

"I'm not sure," McCaffery says politely. "I'll check when I get back. You can call me if you'd like."

144

Four days later, McCaffery returns a phone call from the previous day. He can talk. "I was very impressed with both of them. I like the way they were active on defense. Even when they weren't blocking shots, they were distorting shots with their long arms."

What really impressed McCaffery when he first saw Joe and Jon play made another strong impression: their ability to run the floor.

"And they complement each other," he says. "I see Jon as a 3 (small forward) because of his quickness and offensive skills, or a 4 (a power forward playing inside). I think Joe is more of a 4 or 5 (center). Joe works so hard and plays so hard, especially on offense, and his offensive skills will develop."

He thinks that as the twins work in the weight room they will grow to 225 to 235 pounds before long.

McCaffery has no doubt that both will be better in college than high school. "They have such a good knowledge of the game. And they're tremendous people. They're unselfish."

Almost 24 hours after the Wabash rout, the Norsemen filter into their gym looking relatively fresh and seeking their tenth straight victory against a team beaten by 34 points the night before.

Southern Wells comes into the contest 5-6 and doesn't figure to pose any problems at all for Steve McClure's team.

In the locker room, he has posted an article from the *Indianapolis Star* on Pat Graham, last season's Mr. Basketball. A prolific scorer, Graham is warming the bench for Bob Knight's Indiana University Hoosiers. The thrust of the article is that Graham's attitude is outstanding.

The last sentence -- a quote from Graham -- are underlined in red: "The thing you just have got to keep in mind is, after every game there's always another step to take."

As in taking another step up McClure's ladder.

On the blackboard he has written just seven words in large letters:

What Type of Habits
Are You
Developing?

That will be his theme tonight. Habits, he will tell them shortly, should be great ones, no matter what one does in life.

145

In his prayer, McClure asks the Lord for forgiveness "when we don't handle things too well ... and help us to be in your image in our behavior on and off the court."

Northfield opens by playing tough defense and moving the ball nicely on offense. But the Norse hit only two of their first 10 shots for a quiet 8-6 lead after one quarter.

Troy Miller, who has been relegated in favor of Noi Chay, opens the second quarter and almost immediately hits a trey on the out-of-bounds play McClure worked on two weeks ago in practice.

For the first time this season, Jon Ross shows he's human. His shots won't fall. His touch is missing. But he does not force his game offensively, and on defense, he's a monster inside, batting away shots along with brother Joe.

As Northfield starts to heat up, the margin slowly builds to 28-17 at the half. Unlike the night before, when they had 14 turnovers at the intermission, the Norse have nine tonight. McClure's not thrilled, but he's not unhappy; he knows his team is playing well overall.

"You're workin' at it," he says, pointing to the word "habits."

He tells them they are playing "good defense, not great defense." Offensively, "don't let your shooting affect you. Just stay with it. You're takin' good shots."

The atmosphere is downright relaxed as McClure concludes, "Just bring it up a notch."

And they do.

For the third straight game, Hampton is leading the charge on the fast break, resulting in easy buckets and six straight free throws after getting fouled while going up.

It is 50-23 after three quarters, and McClure starts clearing the bench shortly after the final eight minutes begin.

Pefley, as usual, has the crowd going, moving his bulky linebacker body through the press and looking to unload a bomb. On one occasion, he drives down the middle and puts up an off-balance 12-footer that goes nowhere, prompting McClure to yell, "Don't get so close," and Pefley flashes back a grin.

The final is 71-38, and it has been fun tonight -- especially, it seems, for Joe Ross, who has avoided foul trouble and roamed the court as if he were on a playground, swatting away shots, clearing the boards, putting up an occasional short jumper, feeding off the post.

Hampton's 14 leads the scoring, as Jon is held to 10 on only three field goals.

But, as usual, Hampton has suffered an injury -- a sprained right ankle with six minutes left in the game. His dad, who has driven eight hours from a work assignment in Pennsylvania, wonders what's going on. Yes, he wants Brad to play more aggressively, but he's tired of seeing him get hurt game after game.

McClure is pained, too. "We had a sub for Brad waitin' at the scorer's table for 45 seconds," he moans in the locker room. "And then Brad goes down."

Outside the visiting team's locker room, Southern Wells coach Flava Sirk waits for his team to dress and board the bus home.

Is Northfield the best team his club has faced this year?

"Probably all around," he says, his voice raw from shouting during the game. "We've played three excellent teams this year."

One of the other two, he says, was Woodlan, near Fort Wayne.

"They've got a 6-9 kid by the name of Lloy Ball, who is just an absolute great player, and a 6-7 kid by the name of Jim Mosher. And to me, they're a little more active than the Rosses."

The guy who "makes Northfield obviously a regional-contending team and possibly in the semistate" is Hampton, he continues. "Because, you know, we held the Rosses to 10 points each. And Noi Chay is just a sophomore, gets 13."

Those who have watched Northfield the entire season would agree to some extent with Sirk's comments. Hampton is perhaps the vital link -- as he has shown in his last three games. But the Rosses have carried the Norse all year, particularly Jon, who Sirk has seen play his weakest game of the year.

All of which means nothing to McClure. He knows the Rosses carry the big load. He knows Hampton's his best defensive player and runs the fast break well. He knows Noi and Peck Chay do wonderful things when in control. He knows Troy Miller delivers key three-pointers and Nathan Winegardner provides important back-court relief. And he knows Bob Bratch muscles for rebounds in short stretches on the front line.

Most important, he knows that after 13 wins and one loss, his team is starting to jell, is nearing its peak, is playing the kind of basketball people expected.

He alludes to all this in the locker room before the assembled squad: "Troy has matured to the point where he realizes, I got a few weaknesses, and he's worked on them. But he came in and shot the ball for us when we weren't hittin'. We need things like that."

Remember a week ago? he asks, referring to Eastbrook. "Aw, gosh, it felt like we were in the middle of somebody's hog pit. And today, I think we're on the rise up."

Then, out of the blue, he asks those who have dates to raise their hands. None go up. If that's the case, he says, he'd like a half-hour meeting at his house to discuss the Cloverdale trip the following weekend.

Cloverdale High is not on the Northfield schedule; a team retreat near the school is. McClure's brother-in-law, Dr. Brad Thurston, has invited the squad to his hunting lodge after Northfield's home game Friday night against the Eastern Comets.

Northfield will go into the game with some awesome statistics. The Norse have scored 303 points in their last four games while holding the opposition to 159. The average victory margin has been 36.

The practice jerseys are safe.

And Steve McClure will celebrate his 37th birthday.

Chapter 13: Stretch Drive

February arrives on an ugly Thursday, a misty rain and cold air creating a rawness that cuts to the bone. In the parking lot, a gloom pervades the mind under the flat gray sky.

Inside the warm gym, though, the mood changes quickly as "Pump Up the Jam" (known to the players as "Pump Up the Gym") by the Technotronics blasts forth while partner drills open the day's practice.

January and the Northfield schedule have something in common this year: They've both been soft. Weather-wise, the first month of the year is often the toughest, steeped in freezing temperatures, snowstorms and occasional "whiteouts" that make driving impossible. Basketball-wise, the first month is generally a turning point in the schedule, featuring tougher opposition that gives teams a true reading of their strength.

This season, though, while northeast Indiana has basked in mild temperatures and little snow, Steve McClure's team has basked in lopsided victories over teams not particularly strong. The Norse have scored the triumphs in the wake of important victories over Whitko; Oak Hill; Wellston, Ohio; Manchester twice, and Wabash in the county tourney. All of which leaves some observers wondering just how good Northfield is.

McClure, though, shows no signs of wondering in the waning days of January. On Monday, the 29th, he greeted the squad in his usual upbeat style, glowing, in part, because of two off-court occurrences that might seem minor but are major to Steve McClure.

On Sunday, the team gave McClure a birthday present by attending services at his church, Wabash Friends, on the city's south side. He received the same birthday gift the previous two years -- and while he was not really surprised this time, as he was the first time, he was just as thrilled. After services, the team treated him to early-afternoon dinner at Ponderosa and wanted to treat Lisa and the kids, but McClure said, "Nothing doing."

The other occurrence was the latest Northfield honor rolls. Three seniors -- Jon Ross, Allen Strait and Nathan Winegardner -- have made the "All A" list. So, too, has sophomore Scott Kunkel. Noi Chay and Troy Baer are on the "All A and B" list, and junior varsity players Matt White, David Pfanstiel and Jason Wesco have achieved academic excellence, too. "How about that!" McClure says, sounding like sportscaster Mel Allen.

As he has done at key points in the season, McClure started the week by easing the pressure that has ebbed and flowed with his team all year. He spent most of the two-hour practice in relaxed shooting drills and working against a 1-3-1 trap defense.

On Tuesday, the weekly Associated Press poll has Northfield 10th, the first time the Norse are back with the elite since dropping out after the pre-season ranking because of their late start.

There was no talk about polls, though, as McClure focused on defense, seeking to overcome the tentativeness that has plagued the Northfield press all year. And, knowing that Brad Hampton's swollen right ankle might keep him out of Friday night's Eastern game, McClure tried various rotations in a scrimmage against a junior varsity team that has improved vastly under Steve Desper.

With Hampton, his best all-around defensive player looking more like a casualty for Friday, McClure stayed with defense on Wednesday, pounding away at getting people to be in the right place at the right time. As McClure says, basketball is a teachable sport; the court is no different than a classroom. A player must always be thinking as McClure -- or any other coach -- calls out offensive and defensive schemes or waves a finger or three in the air.

Now, on this rotten Thursday to start what many Hoosiers consider the rottenest month, McClure is back to offense, running a rebound-outlet drill. It's one of the players' favorites -- not because of the run and gun element, but because it teaches teamwork in a full-court situation.

"One thing I noticed in the films is that we're not lookin' deep enough when we're in a pressure situation," McClure says. "On the rebound we're throwin' our outlets too short, and we're throwin' a lot of those away. And even when the other team scores, when we take it out, we're only lookin' 15 feet in front of us."

The rebound-outlet drill incorporates a change in McClure's strategy. All year he has had his big people running deep, but with Winegardner probably starting in place of the injured Hampton, McClure has gone to the "curl."

While the team "rinses out," McClure explains: "People are on to us sendin' the big kids, so we're gonna fake them deep and curl them back to the ball, so they're meetin' a pass against a press; and then we're gonna send our guards down court."

The starting guards against Eastern will be the Chay brothers, Noi again replacing Troy Miller. Sure, Charles Miller says about his son, he was a little disappointed when he learned he was not starting anymore. "But yet," Miller adds, "he still feels he can make a contribution and the best way to do that is to keep a positive attitude and do the best that he can. And that's what he's doing."

Hampton is not indestructible, after all. He won't even suit up for Eastern, which comes in at 5-9 but has two 6-5 starters who have played well lately. The ankle he twisted against Southern Wells has improved, but it's "only about 50 to 60 percent," the youngster reports while sitting in the stands before the junior varsity contest.

"The ankle has a little catch in it," McClure says. "We're not going to take any chances with it. No one game is bigger than the health of the players."

McClure originally planned to tape Hampton's right ankle and have him warm-up, so he could get a little exercise. But the coach abandoned that idea, figuring that with the flu season in force, it would be unwise for Hampton to work up a sweat and then let him cool off on the bench during the game.

When the players enter the locker room, they find the blackboard empty, save for a few plays diagramed from a week ago. McClure has no message tonight. But Jon Ross does. He steps up to the blackboard and writes:

Excellence
Comes From
Within!!
You've Got to Want it!

Brother Joe's custom-made feet supports have arrived from Indiana Brace, a firm associated with Dr. Ahlfeld. And, fittingly, they're in Northfield blue.

McClure tells his troops to open the game with the pressing, clawing defense it worked on in practice during the week -- and they do. The result is some easy baskets and a 20-4 lead after one quarter.

McClure goes to his bench before the intermission. With a minute and 45 seconds left, the Northfield lineup consists of Bob Bratch and Allen Strait at forward, Joe Ross in the post and Peck Chay and Troy Miller at guard.

151

At the break, it's 42-11. In the coaches' dressing room across from the locker room, McClure is extremely pleased. "They've done a great job of preparing themselves this time," he says. "I really haven't been into motivation this week."

He hasn't been motivated this week?

"I've just mainly taught. You know, the last couple weeks I've been driving 'em hard, askin' for more. I just told 'em right before we came in, the moment I see ya gettin' comfortable, I'm gonna ask for a little bit more to squeeze out."

So no, he's still motivated. But the team has motivated itself this week, he feels, "and that's just great to see ... self-discipline out there, 'cause I can't do it for 'em on the floor. When you see signs of that type of maturity, look out."

In the locker room, he says little, ending with: "The big challenge now is to take every possession, offensively and defensively, and do somethin' with it. Just keep playin' basketball."

McClure cannot -- does not, in fact -- expect his team to duplicate its first-half awesomeness. But still, it is 67-20 after three quarters. Northfield has been a machine tonight, meshing on all cylinders -- but against a mediocre opponent.

The final is 83-42, and obviously there's an air of frivolity in the locker room as the troops march in. McClure yells out, "Hampton's job's in jeopardy!," and the big, easy-going kid flashes a wide smile beneath his glasses.

The Brothers Ross and the Brothers Chay have taken it to Eastern, scoring 65 of Northfield's points among them, Joe's 19 leading the way. Peck and Jon added 16 each, and Noi was good for 14.

In the post-game radio interview, Bill Rogge suggests that next Friday night's game on the road at Maconaquah figures to be a stiff test.

"That couldn't be a better situation for us at this time of the year," McClure says with relish. "Maconaquah has a great team -- I think something like 10 and 6. But out of those six losses, I think five of 'em came when they had players injured. They're back at full strength now, and they got a great ball club over there.

"Two years ago we were totally embarrassed and humiliated in that gym. For this time of year to play that type of team with that type of ability and in their hostile gym, we couldn't ask for more."

What McClure does not know is that Maconaquah, back to near-normal with the return of its top player, Latura Coleman, has just been upset, 76-74, at Southwood. And Southwood played without two injured starters, Tim Mohr and Rick Mahan.

The outstanding victory over Eastern has topped off a good week, setting the stage for the team retreat. Lisa McClure hatched the idea. Her sister, Karen, is married to Dr. Brad Thurston, a plastic surgeon.

The retreat will give the team a weekend alone, "where they can say some things amongst themselves," McClure says. "We felt the trip to Ohio was most beneficial in drawing our team together. And that's the whole idea of the retreat, just let 'em have some experiences together. I just want to get away from talking specifically basketball."

On Saturday morning, 10 varsity players, two senior managers and the five McClures pile into the McClure van and another owned by the school for a three-hour trip. The Thurstons' hunting lodge sits in a 700-acre woods.

It is another bleak day, foggy and damp, but the players are oblivious after they arrive at the lodge and sit down to a lunch of soup and hot dogs. A game of football in the mist and mud will come later, along with skeet shooting and a few cases of sniffles.

The highlight of the weekend is watching old film of McClure as a 1970-71 guard for Rising Sun High School. It gives the youngsters an opportunity to reverse roles and unload on the coach, pointing out all the mistakes he's making -- the same mistakes he points out to them.

On the return trip Sunday, McClure changes his route, taking the team into downtown Indianapolis for a stop at the Hoosier Dome.

"Forty-eight days, we're gonna come back here and get the job done," he says.

But first, there's Maconaquah, and so on Monday, it's back to work with the stress on defense. McClure introduces something new -- the 5 Jump -- designed to combat a team that holds the ball.

"We got confidence in our man-to-man defense, and we have our general concepts of any defense down pat," he says during a break in the scrimmage. "Our 5 Jump is match-up where we just step people in the passing lanes, and if the opponent dribbles toward you, you just jump and rotate and trap. Like a 1-3-1 trap in certain areas.

"See, if we ever run into a team that tries to hold the ball, they'd better be awfully good ballhandlers, 'cause this could be a deadly defense against 'em with our size and quickness combination."

153

The defense is similar to the run-and-jump he tried at Eastbrook, but it's a half-court concept instead of a full-court scheme.

"You gotta be a little smarter and little quicker reacting, probably, to do it half-court," he says. "That's what we're tryin' to do with this. We don't want to leave ourselves exposed to something later on. Just tryin' to take our defense to a higher level."

And if this wrinkle isn't enough, on Tuesday he introduces aerobics to his team. He's brought in the cheerleaders, teachers Lottie Waggoner and Iris Wion and Waggoner's friend, aerobics instructor John Dunphy, to conduct 30 minutes of exercising to music.

"It's not your normal conditioning," McClure says with a grin, "but it's just to break the monotony. Mentally, I think it's good for 'em to do something that makes 'em a little uncomfortable. And I think physically it has some benefits. It's a challenge for some of the shy kids to get out there and dance with the girls, so to speak."

On Thursday, he stresses the 5 Jump as practice draws to a close. As is often the case, the entire McClure family is in the gym, and during the last rinse, Katy skips out to center court to hug her dad.

With five games to go, what's going through his mind? McClure is asked.

The standard line, "We're just taking things one game at a time," doesn't tumble automatically from his lips. Instead, he says, "Right now we're gearin' everything toward the tournament. We're lookin' to have everything in and doin' it well by Sectional (which opens February 28).

"We have enough in now offensively that we're just gonna make sure we get it down pat, that there's no hesitation. We're very diversified now in what we can do. We just got to do it as more of a reaction and not have to think too much."

As McClure goes back to conducting the final minutes of practice, Lisa finishes soothing Cody.

"His brother insulted him," she explains. "Cody lost 50 cents in the pop machine, which he shouldn't have gone to in the first place, and Brady said, 'Nice going, Slick'."

Lisa knows about insults. Two years ago, Maconaquah pounded Northfield by more than 20 points, dealing the Norse one of the six losses McClure's squad suffered that year.

"I still have a bad taste in my mouth," Lisa says, feisty as ever.

154

It's a 45-minute ride to Maconaquah High, a "rich school" located off U.S. Highway 31, a few runways from Grissom Air Force Base. Named after the late Hoosier astronaut Virgil "Gus" Grissom, the base houses one of four NEACP planes -- National Emergency Airborne Command Post -- designed for Presidential use in case of nuclear war. And the base has other key functions that require a significant number of military families, which compute into lots of federal cash known as impacted aid. Thus, teacher salaries are handsome and facilities first-rate at Maconaquah.

The gym seats 3,600, and the largest crowd of the season is expected. It's Senior Night and the final home game for the Braves.

As usual, the Rosses have drawn interest, too, but Maconaquah fans might see only one "Tower." Jon, like brother Joe, has developed a foot problem. For two weeks he's been having calluses shaved off the ball of his right foot to reduce the pain. On Thursday, he was fine. But at 1:39 this morning he awoke in pain, the foot swollen. Unable to walk on the foot, he visited a local physician who diagnosed a bad bruise to the bone underneath the ball of the foot.

"It's caused by my arches," Jon reports before boarding the bus. "I need orthotics like Joe has." So starting tonight, Jon will wear the temporary orthotics Joe used until his custom-made pair arrived.

Jon is not worried about his team missing him. "If we play the way we did last night -- Thursday -- we'll beat 'em by 30 points easy. We practiced very well."

By the time the team bus pulls up at 5:40, a good crowd is already on hand, and there's a warm feeling in the air. But the home crowd's mood is dampened 90 minutes later after Scott Bumgardner's three-pointer with five seconds left gives Northfield a 46-44 JayVee victory.

Meanwhile, McClure has gone into the locker room and written on the blackboard

Play To Our
Limits

That will be possible, because Jon Ross will not only play, but start.

McClure gathers the team in a tight circle before the blackboard, says, "I hope you didn't put a lot of stock in Southwood beating 'em."

But at least two players have -- the Chays. Before the junior varsity game they sat in the bleachers oozing with confidence as they talked about the Southwood score. Never mind that McClure has warned against "Scoreboard Scouting" all season.

Now McClure tells his team, "We're in a hostile arena tonight. But we can handle it all."

Looking at the blackboard, he says, "Earlier in the year, we had to put up defenses and offenses, but we don't have to now. We're solid through and through. The key to the game is our initial defense and blocking out."

He compares Latura Coleman to Wabash's Gary Cooper -- both like to wiggle their way inside. The big difference is Coleman's left-handed and always goes to his left.

Switching gears abruptly, he admits, "We've had a little less competition. And I think you knew and predicted that you would pound Eastern like that. Well, this is a little different story -- but then, again, there isn't any reason why you can't go out there and pound these guys if you'll just play together and get totally involved in what we're doin'.

"Rev up the race car. Play hard and have fun."

A few minutes later, the JayVees roar into the locker room whooping and hollering, overjoyed with their victory in the dying seconds. Their exuberance figures to give the varsity a lift. But the varsity will have to wait, because Maconaquah is honoring a veteran coach who is retiring.

Shortly before game time, some 3,000 people are seated as the Maconaquah Braves' mascot and a version of the "Chicken" frolic on the floor. The public address announcer promotes scoops of ice cream on chocolate chip cookies for 75 cents; the Maconaquah band lets people know it has a drum or two; the hootin' and hollerin' is under way in the stands. The place is alive. It figures to be a fun night.

The fun begins immediately for Dee Morgan, a 6-1 senior guard. He pops for three treys early on, the last one coming from the top of the key, hitting the backboard and going in. It is an omen for Northfield.

Morgan's third three-pointer has given the Braves a 16-11 lead, and during a brief break, McClure calls the Chays over, rips them for a lack of defense.

Another omen occurs as the first quarter slips away. Winegardner saves a loose ball on Northfield's offensive end, right in front of one official. But the other official, across the court and far out of position, blasts his whistle and waves possession to Maconaquah. "What's the call?" McClure pleads. The official ignores him.

It's 22-15, Maconaquah, at the end of the first quarter, and it's clear that the Braves were a tough ballclub before Coleman was injured. In the huddle, McClure tells his troops, "Not a one of you are doin' the job down here," referring to the area around the rim. "I don't care if you do foul out, start blocking out and rebound!"

The first bad call is just that -- the first. When others occur in McClure's eyes, he calls time out with 5:45 left and the Norse down 26-19 to express his displeasure. The object of his wrath glowers back, says nothing.

Northfield finally gets even, 27-27, at 3:51, thanks to Jon Ross' jump-shooting. But four seconds later, brother Joe is tagged with his third foul and must come out. McClure slaps him on the left leg, says, "Good job."

Forty-three seconds later, Jon gets his third, too, and so both Rosses must sit. Without the twins, Northfield's offense is out yonder, and so Maconaquah surges to a 35-27 advantage. But at 1:17, Coleman, who has played so-so thus far, collects his third foul. And Northfield gets a hoop just before intermission to make it 35-29.

"You guys are a bunch of cowards," McClure growls immediately after the team assembles in the locker room.

"Homestead'll beat you to death," he continues, referring to the team that figures to be Northfield's toughest foe for the Sectional crown. "Anybody's that's supposed to be any good, you pull in the horns and you stop executin'."

He pulls off his glasses, inspects the floor, resumes: "Remember 'Forward March'? You're phony. I have to scream and yell to get you to do it every time, 'cause you don't have the guts to motivate yourself and compete like a champion when the chips are down."

Why is it, he says with pain, that when he calls for a match-up defense, they fail to get into the right positions? "Now you tell me how many times we've worked on that. Come on. I wanna hear it. You tell me how many times this year we've let a guy stand right here (the top of the key) and seen him shoot. What do we do with every zone? Can somebody answer the question?"

"Match up," Hampton says.

"Then why don't we do it when it's a big game? 'Cause you don't have it up here," and he points to his dome.

"I ain't gonna get mad," he continues. "My health isn't good enough to get mad, and, by God, when you guys just won't come out here and play hard, it isn't worth it to get mad."

Then it's back to strategy: "We gotta play zone, keep some people outta foul trouble, and they'll probably hold the ball and win 35-29."

Then it's back to the mind: "I'm gonna show you a letter from Randy Keaffaber one of these days. He misses it, and realizes what he let get loose last year. And you guys don't."

And back to strategy: "We're goin' 32. Jon and Joe, if they ain't got ya beat on the sidelines, rotate and we wanta trap right here off the lane. Joe one side, Jon the other. You three guys, you'll be up front. You just drive 'em nuts comin' up the floor. Brad, you're in the middle, you cover up the likely passer. You gotta assume that the ball's goin' into the basket, 'cause that's where they're dribblin' to."

McClure's halftime talk figured to center on defense. The Norse shot 52 percent, but Maconaquah was better at 57.

A minute and 49 seconds into the second half Joe is called for his fourth foul and comes out. Fifteen seconds later, Maconaquah opens a 10-point gap at 41-31. Another 19 seconds later Coleman commits an obvious traveling violation, and when it isn't called, McClure can't hold back. He's called for his second technical of the season, resulting in a few Northfield fans tossing debris on the floor.

Northfield keeps scratching back, and after three quarters shaves the Braves' lead to five at 47-42. And Coleman has picked up his fourth foul shortly before the end of the third quarter.

McClure keeps Joe seated to open the final eight minutes of play, which start with Morgan getting another trey.

The crowd has been into this one from the beginning, sensing it would be a typical Hoosier barn-burner, and after Jon sinks two free throws to make it 51-50, Maconaquah, the noise is deafening. Northfield has the momentum.

Then Jon fouls out. He has taken a charge at mid-court, it appears, but he's called for the block. McClure is steaming, but controlled. Debris comes flying out of the Northfield stands. Jon and his sore foot leave with 17 points. Six minutes and 26 seconds remain.

Morgan, who has played a great game, gets his fourth foul, hacking Noi with 4 minutes and 50 seconds left. Noi hits both free throws. It's 55-52, Maconaquah. Jon leaps off the bench, turns to the Northfield crowd and motions to the fans to jack it up.

Peck's jumper gets it to 55-54 at 4:31. When Noi is fouled at 4:13, Northfield has a chance to take the lead. And does, 56-55.

Morgan, who will finish with 30 points, including four treys, answers with two free throws. But Troy Miller gets his second trey, so it's 59-57, Northfield, with just under four minutes to go.

Maconaquah promptly scores three straight times, twice on rebound baskets by Morgan and Matt Kunkle, for a 63-59 advantage. Joe counters with two free throws for 63-61, but that's the closest the Norse will get.

Noi, Hampton and Joe foul out, the latter with six seconds left. After McClure says something to an official as Joe leaves, he's hit with his second technical, meaning that in one game he has doubled his previous total for the year. And with that, the Maconaquah band strikes up Bob Hope's theme song, "Thanks For the Memories."

The final is 79-71. Northfield has been called for 27 fouls, Maconaquah 16. The Braves have made more free throws, 23, than Northfield attempted, 22. And the likable Chays, who have played so wonderfully in spurts this season, have committed 12 of Northfield's 17 turnovers.

Maconaquah has been a game Northfield should have won, despite the officiating, but lost because it couldn't overcome the officiating.

It has been a game in which the Norse took the lead with four minutes to go, but played the next two minutes as if they were still behind. Instead of being patient and making Maconaquah panic, Northfield panicked. It's likely that when Northfield finally got on top, Maconaquah was thinking, We led this whole game. Now, all of a sudden, the better team is leading. We're in trouble.

But the better team didn't make better decisions offensively.

In the locker room, McClure is wrung out. He doffs his blue sweater and removes his red tie. Then he goes into a rambling 43-minute speech, punctuated at times with patches of silence as the players sit, many with heads in hands, all with heads down.

He does not mince words: "You don't have the guts, you don't have the mental toughness, you don't have what it takes."

He mentions last year's Sectional, saying Northfield "just happened to be good enough (to win), 'cause Homestead wasn't. This year they're good enough to whip ya. And that (tonight's game) was the last chance to see how you measure up to a good ball club, and you flubbed it.

"I mean, the fouls, all that stuff's incidental, because if you came out to play ball when you got off the bus, you wouldn't have had to get to that point. And I'm outta tricks. It's pathetic."

McClure stoops to his briefcase. He fishes for Randy Keaffaber's letter, printed on a sheet of classroom notebook paper. It is addressed simply to "Coach," and is one long paragraph that fills the sheet.

McClure reads every word, starting with, "Congratulations on winning a third TRC championship."

Keaffaber wishes he were still on the team, he writes, adding that he can remember almost every situation the squad was in. The three years went by quickly, and he will cherish them forever, "not because we were so successful, but because I spent them with you and your family. You guys are a big influence of my life and there's nothing I wouldn't do for any of you."

He says he still cries about last year's Regional loss to Marion.

Continuing, he writes, "You taught me more than basketball, you taught me how to be part of a family and how God wants me to be. ... I think I can speak on behalf of everybody that has ever played for you and say we respect you for more than a coach, we love you as a friend. You'll always be like another father to me. I love you and thank you for everything."

The letter is signed, "God Bless You, Randy."

Looking up from the sheet, McClure says, "You're gonna feel like that." He is referring to how Keaffaber feels about the Regional final.

Dead air follows before he points fingers, some specifically, some obliquely: "You guys have played three years. You look at the big games and how many minutes you've played and how well you've played in the big games. Noi, you play like a sophomore; you're not a sophomore anymore."

He belittles them with straight talk: "You can go around and say, 'Hey, baby, let's get 'em, guys, come on.' It's all phony. It's on the outside. 'Cause it doesn't burn on the inside, 'cause if it did, you would have beat them to death."

McClure does not see anything positive in a defeat. "You might say," he tells them, " 'Well, we got beat and now we're ready to go.' No, you're not. You aren't ready to go anywhere but to Marion March 10th and watch somebody else play (in the Regional). You

160

probably think I'm sayin' that to rouse your feathers, don't ya? No, 'cause I know what'll happen the next time we get against a good team. You'll wimp out."

Turning to Saturday night's game against Marion Bennett, he claims, "The team tomorrow has got more talent than these guys have. They're gonna get after your hide. You can say, 'But, coach, we'll be ready for Bennett.' "

He pauses, then gets sarcastic and contradictory at the same time. "Bennett's a great power, aren't they. They beat (winless) White's by 15 and Lakeview Christian by three. Boy, they play a lot of tough people."

One senses that he wants to let them shower and dress for home but can't drop tonight's game, just can't. And so, more silence.

"I *wanted* this game," he says, sounding almost like a youngster about to cry.

"I was gonna have practice tomorrow morning before Bennett so we could see what it's like playin' twice in one day for the Regional. We aren't goin' to, 'cause if you don't want it..."

Silence again as he ponders, then: "I don't know if you're Christian or not. You don't have to be. I hope you are sometime, 'cause that means more than anything. But, guys, Christian or not, you're here for a reason. If you don't believe it, you should. Let's get the blood on our skin.

"I guess I had the feeling I wanted to whup these guys good, get off the springboard and just come stormin' into the tournament. But get my point very clearly. This is about as negative as I'm plannin' to get."

Finally, he ends with a positive, pointing out that last year, Lawrence North lost its final regular-season game before grabbing the state championship.

As the team prepares for the trek home, McClure walks into the near-empty gym. By now, the bleachers have been rolled back, so he and Lisa sit on the floor, in the very corner of the court, alone, she rubbing his back soothingly as they chat softly.

After a few minutes, he's asked if, in retrospect, the easy schedule for the last four or five games had any effect.

"Well, yeah," McClure says immediately. "And that's what disappoints me, 'cause I wanted them to get geared up against our toughest challenge. We didn't do it."

What beat his team tonight?

"Ourselves. Because if you make your breaks, you'll get em. And once we were obviously in a frame of mind to make our own breaks, Maconaquah made some of their breaks. And the refs helped them. We've never had four kids foul out of a game since I've been coaching 15, 16 years. Just look at the totals and look who they were on and minutes played."

What does he do at this point?

"I find myself exhausting myself physically and mentally for ways to motivate them. And if they can't motivate themselves, we're done. I can work up a sweat, I can work up my health, I can throw things, I can go bananas, but until the kids learn to face their toughest challenges like men, we aren't gonna accomplish anything."

Why don't they?

"If I knew, I would rectify that. I really don't know."

He reiterates that there is nothing gained from losing. "But, on the other hand," he adds, "when I run out of ideas for motivation and ways to spur kids on, I think God has somethin' bigger for 'em and ... I, as a human, can't understand and maybe they can't. But He sees the big picture, and He knows what a group of people who are honoring His name need."

Lisa is mum, her face a combination of strain, pain and concern.

"But, you know," McClure says, a little upbeat, "Bobby Knight said that throughout the season you're presented new opportunities and, you know, if you'll just continue to work hard and stay focused, sooner or later, if you're in the right frame of mind, if you're workin' together as a team and all that, you'll be able to take on those opportunities. So we're gonna look for the next opportunity and we're gonna get after it this time."

And a smile sneaks on Lisa's face.

The players file out quietly, bags of gear hanging from shoulders, and board the bus. Jon says his foot didn't bother him, but that can't be.

Junior varsity player David Pfanstiel has brought the food, and so as the bus heads north, past Grissom and the planes that sit in the shadowy dark, it's quiet eating time.

Later, David Pefley says, "When we got ahead at the end, we should have stopped puttin' up the threes and started baggin' it to Joe inside to keep the lead. And make them be the aggressor on offense."

Next to him in the last seat of the bus, Hampton says, "One thing I think the team's doin' is, we're wantin' just to go out on the court and acquire things. You know what I mean by that? Just go out there and it's automatically gonna happen 'cause we're Northfield and we're ranked. We're not really goin' out there and doin' it the way we want to, to our limits. We gotta get mentally tough, just like the coach says, to get in there and kick their butts."

The aroma of vegetable soup floats over the parking lot as the sun falls in the western sky. It is 90 minutes before Northfield hosts Marion Bennett, starting with the junior varsity game at 6:30. But the parking lot is filling rapidly with fans arriving for the 18th Annual Baseball Boosters Chili and Vegetable Soup Supper.

Some 400 boosters are expected in the cafeteria before moving across the hall to the main gym for the Bennett game. Many wonder about Bennett's top player, Toby Ware, others about how the Norse will come back against a very small school with a decent 10-6 record.

Thirty minutes before the junior varsity tap, Jon Ross sits in front of his locker, getting organized. His foot hurts, he admits. He doesn't know if he will play, but he'd like to know one way or the other so he can get in the right mental frame of mind. The coach, he's told, has just headed for a bowl of chili.

In the bleachers, Hampton and others stake out the second row for the junior varsity game. "Coach got another tech today," he says, trying to keep a straight face.

Oh?

"Yeah, some of us were at his house this morning, watchin' the Maconaquah film, and when Jon got that last blocking foul, coach jumped up and yelled, and we called another tech." And now the smile spreads.

Minutes later, just off the locker room, McClure is asked about the film. "I concluded that the officials were even worse than I thought. It's particularly bad when you ask about something and they sneer and laugh at you."

He cites the play in the first quarter, when Winegardner was called for being out of bounds by the official far from the play. "The call kind of set the tone for the entire game."

As usual, the varsity starts to dress as the fourth quarter of the JayVee game begins. Tonight -- appropriately -- they don their uniforms to Soul II Soul playing "Back to Life." And as they do, Jon is limping noticeably.

The blackboard is blank, but not for long. Jon paces for a few minutes, then writes:

Believe in <u>Yourself</u>!
Believe in Your <u>Team!</u>

There are no signs of depression as the music blares, but there is no gaiety either. One gets the impression that the mood is a good sign -- not just for the team's basketball psyche, but for the players' individual mental well-beings.

After doing stretching exercises, Pefley, who has been emerging as a leader, takes his turn at the board, writes:

Execute the basics
and the <u>extraordinary</u>
will be the result.

McClure arrives, low-keyed, glances at the board, says he has something to read and hopes the team "never gets tired of the spiritual undertone."

He takes a Friends Church bulletin from the chalk trough and opens to a poem written by Georgia B. Adams. It reads in part:

"As I stand on the shore of the ocean vast
and listen to the breakers roar,
I know there is more than what meets
the eye. ....
I live one day at a time, but God above sees
the rocks and shoals;
He works out reason and rhyme.
Were it mine to know all that lies ahead, I'd
panic and sink in fear.
He stills the tempest and he still is God for
He is solace and cheer. ..."

Finished, McClure looks up, speaks with a catch in his throat, searches for the right words. "Sometimes, I think -- and it's probably some of me just pushin' all of ya to see the big goal, askin' for more each time that you come out -- we need to just take it day at a time. Yesterday's gone. Today's here, and it'll soon be gone. ... We just gotta trust in God. He sees the big picture. He sees what we can't. And so I guess what I'm sayin' is, let's just focus on the task at hand each time we come out, to do the best you can. Just be ready."

In his prayer, McClure follows up on that theme: "We just thank you, Father, that you care about us and that you can see the big picture. We can't, and sometimes it scares us, Father, but just give us the calmness to just go out and play to our ability."

Another theme tonight is one he has used all season: The opponent has been pointing for Northfield, anxious to chop down the mighty.

Defense and rebounding, missing the night before, must return tonight, he stresses.

As he talks, the Rosses toss in words of encouragement and Noi Chay sits on a soft-drink cooler, head down, inside himself for perhaps the first time this season.

Leaving the locker room, Jon says, "Start concentrating the minute you go out there," and as they stream forth, McClure says Jon has been named the team's permanent captain. It's no surprise. Jon has been emerging all season as the team leader, with brother Joe right there with him.

As they enter the gym, the public address announcer tells the crowd that Joe and Jon have been named to an Indiana all-star team that will play against a Soviet Junior National team in May.

Bennett is a small Catholic school with about 100 students. But it has a solid team, headed by the highly recruited, 6-3, 200-pound Ware. He's averaging more than 20 points and 10 rebounds a game.

Before the contest, McClure, as usual, chats with the opposing coach during warmups. As he talks with Marc Planck in front of Bennett's bench, an extremely attractive woman in a tight dress walks up to McClure, smiles, gives him a sexy "Hello, Coach McClure," kisses him on the cheek, gives him a slight bump with her hips and walks on.

"Karen, good to see ya tonight," McClure says, returning the smile.

Planck's eyes look like quarters, having just taken in the brief scene.

McClure turns to him and says, "Hey, we have great fans here." Then, before heading for his bench, McClure makes sure Planck knows that Karen is his sister-in-law.

165

It's game time, and instead of Ware, it's Eric McMillan, a 5-11 perimeter player, who does the early damage against Northfield. Still, the Norse take a 17-14 lead after one quarter.

Northfield's 5 Jump defense starts to create some offensive opportunities, resulting in Bennett fouls, but the Norse are cold from the line. So Bennett, which has played with discipline, is down by only seven, 33-26, at the half.

McClure is collected in the locker room, but harsh: "You are not a mentally tough group. That's what it is. You got all kinds of ability, but you are not mentally tough. You don't believe in yourself. You don't believe in your team. You can't do basics. The basic is competition. And you won't even compete. ...

"I can't believe it. Guys, when we run a 4 high, what does the wing man do when he passes back? ... Why don't we do it?"

It is late in February, and nothing positive is happening, he says. "A bad, bad sign."

Northfield is winning and has not played that poorly, but there is a pall over the sweaty assemblage. And McClure says, "I don't know what's going on."

On the way back to the court for the second half, he says he is confounded. "Mental toughness," he says. "I'd be thrilled to death if I saw it."

He sees a little the second half -- at least from some players. But he sees something else, too: inconsistent guard play, a bugaboo all season.

Northfield plays better in the third quarter, leaving no doubt about the outcome. If Bennett had any hopes of coming back, they're dashed with 40 seconds left when McMillan turns his right ankle and limps off.

The 12-point lead Northfield takes into the fourth quarter would be greater had the Norse made free throws. But it doesn't matter. Worn down, Bennett folds completely in the final eight minutes and Northfield rolls to a 77-49 final.

Joe finishes with 22, Jon 21, while McMillan leads the Trojans with 17. Ware has been held to seven and just two rebounds.

"They took Toby out of his normal game," Planck says after the game. "He had to change his shots or eat them."

Planck is not unhappy with his team, feeling it played well for three quarters. But Northfield is "definitely the best team we've played. It's going to be tough for anybody to beat them without a couple of 6-5 guys."

Immediately after walking into the locker room, McClure looks at Troy Miller and asks if he didn't shake hands with his teammates.

"I shook," Miller says softly, making a motion with his right hand.

"Well," McClure says, "I heard you didn't shake."

Miller shakes his head in denial, sticks out his hand in illustration again.

"Best thing about this weekend is that it's over," McClure says, moving on. "We'll take Monday off. Guys, White's game, don't you think about it."

There is nothing to think about. White's has had outstanding individuals and teams in the past, but this year is winless.

In contrast to Maconaquah, McClure is exceptionally brief and then walks over to Miller's locker. The coach says a few words softly, Miller nods and McClure leaves for an interview with Bill Rogge.

On the way, he says, "The kids were trying too hard in the first half to redeem themselves. We definitely got the job done defensively. Ware was averaging over 20, we hold 'im to seven."

With Rogge, McClure talks about opportunities, citing Fort Wayne Harding one week hence. "Harding's playin' great ball, especially of late. They have a 6-9 center. So they're gonna be a little different to match up with, and that's gonna be really interesting. We felt like we missed a great opportunity last night to go to Maconaquah and play a good team and execute well. ...

"We've got a lot of people banged up right now. Jon Ross played both games this weekend in extreme pain with his right foot. Joe twisted his ankle tonight. Brad retwisted his ankle last night. Peck twisted his ankle. Troy Miller's got a sore ankle and a little flu. It goes down the line."

When the interview concludes, McClure is asked about the Miller situation.

"Harold Christie told me after the game, 'You might want to just check with Miller. It looks like the boys tried to shake hands and he wasn't very enthusiastic about it.' I like to nip things in the bud, so I just got right up front with him and asked him, and I'm satisfied that Troy's fine."

McClure washes down a bite of ham sandwich with his Coke, then: "We had a situation two or three years ago where a kid was a little unhappy, and we probably didn't jump on it soon enough. So I was just doin' a little preventive medicine there with Troy's attitude and found out he's in good shape. He just wasn't happy with the way he played. But he feels good about bein' on the team and his role."

Lisa McClure is not happy either. "They'll never get this opportunity again," she says, sounding like a teacher scolding her students. "They just get me so mad sometimes when they don't play well."

The mental strain has been clearly evident this weekend -- a strain almost impossible to avoid at this juncture with a team expected to do so much and pushed so hard by a coach constantly driving home tough lessons that go beyond basketball.

Walking into the near-vacant parking lot in the brittle cold of night, one wonders about Steve McClure. Is he for real about God? Does he really not care about losing so long as his kids grow, learn, mature? Is winning really more important than he lets on? Is the pressure inside him really greater than he would admit? Is the man really good for high school athletes?

The answer to all the questions is, probably yes.

For the first and last questions, definitely yes.

•••••••••••

In late January, Steve McClure received a letter from Tim Knight, Bob Knight's oldest son, reporting that Joe and Jon Ross have been invited to play for "Team Indiana," an AAU squad that will face the Soviet Junior National squad May 5 in Fort Wayne.

A Stanford University graduate, the younger Knight handles some of his father's business affairs and promotes events, such as this all-star game.

It's another exciting opportunity for the Rosses, because they will be among Indiana's finest, including Damon Bailey and Eric Montross.

Those two highly coveted stars will also play in the McDonald's All American High School Basketball Game on April 15 at Market Square Arena in Indianapolis.

Morgan Wooten, the legendary coach of DeMatha High School in Maryland and chairman of the selection committee, told the media in announcing the players and other game details: "It is only appropriate that a game with talent of this caliber will be held in Indiana, the cradle of high school basketball. Hoosier Hysteria will be more than satisfied with this McDonald's All American game."

Chapter 14: Key Weekend

The weather is anything but rosy on Valentine's Day as freezing rain knocks power out, makes driving nearly impossible and leads to morning classes being canceled the next day.

Steve McClure is a teacher first, but volunteers that the short school day on Thursday is a plus for his tired, hurting team that faces a pivotal -- and unusual -- weekend.

Northfield will host White's Institute on Friday, and while the Warriors have been tough in the past -- they beat the Norse the year before McClure arrived -- this year, Steve Desper's JayVee team could win by 40.

White's is a boarding school for teens with problems ranging from truancy to drug offenses. It is administered through the same school corporation that oversees Northfield and Southwood.

At times White's has had strong teams for only half a season, because leading players, like the other students, come and go depending on their behavioral status. The normal stay is about one year.

This year, White's has had little talent all year and comes into Friday's game winless in 18 contests.

On Saturday, though, Northfield faces a tough foe -- and perhaps its most important game of the year; another gut-check, for sure -- in Fort Wayne Harding.

For Steve McClure, it will be a new beginning of sorts. Last Saturday afternoon, before the Bennett game, he lay in bed napping with Lisa and talking about the season dwindling to a close.

He had gotten away from making the game fun for the players, he told her. And, of course, that meant no fun for him either.

"Well," she said, "maybe you better pray about it to yourself," and left his side. Returning a short time later, she asked, "What do you think?"

"Well, I've got to forget the possibility of losing," he replied, "and I've got to get back to the game plan of having fun. When you're having fun, you're gonna forget about all the pressure that's on you, you're gonna forget about all the people that are sitting down and you're just gonna play like you practice."

With that in mind, McClure's operative word was "fun" when the team returned to practice Tuesday, February 12. They worked mostly on offense, striving for more consistent execution.

If McClure had planned on intensive defensive drills Tuesday, he probably would have been disappointed and frustrated by day's end. The players' sub-par health and the strain of the previous weekend -- getting upset at Maconaquah, struggling to victory against Bennett -- left them "pretty dead" in McClure's eyes. He could see the discolored faces, hear the coughing, witness the limping.

Wednesday's Valentine's Day practice is nearly a carbon copy of Tuesday's workout, stressing offense and light physical play to avoid aggravating wounds and ills. And outside, the weather grew progressively worse.

By early Thursday morning it is clear that slick roads and patches of fog are too dangerous for buses, so students get to sleep in. When the team arrives that afternoon, McClure keeps things light, holding shooting contests and a two-ball competition that tests dribbling skill. He closes practice with the players' favorite drill, the 11 Man fast break exercise. By five o'clock, it is clear they have enjoyed the day.

"I think the delay we got this morning was a Godsend," McClure says after practice. "The three-hour postponement couldn't have come at a better time. This is really workin' out well that the kids are gonna have four and half days of school. It gave them some extra hours' rest and got 'em out of their regular routine of gettin' up, go to school, go to practice, go home and study and go to bed."

Now the weekend has arrived, bringing with it one of those opportunities McClure remembers Bob Knight talking about. "It's a perfect time for us," the Norse coach says as the crowd filters in for the JayVee game. "Physically, we've been down. In fact, I misjudged the team physically last week. We had more ankle turns than I was aware of. Jon's infection on his foot was more severe than he had communicated to me. And we had flu, which I wasn't aware of either.

"Some of the kids, I think, wanted to play the past weekend because they knew the Maconaquah game meant a lot to us. But I think they went out there hurtin'. Not to make an excuse for 'em, but after I saw 'em come back Tuesday and they really didn't feel any better ...

"You know, when you're physically down, sometimes your mind goes down with it. I think we had a couple of cases where the kids were mentally tired as well."

There will be two "Senior Nights" this year -- sort of. With White's being the second to the last home game, McClure will open with three seniors who haven't started all year -- Bob Bratch, Allen Strait and David Pefley -- along with seniors Troy Miller and Nathan Winegardner.

"It's kind of our chance to applaud the people who play the less glamorous roles," McClure says. "It's a chance to have their name announced. They've earned it."

In his pregame prayer, McClure asks that "this be a special weekend for the seniors, Father. It's their last home stand. Just let them go out and play some great basketball here at Northfield High School and be able to carry on through the road games upcoming. And Father, this game tonight. It is a little bit unusual, and it's kinda neat in a way."

Unusual, indeed. McClure has taught 13 of the 20 White's varsity and junior varsity players in his health and/or physical education classes. And five years ago, when Joe and Jon Ross were 6-3 eighth-graders, McClure coached White's eighth graders. The other Northfield seniors, save for Peck Chay, were also on that squad. White's seventh-grade coach then was Clyde Lovellette, and during the game against Northfield, McClure turned to him and said, "I sure like the little red-headed kid."

The "little red-headed kid" is now the 6-5 Brad Hampton, and, as usual, he's upbeat and loose as he laces his shoes.

The crowd is the smallest of the year, as expected, despite almost the entire White's student body of some 100 students being on hand.

The game, of course, is never a contest. By the half it's 53-13, and at times in the first 16 minutes, McClure and White's coach Larry Vaughn -- a fellow physical education teacher -- joke with each other despite being separated by the scoring table.

McClure plays everyone except the Rosses. Hampton sees action only in the third quarter, primarily because his father is home for the weekend from Pennsylvania.

The final is 102-32, but, of course, the score doesn't matter.

What will matter will be tomorrow night. Can Northfield pound a tough team the way it has pounded some patsies on the second-half schedule?

On Saturday night, McClure has no doubt in his mind. Using a simile as he does so often, he tells the squad in the locker room, "All season long, it's like you've been under nuclear attack. Now the dust is settling and our Minuteman missiles are intact."

In his prayer, he doesn't forget the White's kids: "They have more challenges than we do, Father."

Harding's Hawks come into Northfield's finale after capturing their second straight Summit Athletic Conference championship on Friday night, which means they are Fort Wayne's top team. Their record is 14-6, including a win at home against Manchester.

Coached by Al Gooden, a former Ball State standout, the Hawks have a quick club that plays tough defense and has an outstanding all-around player in Ray Moon.

McClure and avid Northfield followers realize how important this game is psychologically. If the Norse fall behind, will they have the grit to come back? Can they deal with the pressure the way they did in the home opener against Whitko, which has lost only one more game since then? Can they motivate themselves like they have in past big games?

In the locker room, David Pefley has provided the music -- fittingly, a collection of rock he taped and labeled "We Are the Champions" after one selection by the group called Queen.

On the blackboard, McClure has written:

End
Or
Beginning

He has abandoned a sweater for the second straight night, choosing instead a neat gray suit to go with his favorite red-knit tie.

He begins by saying he doesn't want to make "a big deal about the seniors. But you know, the thing you gotta look at is -- this is your commencement really in basketball. What does commencement mean? Beginning. Okay.

"You seniors, in May you'll have commencement. And some people see it as the end, the people who are just gonna stick around town and, you know, have three jobs a year, come to the ballgame on Friday night and complain about it. Your general NIOP.

"And then some people go on to college and military service or other mission or something worthwhile, and they move ahead with their life and they just use commencement as a start.

"And as we look at our basketball team, you gotta think, Is this the end of it? Is this what we've worked for? Is it to have senior night?

"We told ya in October it would come, and it certainly did. But the thing you gotta ask yourself is, Have we worked to get up here February 7th to just have an emotional night at Northfield?"

He acknowledges that they have had "pressure galore," and then he lays himself naked: "I'll admit that at times I've wanted to run from it. At times I've just wanted to pack it up and hit the road. I've asked God, 'Why did you put me in this stupid, idiotic profession?' "

"You love it," Hampton says.

"You bet," McClure responds, "because I'm a pressure man. And God doesn't give you somethin' unless he's gonna see you through it."

Seconds later, he changes tone, injecting a lightness that shows fun is really on his mind.

"Guys," he says, "let 'er fly. You want to pull up and shoot a three-pointer -- pull up and shoot a three-pointer. Pefley, if you want to go behind your back (with the dribble), pull up and shoot a three-pointer, blow to cool off the gun and stick it back in the holster. I'm sayin' to ya, turn it loose.

"I want you to have a great time. Make as many turnovers as you want. Make 30 on the 11-man drill. If we have five possessions without a turnover, kick one out of bounds."

And they laugh.

But turnovers are not funny. In the two games the Norse lost, they committed a total of 50, including 33 against Tippecanoe Valley.

The films show that McClure's team has a tendency to stand around too much offensively, and that's what practice has been about all week, moving without the ball, looking for entries into the big men, running the break.

McClure closes his pregame comments with a few minutes of X's and O's that stress one-on-one coverage outside the three-point area, attacking the ball inside the three-point area, blocking out, rebounding and running the 11-man drill.

Shortly before gametime seniors from all sports -- including cheerleaders and trainers -- are introduced and walk with their parents the length of the court. An unfortunate -- and seemingly unintentional -- situation has occurred, but hardly anyone in the crowd knows. They will know later; word of such incidents spreads fast in small communities.

Two names are missing from the program listing the seniors and their parents -- Edward and Vahn Chay. The Chays -- faithful fans all season -- have seen the sheet and are not present. When Peck's name is called, he's escorted by brother Pick.

The master sheet put together by Jim Kaltenmark has the Chays on it, but somehow, they are missing from the circulated version. When the error was spotted, Peck heeded friends' advice and, in his warmup attire, went home to get them. But they declined. "My Dad can be stubborn," Peck says later.

Finally, the fans rise for the Northfield school song one last time at home, singing the lyrics while Ross Trump's students play the music to Mighty Oregon:

> *We're the mighty men of Northfield*
> *Fighting for our Gray and Blue*
> *We will fight to win our battles*
> *Northfield High we're all for you.*
>
> *We will use our strength and honor*
> *For the glory of our school*
> *Win or lose we're never daunted*
> *Norsemen we are back of you.*

The game starts inauspiciously for Harding. On the tap, 6-2 center Todd Stubbs' goggles get knocked to the floor, and so with three seconds gone, he has to come out while they are repaired. Ron Hughes, a 6-8 senior, replaces him.

The players are tight in the first quarter, especially Joe Ross, who misses several follow-ups in close, and so after one quarter it's 10-7, Northfield.

The Norse defense stays stingy until the half, yielding just 18 points. Moon, a stylish, 6-2 senior, has 13 of them, including two treys. Meanwhile, the Norse have managed 29 points, the last two on Joe's little hook at the buzzer.

McClure talks defense in the locker room. "We're goin' man, because I think our men are better than their men. Guess who you're guardin', Brad?"

"Number 52," Hampton says jokingly, meaning Hughes. McClure replies, "Yeah, you know better than that," and his grin is wide, and everybody knows Hampton's got Moon for the next 16 minutes.

Turning to the board, McClure diagrams Moon's moves, pointing out he's running the baseline to get open for his bombs.

"Now, what we'll do if we go back to zone," McClure says, "is Brad you're comin' down and you just start on Moon's side, man-to-man. The rest of you -- when Moon cuts through, you guys step up. If you get hung up on a pick, Brad, you scream at the top of your lungs for help. And then the nearest big man goes with him."

It is Geoff McDougal, however, who gets Harding off to a fast start in the second half, hitting a three-pointer with just 17 seconds gone to make it 29-21.

Harding will get no closer.

The second half is an exhibition of tremendous team play -- Jon Ross hitting jumpers from everywhere, brother Joe banging the boards, the Chays picking the Hawks' pockets repeatedly for steals and lay-ins, Hampton working inside with Joe.

Midway through the third quarter, as Northfield pulls away steadily, Lisa McClure writes on a small piece of paper, "Are we having fun yet?", signs it "Lovely, Lovely," and passes it to her husband. It's extremely rare for her to do something like that. The expression is a favorite around the McClure household, and from the beginning of their marriage, Steve has referred to Lisa as "the Lovely, Lovely." Upon getting the note, he looks back and can't help but smile his answer.

After three quarters it's 52-29, and everyone knows it's over.

Defense has been the key. The Rosses have forced the Hawks into altering their shots repeatedly, and after yielding one early three-pointer to Moon, Hampton has held him to just one more free throw.

The defense has created a burst of offense. At 3:31 and Northfield up, 65-31, McClure yells to his bench, "Let's get the gear off!" For the last time at home, the Rosses come out to a standing ovation.

Pefley gets his patented trey with 2:02 left to make it 72-37 and send the crowd into jubilation.

The final is 75-48. Joe has scored 18 points after his poor early start and grabbed nine rebounds, while Jon has contributed 17 and eight rebounds.

McClure walks into the locker room and yells as loud as he can, "You guys having any fun yet!?"

There will be no post-game talk tonight. There will be no practice on Monday. "If I see anybody Monday within three miles of the gym with a basketball, you get fined 500 dollars," McClure says.

He has one final announcement: they need to wear their uniforms to practice Tuesday for the team photo before the Sectional.

It has been a great evening, except for the Chay incident. In the small passageway between the locker room and gym, Lisa is clearly disturbed. Like many coaches' wives, she really is a second mother to the players.

"If it had happened to one of the American kids, it would have been overlooked and the parents would probably be here," she says. "But I think maybe the Chays' culture is such that they didn't feel they should come. They think perhaps they would be hurting somebody's feelings, but, of course, they wouldn't."

Is there an inferiority complex involved, too?

"Maybe," she says. "Probably."

The next day, Northfield learns it has drawn its final regular-season opponent, Southwood's Knights, for the Sectional opener. It will mean back-to-back games for the country cousins.

The host Knights -- 46-point losers at Northfield -- are a crippled ballclub. Tim Mohr, their top scorer before breaking his right wrist prior to that game, is out for the season. Rick Mahan has suffered an injury in practice severe enough to sideline him indefinitely. And a third starter, Chad Larsh, is ill.

McClure, though, gives no thought to Southwood's problems as practice resumes on Tuesday. The emphasis now is on refining, not teaching.

With 15 minutes left in the 90-minute session, something odd occurs: McClure kicks Joe and Jon out of practice -- the first time anyone has been banished all season. It happens quietly and suddenly.

"They were gettin' on each other and practicin' bad habits," McClure says later.

Bad habits?

"Well, it's just that Jon was startin' to shove with his hands, foulin' a lot and stuff. And Joe was startin' to join in 'cause he was a little upset that Jon was upset, I think.

"Jon was obviously very frustrated, and he tends to take some of that out on Joe. And Joe was getting frustrated. When they're not handling things mentally, that's a bad habit, too."

McClure is particularly irritated with Jon. "I'd asked him to be a show-me captain instead of a tell-me captain. And he was tellin' 'em today, so I told him a few things. We're not gonna have it. It doesn't matter if it's from the top person, quote, unquote, or the number 20. The rules are the same for everyone. And the rules I do make I enforce very strictly."

McClure likes to give young people a chance to work things out themselves, learn something about self discipline. But when a situation creates what he feels is a turning point for the team, he will clear the air and take charge.

Are the Rosses feeling more pressure now?

"Naw," McClure twangs, "it's just that Jon, he said he'd been gettin' hacked and gouged underneath and fouled a lot. And we don't call fouls in practice very often, and, you know, after three and half, four years of that stuff, it probably does get a little frustrating."

Even when they're his own teammates?

"Yeah, sure, after all ..."

The two big kids -- first-class people -- are embarrassed, and Joe ambles over to say he's sorry.

"I just told him," McClure says later, 'Hey, you're human.' He felt bad. He blew it, he said. And I told him we're all human, that I blew it a couple of weeks ago, that Maconaquah weekend -- even leadin' up to that. I was hard on people and probably dishin' a little more than people can take at the time. And I said to Joe, we just gotta help each other out."

Before leaving for the day, McClure and the twins sat and talked.

"Joe expressed his frustration, and he was a little choked up," McClure related. "He was really disappointed in himself. He felt like he had let the team down a little bit. And I just explained that on some teams that'd probably be a big deal, this team it's not. And they came out the next day and you don't even know anything's happened."

What's "neat about the whole thing," McClure says, "is seein' that there's love there and an understanding and a forgiving attitude between ourselves, you know. The team and all that. You're just reminded that's the type of group we have."

It's clear McClure is not mouthing platitudes. This is borne out on Wednesday, with another team get-together. George Price, a retired elementary-school principal in the Metropolitan school corporation, and his wife, Cindi, a teacher at Sharp Creek elementary, have invited the team over for a meal. Last year, the Prices, who operate a catering service, had the team over before the Regional. This season, McClure opts to have the dinner before the Sectional.

"It's kinda nice," McClure says, "that George is a school board member and thinks enough of our team to do that. He just says he and his family really enjoy watchin' the kids play and he and his wife want to do somethin' special."

After the meal on Wednesday, McClure went to the Ross home to help prepare a flyer promoting Joe and Jon for the Indiana all-star team that faces Kentucky. The flyers will be sent to newspapers, schools and others who help influence who are chosen.

"We just had a great time at the house," McClure says, "and the practice incident never came up. They just know that the discipline I give 'em is strictly out of love and for their benefit."

Two days later, the afternoon sun is bright at 5:40 as the players board the bus for the 20-minute ride to Southwood.

The Knights' gym is almost a carbon copy of the Northfield facility, the emphasis being on red instead of blue. As usual, the visiting team is assigned the girls locker room. Tonight, though, there aren't enough empty lockers, so players share and clothing is piled on the floor.

McClure keeps his recent theme going. As the players enter, they see
the blackboard message:

Have fun!

Minutes later, an incident occurs that loosens them as they start to dress.

A tall brunette mistakenly walks into the locker room, gulps, says "*Oh!*" and makes a fast turnaround as laughing and joshing break out. Only David Pefley had not pulled his shorts over his jock.

Was he embarrassed?

He shakes his head no, smiles. He's telling the truth.

Strategically, McClure stresses defense on the board. He wants his team to start with Number 2 and run a series. The 2 will be either a 2-1-2 zone or 2-3 zone, and the Norse will stay in it until Southwood scores. Then McClure will go to a different defense and stay with it until Southwood scores again. He will use what he learns in the Sectional opener.

On the bench, as the team warms up, McClure reminisces, as he does each time Northfield plays at Southwood. It was here that he got his first varsity win, and he can remember almost every play that took place, especially the opening minutes when his team turned the ball over eight times in their first nine possessions.

A near-capacity crowd is on hand for Southwood's Senior Night. After the Norse starters are introduced, the gym goes dark save for a spotlight that beams on the Knights' starters as they are introduced. Never mind that their team is 8-11, the home fans' hootin' and hollerin' almost blots out the public address announcer's hype.

Moffett has decided to employ the strategy he used against Northfield in their Sectional contest last season: a deliberate, ball-control game. So after one quarter, it's 16-6, Northfield, and it doesn't figure to be another 50-point Norse victory.

But it will be a Norse win, that's for sure, as Northfield slowly builds its lead to 30-10 at the half. Southwood has scored six of its 10 points from the free-throw line.

McClure tells his team to relax, because halftime will be longer than usual. Then he sits on the floor near the door to talk strategy with assistants Desper and Christie.

Lots of X and O talk follows, in a teaching mode more than a coaching mode, and it's obvious McClure is thinking Sectional four days hence.

It's obvious, too, that Northfield just wants to get this game over with. The Norse play adequately, at best, and after three quarters it's over at 43-21.

With slightly less than four minutes remaining, McClure starts clearing his bench. A short time later, Moffett removes Brad Weaver. A solid youngster better known for his football, he shows why he's considered a class kid, coming down to the Northfield bench to congratulate his opponents.

The final is 49-32, with Jon's 16 points leading the way.

"A block, a weight has been lifted off our shoulders right now," McClure tells his squad in the locker room. "I don't know about you guys, but all year long, I've just been waitin' for now."

He's not worried about a thing, but, of course, he doesn't like the turnovers and he knows they don't either.

"Waitin' " is the operative word tonight. Just waitin' to get the game over with. Now waitin' for the tournament. Waitin' for "showtime." Waitin' to "turn 'er loose."

About the Sectional opener on Wednesday, he says, "These guys are gonna try to lull ya to sleep a little bit like they did tonight. They're gonna come out on fire. They'll run all that patient-type offense and everything. That makes no difference. With Southwood or any other opponent you might be fortunate enough to play."

If teams get only 32 points against them, he says, they will win the state championship.

A short time later Moffett says his team can beat Northfield if the Knights can hold the Norse to 50 points.

"Our kids think we can beat 'em," he says. "We were patient tonight; we just have to hit our shots. Their bench is their Achilles heel. If we can get into their bench, we can beat them. If you had told me before the season that we could play our bench against their bench, I'd have said, 'We'll take it.'"

He has a point, because for several games, Moffett's team has played decent basketball with three bench players.

Still, McClure was correct when he told his team after the victory, "You wanted to get this sucker out of the way so you could get on with the show. Correct? That's all right. It's our show now, guys."

But the pressure valve needs to be adjusted again, so he ends with: "And don't worry how far it takes ya. Just come out, enjoy it. Let's get outta here."

They shower quickly, dress and pile onto the bus, where Jason Wesco is passing out the post-game food he has brought.

Shortly after midnight, snow begins to fall as an Alberta Clipper moves in. It figures -- it's Sectional time.

•••••••••

Scott Kunkel, nicknamed "Skippy," has made the Sectional squad. Each team is required to send its 12-man roster to the IHSAA two weeks before play begins. McClure has added Ryan Dubois, along with Kunkel, and dropped Troy Baer, who was on the original varsity roster.

Kunkel, told earlier by McClure to "earn" his varsity jersey, has done so. "The bottom line is his play for itself," McClure says. "He just came on strong at the end of the year."

Dubois, a lean 6-2, was chosen for his outside shooting ability.

"It was a very difficult choice," McClure sighs. "We considered Jason Wesco, who had a great year as a junior, as well as George Samons and Troy Baer. It was especially tough for Baer, bein' on the preseason roster."

McClure told each player individually his fate. He offered "alternate" status to Baer, Wesco and Samons, meaning they can practice with the team, including the session at the Sectional site, Huntington North High School.

Returning from Southwood on the bus, Kunkel says making the varsity roster is "a big relief. But I can't feel satisfied. I gotta keep workin' harder. There's a saying I heard. I can't remember where I heard it, but it says, 'If you can't win, make the one ahead of you break the record.' And that's the way I feel. I know I'm not gonna be able to start because all the players are established. So I just try to make them better."

One thing Kunkel has gotten better at is free-throw shooting. He got his nickname based on his name and Kip Jones, who started for Purdue last season. Jones was not a very good free-throw shooter, and neither was Kunkel early on. So Scott became "Skippy."

Is he ready for baseball, his best sport, to begin?

"No, no hurry at all," he says, and his smile is cheek to cheek.

Chapter 15: **The Sectional**

It is Sunday afternoon, February 18, and Hoosiers are clustered around televisions in homes, restaurants, offices, businesses and churches for an hour of great importance.

A network of stations around the state is broadcasting live from IHSAA headquarters in Indianapolis the pairings for the 80th boys basketball tournament.

Starting Monday, February 26, sudden death begins for 386 teams who seek the everlasting glory of being crowned the Indiana state champion.

It all begins at 64 Sectional sites, where anything can happen. Teams that have gone into the Sectional unbeaten have been zapped. And teams with absolutely horrendous records have pulled off huge upsets. Steve Desper remembers his brother's 1965-66 Kendallville team going into the tournament at 0-20 and beating Avilla before "getting blown out as usual in the next game." And in 1968, New Market was 2-17 but stunned folks by winning the Sectional for first-year coach Jim Petty. Twin Lakes topped that in 1980, going in at 2-18 and coming out as Sectional kings.

Sectional winners advance to one of 16 Regionals. The 16 survivors move on to four Semistates, and then it's the State Finals at Indianapolis. Unlike the Sectionals, which are played over a week's time, the Regionals, Semistates and State Finals are four-team affairs contested on successive Saturdays. The first game begins at 11 o'clock, the second at 12:30; then the winners meet that night at 8:15.

Sunday's Sectional draw pits Northfield against Southwood in the 6:30 opener Wednesday, February 28, at Huntington North, which can accommodate almost 5,000 fans. The host team plays Homestead, a Fort Wayne-area school, at 8. Wabash has drawn the easiest route to the championship contest, getting the bye game against winless White's at 6:30 Friday, March 2. The second game matches Wednesday's winners, and that survivor plays for the championship Saturday -- almost certainly, against Wabash.

Playing Southwood back-to-back does not displease Steve McClure. "Looking at the draw," he says, "we're gonna have to beat the three best teams in the tournament anyway, or at least two. So we're just gonna go in there and -- like we started in last week -- have fun."

183

Fun is one thing; winning is another. McClure and everyone else knows it. Winning and losing in tournament play can have a real effect in small burgs, where there's lots of idle time and not much to talk about, leaving basketball with a great deal of importance. Post-tournament feelings can range from the blahs, sour grapes, finger-pointing, neighbor hostility and chants of "Fire Coach Doe" to euphoria, community healing, neighbor love and chants of "Coach Doe for Mayor!"

McClure has figured all season that Northfield's chances of winning its second straight Sectional crown and third in four years will probably come down to defeating Homestead. The Spartans, who go into the tournament with a 17-4 record, figure to handle 3-17 Huntington North without much difficulty.

McClure hoped the draw would pit Northfield against Homestead in either the first or second game. "I would rather not play 'em in the final game," he says, "because that would have us playing on Friday night and then playing them the next day without a serious practice in between. Last year we drew Homestead first and had good success, 'cause we had time to practice for 'em."

Northfield played Huntington North -- an unfamiliar team -- for the championship last year without having time to prepare. So McClure's pleased that this won't be the case this year, assuming, of course, his squad can win its first two games.

On Monday, February 19, McClure says Homestead is no cinch to beat Huntington North, a consolidation that included Vice President Dan Quayle's alma mater. Once a long-time power, Huntington has struggled in recent years. But McClure notes that the Vikings are on their home court and have a good, young team that could explode at any time.

And perhaps the Viking boys will be inspired by the Huntington North girls, who, six days after the boys Sectional draw, upset Noblesville and Bedford North Lawrence for a state championship of their own.

The winter weather became so treacherous the night of the girls final that many fans spent the night at Market Square Arena, safe from the blowing snow and frigid temperatures.

The weather forced McClure to cancel the 6 to 8 p.m. practice scheduled at Huntington North, located 17 miles from Wabash. Instead, he held a 4:30 workout at Northfield, followed by dinner at the Pizza Hut.

It is 8 o'clock Wednesday morning, February 28, and the sun is up as David Pefley begins one of the biggest days of his life.

Shortly before the season opened, McClure wasn't certain whether he wanted Pefley for the varsity. Finally, he decided the youngster's positive attitude would be good for the team and added him to the roster, but not in time for the game programs.

Now, though, on this brisk, sunshiny day, Pefley wears his blue and white letterman's jacket over his blue team sweater and blue pants as he heads for his first class, sociology.

Minutes earlier, the Ross twins ambled across the main gym floor, separately, heads down in thought and athletic bags slung over their right shoulders, to start this Sectional day.

Pefley, who at 5-11 and 215 pounds lettered three years as a football lineman, admits this day is huge for him.

"I mean, it's the first time I've ever been a part of the Sectional as a team member," he says with awe. "I know I won't play much, but still, it doesn't matter, you know.

"It's kind of a dream for a guy who went out for the team for three years and didn't make it -- didn't even make the JayVee -- and now you're on the team.

"Yeah, I'd have to say this is a big day, especially being in Indiana. It's everybody's dream to play varsity basketball on a good team in Indiana."

It is the American Dream that teacher Fred Griffith wants to discuss today in sociology. The 50-minute period concludes with a brief discussion on what is success, and when Griffith asks each of the 13 students to define it, Pefley replies, "Achieve self-set goals."

In Jim Wenrich's second-period physics class, Pefley is joined by teammates Joe, Jon, Allen Strait, and the late-arriving Peck Chay. Wenrich has assigned the students to build towers out of plastic straws. Each student has 125 straws and a supply of straight pins with which to build a tower that will be graded on a power factor involving height and the amount of mass it can hold. Pefley has completed his at home, save for a few minor details, and the Rosses are finishing up, too. The "Twin Towers" have not built twin towers. While Jon touches up, Joe attempts to correct a crooked lower section.

It's on to Advanced Composition and Literature with Lottie Waggoner, and there are no signs of Pefley's mind drifting. In fact, in a discussion on freedom of expression, he leads those who oppose the legalization of flag-burning. "You can protest," he says, "but there are certain things you don't mess with -- the Bible, the flag, the Bald Eagle, because they stand for something greater." Waggoner assigns an essay on flag-burning, which isn't due until March 12 "in deference of basketball stuff."

Fourth period is 50 minutes of calculus with Steve Desper, who teaches the way he coaches: calmly (for the most part), methodically, talking easily, using an economy of words. "This isn't difficult," he says after putting problems involving explicit differentiation on the board. Desper, a very popular teacher, has had most of the students for three or four years.

"They're used to my style," he chuckles while they work on problems. "They know my tests."

On the back wall, Desper has posted the entire Sectional draw -- all 64 sites. Students in his three advanced classes -- two in trigonometry and one in calculus -- are invited to pick the winners. Desper will buy breakfast for the student in each class who picks the most winners. "Just a way to break up the routine of school and let them have some fun," he says matter of factly.

In the hallway, en route to lunch in the cafeteria, Pefley passes Brad Hampton. "The Hampster" doesn't look well, but he's his usual happy self as he waves a small, pale green, congratulatory-type balloon attached to a thin wooden stick. "Good Luck" is scrawled on it in black.

The cafeteria is a sight. The cheerleaders have chosen an outer-space theme to pump up spirit, and on the far wall off the main hall they have spread a huge sign: Norse Are Out Of This World. Blue balloons hang from the ceiling. Windows that help partition the serving area from the dining room are soaped with the players' names and numbers; a separate window has the names of the managers. On another wall, 14- by 18-inch cards have each player's name and number, and in the center is "Coach 1." Smaller signs scattered about urge the Norse to "Take it to the top," "Make 'em see Stars" and "Black out those Knights."

But as Pefley eats with Peck Chay and other friends, spirit seems to be missing in this, the third of three separate lunch periods. Perhaps Southwood is being taken for granted, by the student body, at least.

Pefley makes short work of the cafeteria special: breaded pork tenderloin on a hamburger bun -- a Hoosier favorite -- along with mixed vegetables, jello, cookie and milk. All for six bits.

The second half of the day begins with a biology pop quiz, sprung by Jim Wenrich. The 10 questions deal with the heart and blood. For the first time there are signs that Pefley, a B-plus student who has scored 1,050 on the SAT exam, is starting to drift. He answers only four correctly, but it amounts to "no harm, no foul" when Wenrich says the quiz doesn't count. A 20-question test on Friday will, though, he warns. "Got my reptiles and amphibians mixed up," Pefley smiles as he leaves and heads for econ with Rex Price.

The twins, Strait and Bob Bratch are in this class, too, which deals today with competition. While Price lectures on imperfect and monopolistic competition, Joe reads the special Sectional tabloid published that morning in the Marion *Chronicle-Tribune*. Price, a veteran teacher, ignores Joe as he talks about advertising for cars, toothpaste and other products. "Who would want to put that green stuff in their mouth?" he asks about a certain toothpaste, and the class laughs.

The day ends with study hall, where Pefley and Peck are asked to record grades on a chart for Wenrich. But the chore falls solely to Pefley -- Peck's busy rebuilding his tower of straws.

Each of the last three classes has been shaved 10 minutes for a 30-minute pep rally in the gym. So at 2:35, some 600 youngsters, including the junior high students, troop in.

A case of nerves almost keeps two players from the rally. "Me and Troy Miller really felt nervous during choir period," Hampton relates as the students settle into the bleachers. "We both had to go to the the restroom a couple of times. I mean, even though we're playing Southwood, still it's nerve-wracking."

McClure has been drafted to portray wrestling announcer "Brother Love" introducing "the team from Speicherville" and interviewing "Brother Pefley." McClure asks Pefley, "Could you tell these people here what this Northfield team's gonna do tonight, if you would please?" And Pefley, in his best rasslin' voice, responds, "I'd just like to issue one warning out there to all those Southwood Knight fans ... and that's that we're comin' after you!"

Getting through the bit with his coach was easy for Pefley; getting through the day wasn't. After the session he admits, "My mind drifted off during the day worrying about being overconfident. I think Joe and Jon are a little bit."

It is five minutes before five, and as Bob Slee's bus heads east on U.S. 24, the sun is still bright and the sky clear blue on this gorgeous winter day. The highway to Huntington is a sometimes-winding, narrow stretch also known as the Ho Chi Minh trail because of numerous fatal accidents over the years.

By the time the team arrives, most of the 1,100 Northfield fans are in their seats. The school has obtained additional tickets from other schools, and thus sold 125 more than last year.

Northfield has been assigned to the locker room used by the Huntington girls team. A computer-generated sign remains posted from last Saturday -- and it could apply to the Norse:

Defense and Rebounding
Noblesville

The Huntington girls upset Noblesville in the morning game en route to the championship, and now McClure's got to be worried a bit about an upset tonight. Never mind that his team has defeated Southwood twice by an average of 31.5 points.

As McClure tapes Hampton's ankle, Brad says, "This is where one state championship started, why not another?"

"Amen," McClure responds.

In his prayer, McClure thanks the Lord for the team's nervousness, because "It just shows we care. We know that you see the big plan, as in that poem we read a couple of weeks ago. And you know what's ahead of us, Father. We don't." He finishes by asking that the Lord help the team compete for Him in "as many games as you give us or have us play in this tournament."

To counter Southwood's expected deliberate style, McClure wants a full-court, man-to-man press after Northfield scores, a half-court trap after Northfield doesn't. Team defense is what this game is all about, he stresses. "You're givin' up, what, a little over 51 points a game this year? And if you take out the three-pointers, it's 47. So that's your strength. We're gonna get after 'em right away, guys. You saw how they walked the ball up the floor. It took 'em seven, eight seconds every time. We're not gonna waste time, guys. We're gettin' after 'em with the best thing we have to offer -- defense."

He turns motivational: "The only way anybody's gonna get ya is if you allow it. You're like Hereford cattle, shoulder to shoulder. When the storms come, we draw up close together. See, when there's no storm, when things are easy, you can go out and graze ... browse around and explore. That's what most teams have been doin', especially ones you've played. They just figure, what the heck, let's take a wild shot at the Norsemen and see if we hit 'em. You've been hit a few times, and the metal bends, but it sure hasn't broken."

He closes with, "We said 'Forward march!' last fall. This is the reason, guys. I think you can march as far as you want to. But you gotta make sure that you take the first step, and that's tonight."

Rick Mahan's name is missing from the program, but he's on the floor warming up with his Southwood mates as the crowd swells to considerably more than 4,000. Mahan, however, will not start after being out for a month.

As the last of some 4,500 fans take their seats, McClure turns his back on the bench and says, "We're nervous, and we're undefeated when we're nervous."

Minutes later, the nervous Norsemen streak to a 12-0 lead, starting with Hampton's follow at 7:42. Monte Moffett calls on Mahan at 5:38, but Northfield adds another hoop before Mahan's jumper finally gets Southwood on the board after 3 minutes and 40 seconds.

Surprisingly, Moffett has chosen to play an up-tempo game, and it has resulted in a rash of first-quarter turnovers. The result: a 27-5 Northfield lead after one stop.

Northfield's defense, as planned, will not let Southwood into the game, especially Joe Duncan, an excellent ballplayer with a fine shot. With 4 minutes and 28 seconds left in the half, the Norse take a 30-point margin at 37-7. At intermission it's 49-22. This one's over; Northfield has scored as many points in a half as it did the entire game the previous week at Southwood.

Outside the locker room, McClure confers with Desper and Christie. They want to stretch the lead by another 10 points in the third quarter and then play the bench.

Inside the locker room, McClure tells his team that defense is the major, offense the minor.

The Norse add eight points to their lead in the third quarter. But two minor scares occur when Joe and Jon hit the floor hard in separate incidents. Jon falls on his back in fighting for a loose ball, and

Joe goes down after being undercut. In Joe's case, no call is made, and the Northfield crowd is livid.

McClure pulls the twins for the final eight minutes as he starts to clear his bench. At 4:50, Scott Kunkel scores his first two Sectional points, following his own miss, which make it 77-47. Ryan Dubois and Pefley enter a short time later, and with six seconds left, Pefley shoots a "three" that winds up being an air ball. He laughs with the crowd.

The final is 88-57. Northfield has taken step one in what it hopes will be a nine-step march to the state championship. Hampton has led the point parade with 19 and added nine rebounds. The Chays have chipped in with 25 points, and Joe has snared 10 rebounds. Everyone has scored -- except Pefley, who, when reminded, just smiles and says, "That's okay."

As his jubilant troops go into the locker room, McClure says, "You did your job. You established yourself, especially on the defensive end. Now, when they got to hackin' and gougin' in the third quarter, we backed off a little bit. I'm really not too pleased about that."

Still, "It feels good to get Southwood off your back."

And now, "We gotta make sure when we come out Friday we have 32 minutes of what we do best -- defense, rebounding, good decisions on offense, in that order."

Meanwhile, Moffett is telling reporters that, in contrast to the control game he played the previous Friday night, he wanted to run more and shoot three-pointers. "We thought the 'three' would be the equalizer."

Back in the Northfield locker room, McClure tells his team to "stay humble," and then, "Let's pray. Father, we don't know what the big picture is ..."

Twenty minutes later, the team squeezes into a bottom row of seats to watch Homestead and Huntington North, while McClure, Desper and Christie sit separately to scout.

McClure and the team watch only the first quarter, which ends with the underdog Vikings ahead, 14-12, while Desper and Christie stay.

On the bus, McClure sounds like the sick man he has been for the last month, unable to shake chest and throat problems. He's thinking that Lisa's probably right. After the game, outside the locker room, she suggested he not teach tomorrow and perhaps see the family doctor.

McClure heeds her words on Thursday and calls his doctor. He doesn't need to come into the office, the doctor says; he needs a stronger antibiotic.

So McClure stays home, watches film from last night's game and reads about his next opponent -- Huntington North, which has stunned Homestead, 57-55.

While their coach is trying to mend at home, five players and one manager are at the Honeywell Center in Wabash, participating in a day-long discussion on how the world might mend some of its problems.

Taking part along with 11 other Northfield seniors are the Rosses, Pefley, Strait, Winegardner and manager Flo Huber. Sponsored by the Wabash Rotary club, the World Affairs Conference has brought together students from area high schools on the topic "Confronting the Environment of the Next Millennium."

The environment that's probably on the players' minds, though, is the Huntington North gym. It figures to be packed with home folk to see if the Vikings can score another upset Friday night.

And sure enough, when the Northfield bus arrives shortly after the Wabash-White's game has begun, the parking lot is already crowded. By the time the main attraction unfolds, there will be some 4,400 fans in the seats.

On the way over, McClure has reported that he's feeling much better, and the Rosses say they're not hurting. They have been, however, even more quiet than is usual before a game.

After storing their gear, the players head for the balcony with the coaches to watch Wabash dismantle White's, as expected.

What about Huntington North? McClure is asked.

"They're livin' on emotion of the girls," he replies.

An hour later, McClure tells his assembled squad, "Right here on the board, guys, the keys to the game. Not a whole lot's different from what you've heard all year. Defense, number one. And, along with that, we do not want them on the free-throw line. They scored 40 percent of their points against Homestead from the free-throw line."

He points out that the ballhandlers are right-handed, except for Aaron Stroup, so "Make 'em go left. They can't really score very well when they're movin' to their left. (Eric) Ruppert, number 24, he'll go to his left and try and set ya up, and then he's gonna try and reverse pivot and come back hard to the right. Don't get too tight on him when he makes that reverse pivot or it's gonna be a foul and he hit 12 outta 13 (against Homestead)."

Offensively, he says, run the regular early offense, whether Huntington plays zone or man. The key, again, is to strike before the defense can get set. If that won't work, "we need great offensive movement and decisions."

And, "You can't let your body go faster than your mind. Use your tools. You have defense. You have rebounding ability. You have good ballhandlers. You have good shooters. More than that, you have a good mind."

It's two minutes before game time, and the place is rocking with an almost festive atmosphere. The Northfield throng is on its feet, chanting, "Let's go Blue! Let's go Blue! Let's go Blue!"

The Huntington crowd is behind the Northfield bench. Two rows behind the players are Viking boosters Ray Vanderpool, who's in electronic sales, and George Schul, a veterinarian. Close by, a row down, is Maury Pulley, an executive with a fabricating company. They are unusual hometown fans; they call them the way they see them, not the way they *want* to see them. And the three men -- obviously veteran high school followers who know the game -- are there to have fun.

It will not be much fun for their team, however.

As the Norsemen have done most of the season, they open fast, scoring the first 11 points of the game before Huntington Coach Creighton Burns calls time out.

By the quarter, it's 20-6, and the tone has been set. Still, Huntington fans have some hope after Joe draws his third foul on a questionable blocking call with slightly less than six minutes left in the half. "No way," chuckles Schul, the veterinarian.

As has happened in the past, Northfield loses synch with Joe missing, so McClure calls time to tell his troops, "You're too excited out there. Get it in to these guys," and he points to Jon and Hampton. As they break the huddle, he says, "Don't you dare foul!"

Northfield regains its rhythm and builds to 31-14 with a minute and 34 seconds left when Burns seemingly tries to put a hole in the floor. Reserve guard David Scheib has been whistled for a foul during a scramble for a loose ball, setting Burns off. A big man, he stomps on the floor repeatedly with both feet, drawing attention and guffaws from the crowd.

Hampton's drive with three seconds left appears to give Northfield a neat 20-point lead at the intermission, but Eric Ruppert hits a heave from three-quarters court to make it 37-20.

McClure, Desper and Christie confer, mostly on how to ensure Joe will not foul out. When Huntington goes into the post, Desper says, the guards must drop back and force the pivot man to put the ball on the floor.

In the locker room, McClure tells Joe, "You'll get screwed once by the officials. So you got four right now. Keep that in mind."

Turning to his main theme, defense, he says, "Now, 32 can shoot it. 32. Brad, you're probably gonna have him. Guys, it's shell-drill time, man-to-man defense. Try to discourage the ball goin' inside (by forming a shell near the free-throw line). Let 'em move it around the perimeter. We'll be in better rebounding position. But, guys, we cannot let them dribble the ball into the paint."

Except for getting in a hurry once, he says, they have played well offensively.

If Huntington goes to a 1-3-1 trap, he tells Jon while looking at Joe, "you get to the middle immediately and you get the ball if you need to." And Jon smiles, says, "Yes, coach."

After the team leaves, McClure and Desper talk a few minutes about ball-control, taking 25 to 30 seconds each possession, making Huntington North play defense harder.

It is not needed. Northfield opens the half with a run of seven straight points to surge into a 44-20 lead. Even Joe and Noi's foul trouble can't stop them now.

With 22 seconds left in the third and the score 55-28, Vanderpool announces, "We make our move now," and his pals laugh.

Early in the fourth quarter, Joe is called for a technical for hanging on the rim after a monstrous slam. It does not appear to be a good call. But later, the Northfield coaches are reminded that under high school rules, a technical is called on the "hanger" unless the player is being fouled while making the dunk.

With a minute and 17 seconds remaining, McClure calls time out to settle the subs, who entered seconds earlier. "You guys are just runnin' around out there," he says, and goes to the diagram board.

As the team breaks from the huddle, Huntington fan Vanderpool shouts, "Hey, Coach, you told 55 (Pefley) to take a three-pointer, didn't you?"

McClure smiles back. "It's too early."

But with the score at 72-51 and 11 seconds remaining, Burns calls time out, so McClure yells at Pefley in the huddle, "I want a three." And Vanderpool shouts back, "Yeah! Yeah!"

Pefley gets off two treys, but doesn't find the net.

So it winds up 72-51, and Northfield's starting five have achieved great balance in their scoring. Peck and Noi have scored 14 apiece, Joe 15, Jon 14 and Hampton 13.

"Those Ross kids aren't the only weapons they've got," Burns tells reporters huddled around him. "Those two Chay kids are pretty damn good basketball players. They came over from Laos on the boat, so that tells you how tough they are. And lemme tell you, that Hampton is a gutbuster."

Burns doesn't stop there: "They bring Nathan Winegardner and Troy Miller off the bench, and they play pretty good defense and pass well, and they can shoot."

As Burns is praising Winegardner and Miller to the media, McClure is telling them to their faces. They were the needed glue when Joe and Noi got into foul trouble. Earlier in the season, this was not the case. And so McClure has to be thinking -- hoping -- that his inconsistent guard play might be a thing of the past.

Before sending his troops to the showers, McClure says, "That's a great Norse victory. Very simply, it's step two. Doesn't matter who it is, it's step two. No one step is bigger than the next. Step three is tomorrow night. That team (Wabash) has the third highest offensive output against our defense this year. You gotta start thinkin' about that now."

Joe tells his teammates, "We're doing a great job of keeping together as a family," and heads nod in unison.

"See, that's because you're workin' as a team," McClure says. "Because you're in tune with each other. You have paid the price to go to the next step. It's right there in front of ya. You walk up the ladder, the mountain, whatever. You take 'em together. This is the fun."

Outside the locker room, McClure hugs Lisa, says, "We're rollin'."

The press arrives. Duane Schuman of the Huntington *Herald Press*, asks, "Do you thank Joe and Jon's mother every day?" McClure laughs. "I'm not stupid. I would rather have 6-10 than 6-5, you know. They're great kids and great players. They do their job everytime they hit the floor."

Asked if he ever got concerned, he replies, "This is their home floor, and this could have made their season. But our regular season prepared us for games like this," referring to pressure games.

Still, at 11 o'clock Saturday morning, McClure has his team on the practice floor, which he has done previously before championship games the same night. He looked at Wabash game film after getting home from Huntington; now he wants to review some points aimed at stopping Donny Blair from three-point range and Gary Cooper inside. And he wants to add a couple of offensive entries.

As usual, the Northfield crowd arrives early, some 2,000 of what will be about 4,000 fans, while McClure is putting chalk to blackboard. His game plan is simple: defense, rebounding, outlet passes, good offensive decisions. And play "as champions with togetherness."

After the team does its stretching exercises, McClure gathers them to read a passage from the *Everyday Bible*.

> *"We are perplexed because we don't know why things happen as they do, but we don't give up and quit.*
> *We are hunted down, but God never abandons us. Yes, we live under constant danger to our lives because we serve the Lord.*
> *But this gives us constant opportunities to show forth the power of Jesus Christ within our dying bodies."*

McClure tells them that those words say a lot about the lessons they've learned this year, spiritually and otherwise. "You have had your armor shot at, the NIOPs talk about ya, stuff like that. And yet here we stand today stronger than ever. And let's make sure that when we take the floor, that we give glory to the proper authority."

Then, turning to the matter at hand, he says, "Make sure Cooper doesn't get any offensive boards. And Jon, when they go to the 1-3-1 trap, make sure you get to the middle immediately."

He turns to the mind: "Only way Wabash can get into the game is if you open the door and say, 'Come on through'. They have to beat you. They can succeed only if you beat yourselves, and you're not

195

gonna let that happen. Be together and take step three; continue up the ladder."

Both teams start tight, and unlike its previous two contests, Northfield does not race to a big lead. In fact, Wabash opens the scoring with Cooper on a drive after a minute and 28 seconds have elapsed. The Norse look a little tired, and play is sluggish on both sides, resulting in an 8-8 contest with a little more than two minutes left in the first quarter.

Finally, things begin to heat up, and Northfield has a 14-10 advantage after one quarter. Ray Sims' Wabash team has played sound, steady basketball, but starters Nils Dekau and J.D. Hamilton have been called for two fouls each. And Donny Blair has found Hampton impossible to shake.

Wabash's foul problems worsen at 5:31 of the second quarter when Dekau gets his third, but Northfield holds only a slim lead at 21-15. Meanwhile, Joe has two personals.

Hampton's 12-foot jumper at 3:22 gives Northfield its first double-digit lead, 27-17, and the Apaches are starting to tire. So it's 31-19 at intermission. Still, it's a ball game, because while Hampton has shut Blair down in the first 16 minutes, there's no telling when he can get on a roll of treys like Manchester's Andy Holderman.

Noi has not been an offensive threat, Desper points out to McClure outside the locker room, "so we might as well play Troy." Minutes later, McClure tells his squad: "Offense is where we have to do it We're too tentative. Just go there and whup 'em! Lay your guts on the floor!"

Shortly after the second half opens, Wabash's spirit suffers a major blow in a quick sequence of events. After Noi is fouled by Chad Daugherty under the basket, Sims yells for a three-second call. Standing near midcourt and against the sideline, he chants, "Three seconds!" before finally getting called for a technical. Noi makes two free throws on the personal and one of two technicals. Northfield gets the ball, and Hamilton is immediately called for his third foul trying to stop Hampton on a drive. Hampton converts the free throws and suddenly it's 38-19 -- and essentially finis.

From there, the Norse play out the string for a 77-48 victory. With 48 seconds left, Sims shows his class. He comes down to the Northfield bench, shakes McClure's hand and then steps in front of the bench to congratulate the Norse youngsters.

Joe Ross, who has been growing stronger each game, has led the way with 24 points and 12 rebounds. Brother Jon, whose shot has been tentative during Sectional play, has taken just eight and hit four, along with two free throw for 10 points. But he's matched his brother in rebounds, and their combined total is two more than Wabash's 22.

As Sims is leaving the floor, he's congratulated. He says thanks, but adds, "Well, it wasn't good enough. Like I said before, Northfield has a lot of firepower underneath." He starts to talk about free-throw shooting -- the fact that Northfield shot 38 (actually 35) to Wabash's seven (actually eight) -- but before finishing he gathers his seniors to praise their efforts.

Defensive intensity has given Northfield the triumph. Blair has been held to 15, 10 by Hampton. The hard-working Cooper has been held to 10 on 4 of 14 shooting. Once again, Northfield's size has been too much.

So McClure has won his third Sectional in four years and his team has reached another goal for the season.

As the net-cutting begins, Bob Ross is being congratulated. He's wearing a brand-new, blue sweatshirt with white lettering on the back that reads, "Joe and Jon's Proud Dad." His wife ordered it special from the Shirt Shed, the local firm that provided the airplanes for the Wellston, Ohio, trip.

Minutes after the net-cutting concludes, McClure is carried to the locker room for a drenching under the showers.

Joe displays a small Notre Dame medal given to him by his future coach, Richard "Digger" Phelps. The big youngster wore it inside his left sock, for good luck. And while it perhaps brought him some, his skill was more prominent in leading Northfield through the Sectional.

The fun is not over for the night. Not long after finishing the food that Hampton has brought, the players spot two sheriff's cars behind the bus. At Lagro, a small town six miles from Wabash on U.S. Route 24, the cars swing around the bus, sirens blaring. The team goes wild as the escort begins.

At the junction of 24 and Indiana Route 13, a fire truck awaits. But instead of heading north, for the school, it goes south into Wabash. The escort winds its way through Wabash and then slices through the dark countryside before winding up at the car-filled Northfield lot.

A crowd of a 1,000 or so awaits the heroes in the gym. The ceremonies are brief and the team is invited to the Rosses for more food and a dip in the hot tub.

The Ross family has been busy during the weekend mailing the attractive flyer promoting Joe and Jon for the Indiana all-star team. Bob and Andris have spent about $1,000 in production, printing and postage to send 861 flyers to coaches and members of the media.

The flyer includes testimonials from Lawrence North's Jack Keefer and Red Taylor, who coaches the Municipal Gardens AAU team that the Rosses play for with Damon Bailey and Eric Montross.

Keefer says they are "multidimensional players and the Indiana All-Star team needs their size/talent/quickness combination."

Taylor writes: "I've coached 37 Indiana All-Stars and both Joe and Jon definitely belong in this fraternity of high school players."

And they do. But, of course, politics doesn't escape sport. So who knows?

For now, though, the immediate future holds something more important: The quest for Northfield's first Regional Championship.

●●●●●●●●●●

As usual, there are Sectional surprises. No. 2 ranked East Chicago Central is upset, and Kokomo, in the top 20 all year, falls quickly, too. East Central -- a consolidation that includes the school Steve McClure's father attended -- pulls off one of those inexplicable feats. It goes in at 2-17, comes out 4-17 and a Sectional champion.

The big story, though -- as it has been all year long -- continues to be Damon Bailey closing in on Marion Pierce's career scoring record of 3,019, set in 1961 for now-defunct Lewisville.

Going into Sectional play he needed 138, and because of the draw, he could, like Northfield, wind up playing nine times if his team reaches the title game.

The Frankfort *Times*, like other newspapers, focused on Indiana's latest phenom by publishing a "Bailey Watch," showing what he needs to average to top Pierce's mark.

If Bedford North Lawrence, for example, played just three games, getting beat for the Sectional crown, Bailey would need 46 points a game for the record.

But Bedford North Lawrence won its the Sectional, and Bailey pulled to within 53 points of Pierce.

Chapter 16: The Regional

And now, maybe, Marion.

A school with 1,990 students, Marion High has been a "basketball factory" for years. In its December 28, 1989, edition, the *Indianapolis News* named Marion "Team of the Decade." It was an easy choice. Coached by Bill Green and led by Jay Edwards and Lyndon Jones, the Giants did what only one other school has done: win three consecutive state championships.

But before a possible date with Marion, Northfield must face Logansport, like Marion a North Central Conference school rich in basketball success.

The North Central Conference dominated Indiana high school basketball in the '80s. Marion's three straight titles came at the expense of other North Central members, Richmond in 1985 and 1987 and Anderson by 19 points in 1986.

So now Northfield must defeat two powerful North Central Conference schools to achieve its first Regional championship. The Regional will be played in Bill Green Athletic Arena, Marion's 7,690-seat facility.

Logansport comes into the Regional with a 12-10 record, while Marion is 20-2 and ranked No. 6 -- eight notches higher than Northfield -- in the final Associated Press poll. The Giants have won 19 in a row this season and 36 straight on their home floor. One of the victories was a tough, 68-63 triumph over Logansport in the fourth game from the end of the regular season.

Clearly, Northfield faces a formidable task, but Steve McClure is his usual upbeat self on Monday after tucking away another Sectional crown. And, as he has all season long, he adjusts the pressure valve, putting his team through a relaxed practice hour that features offense and a lot of shooting. "Joe and Jon didn't shoot the ball particularly well in the Sectional," he notes.

"We probably wouldn't have practiced today at all," he continues, "but we drew a later time on Tuesday, 7:15, at Marion to practice. I didn't want to go from Saturday night clear into Tuesday night without hittin' the floor, especially with a two-game situation comin' up Saturday."

After Monday's light workout, the team assembles at McClure's house, which has become a home away from home, to talk about the huge Saturday ahead.

The next night, McClure and Noi Chay get a scare.

While scrimmaging in the Bill Green arena, Noi obeys instructions: follow the big guys around and handle the ball for them. Joe Ross obeys instructions, too. He gathers a rebound and spreads his elbows for protection. Pow! Noi takes a shot below the left eye. Ice applied immediately keeps the swelling down, and five stitches close the wound.

On Wednesday, it appears that Noi will be okay for Saturday, but McClure keeps him out of a tough scrimmage. In fact, the entire practice is tough, with lots of full-court drills designed to keep the team physically fit. And for the first time this week, McClure is thinking about Logansport, reviewing and working on schemes he plans to use against the Berries. He is not thinking about Marion.

Thursday's practice is more of the same, followed by another team gathering at the McClures. They have a meal and watch "Come Fly with Me," a Michael Jordan video that, the coach says, illustrates "basketball in its most beautiful form."

By Friday afternoon, nervousness is setting in. "I wish we could play right now," Jon Ross says, sitting on the gym floor and lacing his shoes before practice. He can barely be heard over Tone-Loc's rap best-seller, "Wild Thing."

Practice is brief. After working on seven offensive approaches, McClure turns to the shell drill, which he got from Glenn Heaton. McClure wants to stop the point guard from penetrating on the dribble and from passing in to the post. He stresses "helpin' out each other by rotatin' and kinda formin' a shell."

In the final analysis -- as always -- McClure has no true game plan for Logansport. That is, unless you call "fun" a game plan. Since the brief emotional bout he fought with himself after the Maconaquah game, McClure has made fun his top priority. Which is not to say he doesn't want his team to play aggressively. On the contrary, he wants to establish the pace immediately against Logansport, wants to take the game right at the Berries to see if they can handle intensity and aggressiveness.

When practice closes, McClure is asked if, by now, he's given any thought to Marion.

"Not necessarily," he says, toweling his forehead. "You know, right now our chances of beatin' Marion are zero percent, because we've focused so much on Logan. We realize we have to cross that hurdle, and that's not gonna be easy. They've played in the

North Central Conference and been competitive there. We have a monumental challenge, but to us it's step four."

There are no gimmicks this time of the year, he continues. "You try a gimmick or somethin' like that, you end up gettin' drilled."

Are the kids looking ahead to Marion?

"Hard to say. I'm sure that Marion is implanted in their subconscious somewhere. And I think maybe it's been a motivating factor throughout the season. They feel like they owe themselves a chance to beat Marion at Marion. But, on the other hand, the kids are intelligent, and they understand that there's no Marion until you beat Logansport."

Noi is okay. And McClure volunteers: "One thing I like about Noi, when the chips are down, he's always there. You look at the Huntington game. It may take him a couple of minutes to get ready ... but the problem is, in the Regional, you may not have a couple minutes. So we'll get in his head. He'll be ready to go."

Visibility is almost zero Saturday morning as Bob Slee's bus sits in the Northfield lot under a hard rain and pea-soup fog, awaiting the 25-mile trip to Marion High School.

Steve McClure strolls into the cozy gym with a broad smile, says, "Great day to play some basketball."

Over in the smaller gym, the student booster club has enlisted Brad Hampton's aunt, Jane Cole, and Jeremy Bever's mother, Barbara, to paint youngsters' faces. Jersey numbers in blue on the cheekbones are popular.

Shortly before 9 o'clock, McClure is a picture of serenity. Danielle Chenault, a senior cheerleader, asks the coach to tape her right ankle, and he says, "Sure thing," as if he were talking to Hampton. But, of course, he's starting to churn a bit inside.

As the team boards the bus at 9:10 for its 11 o'clock appointment with step four, McClure says, "Are the Chays here?" and there is laughter, because the Chays are usually late.

The bus is a mass of decorations, signs hanging from the ceiling along with balloons and crepe paper. On some windows, the booster club has taped eight-by-eleven sheets with a blue outline of a megaphone and the team picture inside. The words "Go, Big Blue!!" jump out. The sheets have come from Thursday's editon of the *Wabash Plain Dealer*.

201

Steve Desper is not aboard for the first time this season. He has driven on his own. If Northfield wins, Desper will scout the Marion-South Adams game while the Norse follow McClure's carefully planned schedule. It is an itinerary that starts with the bus trip and ends at midnight. It does not call for Northfield watching the Marion-South Adams game.

"It's gonna be a blowout," McClure tells Harold Christie on the bus. "We're gonna cut out. They're gonna need to rest, not see someone to get worried about."

At various places along the route, 18- by 24-inch signs are staked in the ground. Christie's middle daughter, Carol, a Northfield grad home from dental school for Easter break, made the signs that say "Teamwork," "Defense," "Victory Bound," "Here We Go Norsemen" and the like.

One wonders, however, if the signs are registering with the players, let alone being seen. Aside from McClure and Christie's occasional conversation, the only sound inside the bus is a mixture of engine noise and rain tattooing the big yellow vehicle. The players sit upright, staring ahead, silent, bathed in nerves.

A police escort from the edge of Marion has been arranged so the team can get to the arena without any hassle. But when the bus gets to the bypass, no patrol cars are waiting. McClure, who has a knack for directions, guides Slee into town via a back route.

Suddenly, the coach laughs. "Turtle Creek apartments over there," he says. "Where Lisa and I spent a lot of time during the Blizzard of '77."

As the bus pulls up to the arena, Jon Ross begins to clap -- the sign of his nervousness. Troy Miller's jitters began much earlier -- when he could eat only half of his mother's pancakes.

The Bill Green Athletic Arena is an imposing place, strewn with banners that denote dozens of triumphs. Aside from the fabulous championship run of '85 through '87, the Giants have won three other state crowns, starting in 1926.

In the expansive locker room, McClure's blackboard message and priorities simple:

Defense
Rebounding
Outlet Passing
Offensive Decisions

202

After the prayer -- "There's gonna be winners and losers, and Father, we just pray that you'll be the biggest winner of all as a result of our playing." -- McClure jokes, "Got somethin' new on the board for ya here. You probably never heard this before."

Smiles push forward briefly on game faces.

Peck Chay has been assigned to Corey Champion, a 6-4 senior who is Logansport's big gun this season. He got 32 against Marion, despite various defenses against him. But he'll be hampered today by a sore right wrist -- his shooting wrist -- which is taped. He injured it early in the Sectional final when he was knocked to the floor while going in for a lay-up. Still, he scored 24 after the injury, diagnosed as a hairline fracture.

Aside from Champion's injury, Logansport coach Phil Hershberger wrestles with the dilemma other opposing mentors have had all season: dealing with the Rosses. He knows his team has to keep the twins off the boards. And, too, his club must shoot well, which the Berries did not do in the Sectional championship victory over Caston. In one stretch, Logansport went three for 17, and Hershberger knows that if the Berries do that against Northfield, "we'll be down 30."

Defensive, though, presents Hershberger with his biggest challenge. The Rosses and Hampton team for an average of 45.4 points per game, Jon's 18.6 leading the trio. And the twins average almost 20 rebounds a game.

Rebounding also concerns McClure. That is partly why he wants Peck on Champion. Although earlier in the week he told the media Hampton would get the assignment, now McClure figures that by putting Peck on Champion, a guard who pops from the outside, Hampton can help the twins on the boards.

Rebounding, he says while pointing to the blackboard, is going to be the key factor. He wants everyone -- "*everyone*"-- hitting the boards. "Block out, get the rebound and we take it up early."

Then, out of context -- for no obvious reason -- he mentions the Logansport locker room, saying, "It smelled like a truck stop, urine running down their legs."

Turning to Noi, who's feeling fine, McClure says, "You'll have (Scott) Montgomery. He's 25. He's the other guard, and, actually, he's probably as good a shooter from outside as Champion is."

If you see a press, he continues, the big men should streak while the guards curl. "Noi, don't get too close to Joe." Noi just smiles; hardly a sound comes from dry mouths.

Lesson by lesson, he runs through everything they have worked on -- the fast break, the early offense, the Boiler entries, Jon getting to the middle on a 1-3-1 trap, working against a 2-3 zone. It is like a classroom before a test.

McClure concludes: "You've learned all the lessons. You have been well trained. You have been presented opportunities throughout the season to prepare you for this moment. You've improved a great deal the last three weeks. You're not playin' Logansport. You're playin' to see if you can play better than you did last Saturday night."

Urine might not be running down the Norsemen's legs, but they're plenty nervous too, and McClure acknowledges it. "You're nervous," he says simply. "Think about what our record is when you're nervous. If you guys care enough about a game to get nervous, we win. When you go out there, enjoy it. By God, you've earned this. And there's just one thing I want to see --"

"Forward march!"

"You bet."

About 4,500 fans -- some 1,800 from Northfield -- and seven radio stations are on hand for the tip-off.

Understandably, both teams are tight, which results in little scoring and neither team taking charge early. Northfield finally opens some light at 8-2 after 3 minutes and 15 seconds, so Hershberger calls a timeout. In the Northfield huddle, McClure yells, "Don't let up! Every possession!"

And the Norse don't. By the end of the quarter, they're in front 22-13. Peck, however, has picked up two silly fouls, and so McClure assigns Nathan Winegardner to Champion, who has not been effective.

The defensive pressure McClure wants is evident, but offensively, Northfield is struggling. When Noi misses a short jumper, McClure turns to Miller, says, "You get ready to go for Noi. You'll hit that shot."

With 5:43 remaining in the half, Northfield finally gets the margin to double digits, 27-17, on Jon's three-point play, the basket coming on a short jump shot from the side.

But while Champion is not hitting, Montgomery -- as McClure alluded to -- is. So when Logansport calls time out at the four-minute mark, McClure says, "The key is to play good enough defense."

Northfield has done the job offensively after the initial sputtering. And so, as the intermission approaches, the Norse are in command. Hampton's two free throws give them a 38-21 lead at the break. Champion, perhaps hurting, has just six points, while Montgomery has nine, accounting for 15 of the Berries' 21. Northfield has a 19 to seven rebounding advantage.

Outside the locker room, Desper tells McClure, "Joe will need a minute and half in the third quarter; he's tired." McClure nods.

Inside the locker room, McClure's words are short and simple. "Guys, the fact of the matter is they've tried probably four or five defenses and they can't stop ya. The only thing they haven't tried is man, and you can expect a jock-style man-to-man. If you play defense, it's over. We play each possession. The score's zero to zero. You gotta win this half, guys. Any questions? Let's go."

Before the second half starts, Desper is asked for a reading. "Logan is afraid of us," he says in a tone that resembles a doctor's. "You could see the fear in the faces of the Logan players. They didn't think they could stay with us. It's in their eyes."

Northfield starts the second half with a quick run of six points from three different players -- a Hampton jumper, a "JoeJam" and a 17-footer from Noi -- for a 23-point lead. Time out, Logansport, with 6 minutes and 48 seconds remaining.

The Berries, it turns out, aren't through. Brett Stines, a 6-2 senior, gets loose twice on back-door maneuvers, one of which results in a three-point play. Northfield goes 3 minutes and 19 seconds without scoring, while Logansport adds 10 points. The margin is shaved to 13.

McClure calls time. He's steaming. "We rest between games!" he snarls. And then, to Hampton, who's been on Stines, "You gotta play defense, too!"

Northfield stops the bleeding. And so after three quarters, it's 52-36, and it looks like the Norse will get a chance to face Marion again for a Regional crown.

It is a routine fourth quarter, except for two things: Logansport scores only three points, and Hampton goes down hard on a drive, causing Pefley to leap from the bench, ready to take on the entire Logansport team. But there is no disorder.

With a minute to go, it's 66-39 and McClure empties the bench, saying, "One more step closer to Fort Wayne."

The final is 72-39. Joe has scored 19 and Hampton 18, but the telling stat is Joe's 20 rebounds. Jon has added 13; their 33 dwarfs Logansport's team total of 21.

In the locker room, McClure is calm. "Step four -- nothing more, nothing less. Step five's comin' up, nothing more, nothing less. Your opponents are the game itself and yourself ... your ability to just get yourself mentally ready. We'll go eat. We're gonna rest."

McClure touches only briefly on the third-quarter lapse. He wants to stay positive. "You're movin' forward. And that's all we ask, and that's all we're gonna ask, baby. We're right where we wanna be. Let's pray."

Minutes later, McClure breaks free from well-wishers and print reporters for an interview on Wabash radio station WKUZ. Chuck Adams, whose family owns the station, is doing the honors, because Bill Rogge has kept a promise to his wife: a Florida vacation.

Adams spots Wabash Coach Ray Sims and invites him to interview McClure. Sims, whose Marion background and three encounters with Northfield give him much insight, does a solid job with the "mike."

Sims notes that a lot of Logansport fans -- and others in attendance -- were amazed at the Chays' quickness. Sims wasn't, of course. Everything Sims mentions -- the Norse's tough defense, the good offensive start, Northfield's third-quarter lull -- draws quick agreement from McClure.

Later, after McClure leaves, Sims predicts Northfield will beat Marion by 10. While that might sound like a sour-grapes comment from someone who didn't get the Marion job, it has plenty of validity. Earlier in the week, Manchester's Pete Smith told Phil Beebe, if the Norse are on top of their game, "I feel confident they can do it." Huntington North's Creighton Burns told Beebe, "Northfield's defense can carry them. ... They're as good as anybody we've faced."

Meanwhile, Hershberger is telling reporters that his team played "as bad as we've played all year. Then again, we haven't shot against guys that are 6-9 and 6-10, and that might have had an effect on us. There's no doubt that a lot of what we did or didn't do can be attributed to the Rosses."

And -- no excuse intended -- Champion struggled with his wrist. "We tried to tape it," Hershberger says, "but the tape was getting wet and the ball was sliding off his hand."

Back in the Norse locker room, the team is ready to follow McClure's intinerary, which has the bus leaving Marion at 12:30 for the Wabash Days Inn. It's 12:38 when Slee pulls out from the lot, and the rain and fog are still hanging around, but nobody seems to be paying attention to the time and weather. In fact, like on the trip to Marion, the stillness inside the vehicle is quite obvious.

It's pointed out to McClure that playing Marion would make Northfield the underdog for the first time this season. How does that make him feel?

"I guess you can say we probably are a little looser today. Even though, you know, maybe to the media and all we're underdogs, I think to ourselves we're the favorites. I think we know that if we go in there and play Northfield basketball, we're gonna win the Regional."

Does he think Marion's feeling any pressure?

"I've said this all year long, and I think the same goes for Marion or anyone else, I would rather be preparin' for Marion or South Adams than bein' one of those two and preparin' for us."

When the bus pulls up to the Days Inn on Wabash's south side, McClure says, "Be humble," and they pile through the front door.

The IHSAA provides each team with a meal allotment -- five dollars per person for up to 17 people -- and each team gets $210 for lodging.

The desk clerk greets McClure with a warm smile and says she's a Southwood graduate who's pulling for Northfield. McClure takes six rooms at $38.85 apiece. He tells the players to drop their gear in four rooms; the managers get one. McClure will occupy the sixth room alone until Desper and Christie return from Marion with a scouting report.

But first the team reboards the bus for a meal at the Ponderosa on the other edge of town. The restaurant is quiet in the wake of the lunch crowd. Still, three tables near the huge salad bar are reserved for them -- which makes it easy for Joe Ross to saunter back four times.

Lunch finished, the team returns to the motel for sack and/or TV time, which sounds good on this late-winter day that refuses to brighten.

McClure changes to "knock around" apparel, flips on the TV, puts the tape of the Logansport game in the VCR he's brought from home, and gets comfortable in bed. He will not watch long. Christie and Desper arrive shortly before four o'clock to compare notes on Marion's easy victory over South Adams.

"Now, here's what they ran the first time down the floor," Desper begins, sounding a little like a calculus teacher. "And you know, (Dedrick) Jackson's normally not the primary scorer; he's probably not going to take many shots. But he's going to play on the three-point line. You almost have to stick Brad out there."

The keys, they agree, are to keep Marion off the offensive boards and to stop Jerry Freshwater, the Giants' outstanding point guard, from running the break. "We got to take away the quick outlet pass to Freshwater," McClure says.

"Joe and Jon have to play 32 minutes," Desper notes. "They can't foul out. If they get in foul trouble, we're doomed."

McClure sits up in bed. "The first three minutes -- we gotta watch it. Last year they got that quick eight to nuthin' lead and two quick fouls on Joe."

The discussion is brief, and when it ends, the coaches agree: Marion can be had.

"Didja see that sign at Spiece's in Marion?" Christie asks, changing the subject. He's referring to a well-known, Wabash-based company headed by Tom Spiece, a successful, outspoken businessman who marches to a different drummer. The company, which was started by Spiece's father, specializes in jeans and sporting goods, particularly athletic shoes.

"It said," Christie continues, 'The Twin Towers are in town. Go get 'em Big Blue. Signed, Tom Spiece.' On the other side was an advertisement for jeans."

Later, Spiece is asked if he was concerned about losing business in Marion. The independent-minded Spiece responds: "I wanted to beat Marion and I'll take the consequences. The loss of business I will take. I'd rather have the victory."

There will be no problems with the sign at his Wabash store, which reads: "Logansport first, then beat the damn Giants."

At 4:42, McClure calls his wife at White's, which will be the team's next stop. All arrangements have been taken care of, she reports. "Harold, Steve and Ray are here," he tells her. "Steve and

Harold are wonderin' how we can hold it down against the Giants."
His smile is broad and the laughter is loud.

Outside, rain lashes the motel; inside, McClure strips for a
shower shortly before five o'clock. Desper and Christie turn their
attention to the television set, where Notre Dame is playing DePaul in
a game that has a strong bearing on the NCAA tournament bids.
Never mind Joe and Jon, Desper roots against the Irish, as he has for
years; he has no love for Digger.

McClure's hardly out of the shower and starting to dress when
players start drifting into the coaches' room. It's not even five o'clock,
and the schedule calls for a 5:30 departure from the Days Inn to
White's for pancakes and sausage. By 5:10 the entire team, save for
the still-snoozing Bob Bratch, has crammed into the room.

Twenty minutes later, McClure checks out and the bus heads
for White's.

In the home ec room, Lisa and the Millers whip up pancakes
and sausage while Brady reads *Sports Illustrated* and Cody and Katy
romp around. "This is home ec, where we make men out of boys," Lisa
quips.

The pancakes will provide carbohydrates and are easily
digestible. But not everyone chooses to eat so soon after the big meal
at Ponderosa. And yes, butterflies are fluttering in some stomachs
already.

At 6 o'clock, McClure shepherds his troops into the old, small
White's gym. He walks the starters through plays at one basket while
his own kids shoot around at the other, oblivious to it all. Katy has
brought along her little portable tape player, and now Janet Jackson's
"Rhythm Nation" is rocking along.

At 6:25, the bus rolls out for the biggest date in Northfield
basketball history. "Losing tonight's not one of the possibilities,"
McClure says as the rain rages. "It's all there for us to take it. And
these guys are ready to take it."

He's feeling much better this year at this stage than last
season, when Northfield defeated South Adams before falling to
Marion. Last year, instead of returning to Wabash County after the
first game, the team checked in at the Marion Sheraton, about five
minutes from the school. They ate their dinner and then spent hours in
their rooms before taking the five-minute return trip.

"We thought then that we wanted to give them as much rest
as we could," McClure explains, "but I think you gotta consider mental

rest, too. I think goin' back to the Days Inn was a good move. This gives 'em a 40-minute drive back and a chance to reflect on what they've done. Goin' back to familiar surroundings, familiar food ... gonna be a big plus for us."

At 6:58 -- 77 minutes before game time -- Slee's vehicle pulls up to the parking lot. Just inside the lobby area, a mass of Northfield fans awaiting entry into the arena greet the team wildly as they head for the locker room.

Everything McClure put on the blackboard before the Logansport game applies to Marion, but the task -- especially rebounding -- will be considerably tougher. Marion came into the Regional averaging 100 points per game in mauling two Sectional foes. And in Jason McCain, the Giants have one of the most talked about players in the state this year along with Damon Bailey and Eric Montross. McCain is shooting at 68.9 percent for the year.

McCain's size has drawn more comment than this talent, which is considerable. He is 6-5 and listed at 320 pounds, but there are reports that he actually weighs closer to 360. Whatever, he has played exceptional basketball all year, moving his bulk with amazing grace while averaging 16 points and almost eight rebounds.

Complementing McCain up front are Travis Kirby and Dedrick Jackson. Kirby, a 6-4 senior, scores at a 14.3 clip and is dangerous from deep. Jackson leads the team in rebounds with almost nine per game while averaging almost 12 points.

"Outhustle 'em," McClure begins his pregame talk. "You know, I'd rather be sittin' in this locker room right now after what's transpired today and the last few weeks, as compared to theirs. They got some questions they gotta be askin' themselves, guys.

"You can go out there and just let 'er happen, baby. There's only probably 12 people in the state of Indiana that expect us to win. It so happens they're right here in this locker room. And that's all we need really.

"When was the last time you think they've been behind 10 points? They get behind, how they gonna react? They like things easy. They like it when teams come in here and belly up and bloat and stink, and you step on 'em, all the gas goes out and it stinks. That's not us, though, baby. We're full of life tonight. Enthusiasm. Let's have it. That's all we've done the last month, since the Harding game -- thrown in a little enthusiasm. That's God within ya. It's there. You let it out and enjoy it. Let people know we're full of life. ...

"They're hopin' that you're not as good as you looked out there today. We're better than we were this morning, 'cause we've had a chance to prepare. And this is the next step."

McClure's pregame talk ends eight minutes before the teams are allowed on the floor, so he tells them to just relax, which is not easy. In fact, he's having a tough time himself as he paces along the wall that partitions the shower area from the lockers.

"Ring, bell, ring," Jon says, walking nervously and reaching to the ceiling with palms outstretched.

Finally, it's 7:48, and the bell signifies it's time to take the floor.

The place is nearly packed, and a local cable television station has joined the electronic contingent.

Now, for sure, Marion.

The big question on many people's minds is whether Northfield will be intimidated by the basketball factory. This year's product, thanks in large part to McCain, has received its usual share of heavy publicity. The opening minutes -- nay, seconds -- will be crucial.

The Marion crowd outnumbers Northfield's aggregation of 2,000. But it's hard to tell who's winning the cheer war, because seconds before the tipoff, the noise blurs into an indistinguishable roar.

Shortly after Joe gets the tap, Hampton tries to draw first blood with a 12-footer from the right wing. But Kirby sails out of nowhere to swat the ball into the stands, as if to say, "Take that!" The crescendo reaches new heights in the Marion section. A sense of arrogance emanates from the mass of student rooters. Understandably. They are the Giants and supposed to win. See all those banners on the wall?

But it's part of the fun.

Not all is fun, though. Midway through the first quarter a close call goes against the Giants, bringing chants of "Bullshit! Bullshit! Bullshit!" Some of the special flavor of Indiana high school basketball is soured -- and never mind that this kind of crudeness takes place at other schools, too, this is the Regional championship.

It is clear, by now, that defense will dictate. The pressure on both ends is fierce, and so with more than half the quarter gone, it's only 7-4, Northfield. By now, too, it is evident that Northfield, led by Joe, is not intimidated.

In a game in which breaks will be crucial, Northfield gets a major one when McCain is called for his second foul with more than two minutes left in the quarter.

When the first eight minutes do end, Marion's on top, 13-11, although Northfield led most of the way. It stays nip and tuck through the second quarter, with Northfield creeping ahead by five until Kirby unleashes two straight three-point bombs to put Marion up, 27-26. Jackson follows with a free throw a short time later, but Jon's jumper squares matters at 28 before the halftime buzzer.

Northfield has shown no signs of cracking, and the twins have contained McCain. Marion has hit just 10 of 30 shots, but Northfield is not much better at 10 for 25.

Outside the locker room, McClure says, "The game's going our way; it's low-scoring." Desper points out that Kirby's got 13, but more worrisome is Marion's 12 offensive rebounds.

So McClure's first words inside the locker room are: "Defensively, we're not talking at all. We got to get on Kirby. They are in the ball game because of rebounding."

After briefly going over X's and O's, McClure says, "We've come too far. This game is in your possession." And that's it -- no long oration, just an attempt to keep his troops calm and collected.

As he did in the first game against Manchester, McClure had chosen to have his defense in front of his bench for the final 16 minutes. He figured this game will come down to "D" when all is said and done.

If the Marion crowd had been hoping that the "hicks from the country" will crack, they are mistaken. Forty seconds into the second half, Joe opens with a short jumper and comes right back for a bunny to make it 32-28.

The feeling-out process that opened the game has turned into heavy hitting in the opening minutes of the second half. Northfield maintains the edge, and with 3:18 left in the third, takes an eight-point lead on Jon's bucket in close. But a short time later, each Ross picks up his third foul.

Northfield calls time out with 2:22 remaining. In the huddle, the crouching McClure looks up at his troops, yells, "You gotta suck it up." There is not much more he can say, strategically or emotionally. Everyone knows what the game plan is; everyone is in this one mentally.

212

When Joe sinks a short jumper at 1:50, it gives Northfield a 10-point bulge, 46-36, and now it's a question of whether *Marion* will crack.

But Northfield suffers a blow with 40 seconds remaining when Peck goes down at midcourt in front of the Marion student section. He is in severe pain with cramps in his legs. There is no sympathy from the nearby onlookers; in fact, there is derision. Nathan Winegardner, whose mental toughness McClure has questioned all year long, enters the fray.

The quarter ends with Northfield holding its 10-point margin. And yet ...

Shortly after the final eight minutes unfold, McCain is called for his third foul, trying to stop Jon. The big Marion kid has had his hands full all night with the twins. They have forced him to alter his shots -- Joe has blocked two -- and taken it to him offensively.

Jon converts the first, misses the second, so it's a 12-point game at 50-38. Marion cuts it to 10, but Northfield maintains its momentum on Jon's two free throws after McCain collects his fourth personal. Six minutes and 28 seconds remain; lots of time. That fact becomes more evident at 6:02 and Northfield up by 10 when Jon gets nailed with his fourth.

Then each team loses a starter. Johnnie Williams, the Giants' talented, 6-4 forward, hurts his foot and retreats to the locker room for repairs. Peck, who returned a short time earlier, cramps up again and is replaced by Winegardner.

With 3 minutes and 50 seconds to go, the moment of truth arrives for Northfield. Marion has been sneaking back, and when McCain, who has refused to quit, scores from underneath, it's 56-52. What's more, he's fouled on the play by Jon, his fifth.

Time out, Northfield. As Jon nears the bench, he looks at brother Joe. "You've gotta do it," Jon says, and Joe nods in silence, as if to say, "Not to worry," but in his mind, he doesn't know what to expect. McClure hates to see Jon go, of course, but he feels fortunate to have an experienced Troy Miller going into the game.

McCain, a good free throw shooter, is at the line now. No good.

Winegardner provides some breathing room by hitting a jump shot from the right wing to make it 58-52.

And then Joe, Northfield's best clutch player all year, takes command. He makes both ends of a one-and-bonus situation, pushing the margin to 60-52. He immediately sprints down the floor and blocks Jackson's baseline jumper. Then, at 3:02, he follows with a psychological blow, a monstrous slam from the side for 62-52, unleashing insanity in the Northfield bleachers. In stark contrast, Marion cheerleaders sob, thinking their invincible Giants have lost. But there's plenty of time left, as basketball *aficionados* on both sides know.

Kirby's trey at 2:40 makes it 63-55. But it proves to be Marion's last gasp, and at 1:28, Christie shouts, "It's over!" Winegardner and Miller make sure, converting free throws down the stretch and holding things together. So much for mental toughness.

In the stands, it's not yet over for McClure's good buddy from White's, Sherm Knight. He parodies the "fat lady" expression, saying, "It's not over until the fat man plays," referring to Pefley.

Inside a minute, McClure starts substituting, and as Hampton comes toward the bench, he raises clenched fists. The Northfield faithful return the gesture with a roar that echoes through the arena, now baking at 80 degrees.

Pefley takes the floor with 13 seconds to go, and the smile on his face matches his girth.

As the clock dies, McClure spontaneously drops to his knees in thankfulness for the biggest basketball victory of his life. He had played this scene in his mind so many times, he lost track. And now, it has actually happened. Later, he says, "It was just my way of tellin' God that I still understand the priorities and that he's Number One and Jesus' victory on the cross is still the biggest."

The final is 73-64. Northfield has achieved another milestone for the season. Joe has tossed in 18, Jon 16, and Noi 15 to help boost Northfield's second-half shooting percentage to 56.5. The Norse have hit 17 of 21 free throws in the fourth quarter. For Marion, McCain has dumped in 16, while Jackson has played a great all-around game, scoring 12 and hauling in 18 rebounds.

The victory gives Wabash County a Regional title for the first time since 1956. It is only the second time in the last 16 years that a school other than Marion has won the championship.

McClure and Desper embrace in a bearlock as Northfield fans storm the floor, engulfing players. The Giants beat a hasty retreat. Media people fight their way to McClure, who can barely see. His glasses are steamed and the sweat is rolling in thick droplets down his forehead.

"Not too many people believed in us," he says, still almost breathless. "But as long as you believe in yourself, you can get it done." Trite, but true. And then: "But I want to emphasize that, you know, there's bigger things in life."

Whatever he said in the huddle after McCain's basket cut the margin to four must have worked, he's told.

"We knew we were gonna have some nervous kids out there," McClure responds. "We had a little quicker lineup in there, and I just told 'em, 'Go to the hoop. Just play to win.' And that's what they did."

You have to be pleased with the Twin Towers, he's told.

"Yeah, the Twin Towers ... and I'm pleased with Nathan Winegardner and Troy Miller. They came in in a very difficult situation and performed like champions." True again.

How much did the Rosses and Hampton benefit from playing in this game last year?

"If anything, it helped us get off to a good start. And it helped when Marion made a run late. Then the free throws at the end (Hampton hit five of six), I think, were also a result of experience."

What was your strategy coming into the game?

"Just to worry about what Northfield can do, and you can't be concerned about Marion. You come in here scared, you get kicked on your butt. And our strategy's just to focus on what we can do... play good defense... rebound. And make good offensive decisions."

Finally, the net-cutting completed, McClure staggers back to his locker room. Peck is flat on his back, lying on a wide slab of cement that serves as a bench for the lockers. His cramps have spread through his body, and he cannot hide the pain as his brother tends to him.

"I'm so exhausted," Hampton sighs. "Exhausted. I don't have an ounce of energy left, I don't think. I gave it all. We all gave it all."

Down the way, Joe inspects his left foot, which has developed a bad blister. He, too, is in pain but tries not to show it. "Don't neglect that," Desper tells him.

Thirty minutes later, the happy campers board the bus, and when it reaches LaFontaine, two fire trucks and two police cars begin the escort. A window is opened in the rear. Whooosh! Hampton's glasses blow off his head and into the cold night air, lost forever or shattered beyond repair.

The bus finds the Northfield parking lot is crammed with cars. Inside the main gym, some 1,500 fans await their heroes. When they do arrive, it's bonkers time as the cheerleaders dance to piped, upbeat music.

"Do you believe these guys?" McClure says, pointing to the team standing at center court. The crowd rises to its feet and goes a little nutty, clapping and stomping feet.

Twenty minutes later, after others have also spoken, the faithful head for their cars. The talk turns to Saturday's semistate at Fort Wayne, where victory means a trip to the Dome.

For Steve McClure, the monkey has to be off his back as he shepherds his family home. Sure, a small band of critics will take potshots no matter what Northfield accomplishes. But the extra burden McClure has carried with him all season -- and played down -- has to be back in Marion now. Or perhaps lying alongside Hampton's glasses on the blacktop of State Route 13.

Chapter 17: The Semistate

Like any malady, advanced stages of Hoosier Hysteria can cause a sense of irrationality in some people that requires others -- such as those who deal with ticket sales -- to guard their own sanity.

On Monday, March 12, Jim Kaltenmark, who has been athletic director for 13 years, finds he is suddenly one of the most popular guys in town. It doesn't surprise him. Troy Miller's mother, Judy, and her co-workers in the administration office, Louise Yentes and Sharon Harris, are perhaps the most harried. They are not surprised either. Or are they having a lot of fun when hostile, irate people demand ducats.

"It's the biggest challenge I've had in 13 years, but I've enjoyed it," Kaltenmark says. "It's nice to have these problems."

For some people, it's not a matter of obtaining highly coveted tickets -- they consider getting them a "right" -- but *where* their seats will be in the 10,000-seat Fort Wayne War Memorial Coliseum.

Northfield has been allotted 1,404 tickets, but by obtaining additional ones from two other Semistate teams, South Bend Riley and Whitko, Kaltenmark's office will wind up selling 1,857.

"It's just a ticket to a ball game," Kaltenmark smiles, "but for many people it's a lot more. I think everyone feels very entitled to a ticket because they've done something for the school or been involved at some time previously, and they think this is payoff time."

Ticket demand has been heightened even more by the combined record of the four Fort Wayne teams, 91-9, which is the best of the four Semistates.

Before the week is out, the hunger for tickets becomes comedic. Sharon Harris takes a call from a man who says he is good friends with Steve Desper, Kaltenmark "and Greg Winegardner," meaning, of course, Craig Winegardner. "So we were a little suspicious of that fellow," Kaltenmark deadpans. "It's just amazing."

The requests for tickets followed Kaltenmark home. His wife finally took the phone off the hook, so she could get things done.

On Tuesday afternoon, Steve McClure is busy, too, despite his worsening throat problem. He's visited the doctor that morning and been ordered not to yell -- preferably not even talk -- and to take his medicine.

"We both kinda chuckled about the talkin'," McClure says as he watches a rebound/outlet drill. "We both knew that probably ain't

217

gonna take place for two more weeks. But, you know, I've had this for about six weeks now, and we tried three different medications."

He shows Noi where he should be as eight defensive players pressure the five starters, except for Brad Hampton. He's gone home, feeling dizzy after wearing an old pair of glasses. New ones are due Thursday.

During a rinse, McClures volunteers, "The doctor described my larynx as lookin' like a young boy who had bare feet runnin' sprints in sharp gravel. And that's just from irritation from the cold in my chest and the screaming and yelling on the weekends. But he said, just tone it down as best I can and to inhale some steam to kinda soothe it. Nothing major."

What is major is South Bend Riley, a school of 1,431 students that compiled a 22-4 record. An explosive outfit, the Wildcats won their Regional, 81-63, over LaPorte, after defeating Valparaiso, 112-100. Although ranked just 19th in the final AP poll, Riley is seen by some experts as a major threat to win it all.

Northfield is not. When the Northfield-Marion score was announced at Hinkle Fieldhouse during the Indianapolis Regional, the crowd went wild and was abuzz for several minutes. Still, the doubters are plenty, including the media mavens who argue that another small school from the boondocks can't win it all again.

Riley coach Bob Berger knows better, and it's not just coach talk when he says, "We have not played with (against) size that can play the game. Hampton really complements Joe and Jon Ross. If you don't keep a close eye on him he'll kill you."

Riley's biggest starter is Jeermal Sylvester, listed at 6-5. But the Wildcats might be the quickest team in the state. "We want an up-tempo game," Berger says. "And they want to get the ball under the basket." No mysteries here.

McClure doesn't say so, but the Wildcats' quickness has to be worrying him. Marion was the quickest team Northfield has faced this year, but the Giants' guards can't match Riley's.

"Riley doesn't have a Jason McCain," McClure says as Tuesday's practice winds down, "but they have four kids who scored over 300 points this year. And they'll press ya to death. I think our biggest challenge -- like we told the kids yesterday -- is, are we gonna look back at Marion and concentrate on how that felt, or gonna concentrate on steps number six and seven? That's the million-dollar question this week."

McClure has already answered it in his mind. "We took Monday off, but the kids are probably emotionally tired. But I'm sure they'll be ready Saturday."

Joe and Jon will be, that's for sure. On Sunday night, they stopped at the McClure home to express their concern that the post-Marion euphoria might obscure the task at hand. McClure, well aware of what the twins were thinking, held a team meeting Monday to emphasize that all the congratulations and clippings must be put aside. "You can read 'em later this summer," he told the squad, "when it's all over. Let's just keep takin' one step at a time."

McClure, once the youngster who couldn't define the word "defense" as applied to basketball, has a love affair with the word now. So on Wednesday and Thursday, he focuses on defensive drills, pounding away at execution and fundamentals, using the word "rotate" in some verb tense repeatedly. He knows -- like anyone else who follows the high school game -- that Riley's offensive thrust comes entirely from its starters. They have accounted for 73.8 of the 79 points per game the Wildcats average, led by Sylvester's 21.6.

Friday's practice is held at the Coliseum before a banquet that night honoring the four teams. The session opens on a sour note as some players complain about dead spots in the floor and the rims not seeming right. McClure blasts them out of their negative thoughts, telling them to "major on majors, not minors." By the time the session ends, he's happy with what he's seen.

Instead of staying in Fort Wayne that night, McClure chooses to take the hour-long ride back home. Before the Regional, Northfield did not make motel reservations in Fort Wayne, but the Norse will have accommodations Saturday. Marion has offered the rooms it booked and Northfield has gladly accepted.

As he did before the Regional, the well-organized McClure has handed out a typed intinerary for the Semistate. The schedule starts with the bus leaving at 8:30 and ends with its return at 12:30 Saturday. At the end of the itinerary he's written: "Crome (sic) Dome's Home is the Dome -- and We're Going Home!!!"

Unlike a week ago, Saturday dawns with sunshine that takes the edge off a nip in the air. It is 8:29 as the team boards, and McClure asks, "Allen, you got your 'Walkman'?" The shy youngster nods yes. It has become a standard question -- ever since Strait forgot his headset for the trip to Maconaquah.

Sheriff Larry Rice will escort the team the entire way to the Coliseum, with Deputy John Blakely, father of junior varsity player Doug Blakely, guarding the rear. At this level, the best get the best treatment. And it's fun duty for the law enforcement officers. It is particularly pleasing for Rice, who was graduated from Urbana High School before it was folded into the Northfield consolidation. In a sense, he's taking his "alma mater" to the Semistate.

The situation is the same for Harold Christie, who not only was graduated from Urbana, but got his first coaching experience there after college.

Pockets of people, some holding signs, cheer as the bus winds through the countryside that's starting to rebound from winter.

As Bob Slee follows Sheriff Rice through two red lights on the Huntington bypass, McClure is asked if playing Wellston in the big Ohio University arena will be an advantage?

"Very much so, and we remind the kids of that -- that they've conquered the unknown before."

Is his team healthy?

"I think so. We've got some kids with sore bodies. And that's probably common after five months of bangin' around with each other. But their mind's healthy, and that's the main thing."

Now that you've thought things all the way through, what do you do against Riley?

"We have to just be able to beat their press. I feel like if we do, we'll beat 'em decisively."

Upon reaching Fort Wayne, the bus stops at the Carlton Lodge, where McClure checks on arrangements and a Fort Wayne city police car hooks up with Sheriff Rice. Six minutes later, sirens wailing, they push traffic aside in leading Slee to the Coliseum unhindered. People in cars pay little attention to the hubbub. It's old hat to them -- a way of life in the Hoosier state.

It is 9:50 as Slee pulls into the parking lot for the 11 o'clock encounter. Just inside a back lobby, Frank Swinford, a childhood friend from Rising Sun, greets McClure. Now a junior high school teacher in Fort Wayne, Swinford is helping Wayne High School host this year's Regional. Two others from Rising Sun -- population 2,500 -- were at Friday night's banquet in official capacities. And now McClure sees the connections with his past, which he treasures, as good omens.

The Coliseum locker room is small and spartan, but the ghosts of yesteryear -- George Yardley, Fred Schaus, Mel Hutchins, Andy

220

Phillip, Larry Foust, who played with the professional Fort Wayne Zollner Pistons -- can be felt.

How does it feel to be here? McClure is asked as his team dresses in eerie silence.

"This rewards those who are not afraid to dream and are bold enough to back things up and get here. I can remember Christmas shoppin' over at Tepe's, right across Parnell Avenue, and just starin' at this place and gettin' a tear in my eye. I'm just happy to be blessed with a bunch of good kids able to get us here."

He seems less tight than a week ago, because while he wants to win badly, the monkey is missing.

Desper and Christie watch quietly from just inside the doorway. "Steve has really made them believers from day one," Christie says softly.. "He's a very motivational person, and he really believes in the service of the Lord, which is not to say other coaches don't do the same thing. But I think that's a big uplift that the kids have needed."

Desper, staring intently at the troops, says, "I think the players have their game face on. They're getting mentally ready and serious to play the game."

At 10:05, Jon, now dressed, starts his nervous clap, a pop-pop-pop as he moves around the cramped quarters. Noi is wearing his nerves on his sweats; Peck is relaxed, lying back in the open locker stall.

Sixteen minutes later, McClure yells, "Nathan, get off the pot and let's go!"

They gather, and McClure begins,"You have seen 'Rocky', I'm sure. I'm not sure which one it was -- two or three or four -- the night before he couldn't sleep and so he walked down to the Spectrum, and he looked around and just kinda stared. His stomach was fluttering and all that stuff. And he went back to his wife and said something to the effect, 'Am I crazy?' And she just kinda patted him and he went back to sleep. Then he came out and did the job when it was prime time. And that's what I see you guys doin' today."

Riley has quickness, jumping ability and athletic skill, he continues, switching reels. "But what do they have that we don't have? What do you think they're gonna do when they come out there and look at us? We got quickness. We got size. And most of all, guys, we've taken everything that you 12 can possibly put together and blended it for one.

221

"I love your attitude right now. I just think we had a great bus ride up. I know it's gonna be a super day. All you gotta do is go out there and make it that way, not a worry in the world.

"You know, our 350 students or whatever will take on their 1,400 in a basketball game, in a fistfight, anything they wanna do, because we're doin' it together. You go out there and be the aggressors. You don't feel anybody out. You let 'em feel what it feels like to get thumped early."

He turns to basics, reminding them to control the boards, beat the half-court defense, stop the guards from penetrating and stay tight on the three-point shooter.

"They run faster to the offensive end than they do the defensive end," he says. "I noticed that. They must be related to me or somethin', cause that's the way I used to do it. If you get down and see a three on two, make 'em pay. If you see anything other than that, get it out to the side. Don't throw it to Joe or Jon if they're trailin', unless they got a lay-up. Just move the ball, reverse it, 'cause they're not gonna go to the strong side and try to steal it from ya. Big men curl, guards streak on fast break."

One minute to go, Christie announces. And so McClure wraps up: "If you'll do what we've told ya, you'll beat 'em to death. You'll get 80 points and they won't get 50 on ya "

The teams take the floor to a nearly packed arena, although gametime is 30 minutes away. Lisa and the kids, along with others, sport the latest Northfield T-shirt, which features a montage of newspaper articles proclaiming the Norse triumph in the Regional.

It is a big-time atmosphere, what with almost 10,000 people on hand, television cameras all around and a full press section. And yet, five minutes before tipoff, it seems like just another high school basketball game as the students stand and sing their school songs to taped music over the P.A.

Northfield starts on the right feet, Joe following Hampton's missed jumper for a 2-0 lead 20 seconds into the contest. But Riley promptly answers with eight straight points, beating Northfield's zone from outside. Timeout, Norse, with 5:48 remaining.

Perhaps the big question going in has been answered immediately: Northfield won't be able to handle Riley's quickness, which is awesome. And the Wildcats haven't even shown the press yet.

In the huddle, McClure is calm in the sea of bedlam around him. "They're streaky, guys," he says. "They gotta start missin'."

Riley resumes play by scoring seven more points to make it 15 straight, forcing McClure to call time again with 4:11 remaining. The match-up zone has to go, he realizes, in part because his people are standing around too much. "Guys," he says in the huddle, "we're goin' man to man."

Joe's follow at 3:01 stops the hemorrhaging, but only briefly. And when Riley surges to 21-4, McClure mutters to Desper, "They keep hittin' like that, we don't have to worry about a thing. We're out."

But Peck, cold early, unloads two straight treys, giving the Norse a huge psychological lift. Berger now knows he has to quit cheating inside on the Rosses and put more pressure on the perimeter. The quarter ends with Riley thoroughly in command, 31-21. So much for holding the Wildcats to 50 for the game.

"They can't keep shootin' like that the whole game," McClure shouts in the huddle between quarters.

But Sylvester, who at 6-5 looks like 6-7 and plays like 6-9, is unstoppable. He scores the first two baskets of the second quarter, and it's back to 14.

As the clock dips under the six-minute mark, Hampton gets loose in close and is fouled by Eric Ford, Riley's outstanding junior guard. Hampton converts the three-point opportunity, and seconds later, Joe hits a short jumper to reduce the margin to nine. McClure slumps back on the bench momentarily, thinks, If we can be within 10 by the half, we can win.

Jon gets loose close in for an easy hoop, and now it's down to seven. Noi's short jumper slices the lead to five. Timeout, Riley. After setting the building on fire in the first quarter with 13 for 16 shooting, the Wildcats have found Northfield's man defense tough.

"Stick the defense on 'em right now!" McClure yells, as if his team hasn't been doing just that since abandoning the zone.

Play resumes with Jon collecting two free throws and Hampton scoring on a fast break. It's 35-34, Riley; Northfield has scored 13 straight points.

When Hampton hits a short jump shot at 2:03, Northfield has the lead, 38-37, for the first time since Joe's opening hoop. And when Peck unloads his third trey of the half, it's 43-40. A Ford free throw makes it 43-41 at intermission, and McClure is ebullient as he hustles to the locker room.

Riley has gone from 13 of 16 in the first eight minutes to four of 14 in the next eight. Most of the Wildcats' damage has been done by two players: 5-9 guard Charles Adams, who has burned Northfield with his quickness for 15 points, and Sylvester, who has soared above the Norse outside for 13.

"Ya got guts," McClure says as his troops file in, whooping it up. "Ya got 'em on the run. Ya got composure. You tell me, guys, what do we need to do?"

"Pick up the defense," Hampton says, drawing immediate concurrence from the Rosses.

"Right. They played the second quarter about like I expected 'em to. Did we tell ya they would put it on the floor and dribble? Ya gotta rotate, guys. We're stayin' with man to man, but, I'll tell ya, ya gotta come to the ball's side. We gotta stop the dribble penetration and we gotta get the rebounds. No reachin' inside. Let's don't get 'em to the line."

He tells them what they surely know: Riley has quick jumpers, "so you gotta lay your body on 'em and get your hands up. See, a couple of those rebounds went over our heads 'cause our hands weren't up."

Rallying from such a huge deficit was outstanding, he says, "but that's past history. We can't be lookin' back now. You gotta move forward. The possessions starting the third quarter are crucial. They know you're for real now. They're thinkin' about ya. See, the reason they were shootin' so relaxed early is they thought it was gonna be easy. We made 'em a pretty good team."

He asks for stats on rebounding, is told Northfield got 16 to Riley's 15. "We can't afford to break even with 'em on the boards. We gotta stuff it ... one shot only."

McClure notes that the Wildcats are in some foul trouble, so he wants to take it to them inside. "If they have to bring the bench people in, they're Tuna of the Sea. They're fish. They aren't any good. You're gonna be in great shape. Your body will follow your mind."

Surprisingly, Riley has not pressed, but McClure warns his team to expect it the second half.

Hampton is on Adams as the final 16 minutes open with Joe getting called for goaltending. For all intents and purposes, it's a brand new ball game at 43.

It becomes a real dogfight, and, in some ways, a personal duel between Sylvester and the Rosses. The Riley star is practically impossible to contain from outside, skying for left-handed, 15-foot jumpers from just past the free-throw line. Meanwhile, Jon is finding room in the high post for 12-foot jump shots and Joe is dominating play inside. The result: 59-58, Northfield, after three quarters. The venerable Coliseum is reverberating and there are more than a few dry mouths.

In the huddle, McClure points to Hampton, shouts over the noise, "We gotta rebound," and Hampton, drenched in sweat, blinks and nods.

With 6 minutes and 25 seconds remaining, Riley edges into a four-point lead, 65-61, as Sylvester refuses to be stopped. Now the question is, which team will crack first?

The answer comes quickly: Riley.

Jon, who has clearly recovered from his brief shooting slump, hits a jumper from inside the paint. Peck adds four straight free throws. Jon finds himself open for another jumper in the lane. It is a 10-point run before Riley can score again. Now up by four, Northfield plays with great patience, using the clock and looking for easy buckets. Noi and Peck each get a field goal and Hampton adds two free throws. It is a 16-2 blitz now, and the Norse crowd behind the bench is on its feet, cheering and stomping nonstop. With 2:25 left, Berger calls time out, hoping he can regroup his forces.

But Riley, lacking depth, is out of gas. The Wildcats' tremendous first quarter play has deteriorated gradually. And so with 1:36 remaining, it's 79-68 after Joe knocks down two free throws. Seconds later, Jon takes a long pass from the rebounding Joe to score on a fast break, ending any doubt that Northfield will advance to the final eight.

After falling behind by 14, the small-town kids have rallied for an 81-72 victory over the kids from the city, led by Jon's 28 points. Joe has contributed 17, and, like his brother, gathered eight rebounds. Peck has gone five from nine from the field and added six free throws for 19. That combination has overcome the efforts of Sylvester and Adams, who scored 26 and 21 points respectively.

In the locker room, McClure calls for prayer. The air is soaked with emotion as the players huddle tight, some head to head. McClure's words tumble out with feeling: "Father, I just thank you for these guys... for their composure, being able to compete under adverse conditions. Just thank you for your love, and we know we're a team of destiny. ... Help us not be satisfied. Help us to continue marching forward with your cross at the forefront. ..."

Now, as they sit in their locker stalls, McClure warns, "Guys, step six is finished. Over. Done. And you're gonna play for a chance to go to the Dome. You gotta go back (to the motel), get off your feet. And when we come out tonight, the only opponent is us, our minds."

Back on the floor, the next would be opponents-in-the-flesh -- Whitko or No. 1 ranked and unbeaten Concord -- are concluding their warmups. As he watches them from his guard post in the small channel that leads to the locker rooms, Frank Swinford is overjoyed.

"Steve's older brothers kinda teased him a lot, picked on him a lot like older brothers do," Swinford recalls from the days he buddied around with the McClures in Rising Sun. "But Steve was such a nice young man, always polite.

"He was always doin' things in sports. It's fun to watch someone you grew up with be so successful, especially when you come from a small town where there's 250 in the whole school system."

By now, the polite kid from the sticks has been ushered into the press room, where a gaggle of announcers and reporters, including representatives of the Indianapolis newspapers, are asking questions.

Was the turning point the defensive switch?

"It had to be. We feel that's our team's strength, as well as character. When we get down in a good athletic stance and get more aggressive, then things seem to happen in all phases of the game."

It's suggested that Northfield's strength -- size -- simply took command the last three quarters.

"You know, in the three years we've had the Ross boys in there, you can cite several examples where teams worked so hard the first half to defend them, and their legs go. And yet Joe and Jon don't get any shorter. The first quarter, Riley's legs were there. They were very active on defense and did a very good job of keepin' the ball out of Joe's and Jon's hands."

Why did he leave Joe in after he got his fourth foul with six minutes and seven seconds to play in the third quarter?

"We're used to it. Phil (Beebe) can tell ya that. Joe's been in foul trouble a lot this year, not a lot lately. You know, they were just rebounding fouls. We realize we're not gonna be a good team without him. That's not a knock on my bench, because they won the Marion game for us practically -- Troy Miller and Nathan Winegardner. But today we just felt like, as well as the team was playin', we had to let 'em go as long as they can."

What about the two "threes" by Peck Chay?

"Saved us. We were on the brink that, you know, another onslaught like that and it's probably gonna be out of reach with only 24 minutes left. We obviously look inside first, but if the defense isn't gonna give that to ya, you have to take what's left."

During his time with the media, Berger says he's glad the Rosses are "moving to my town. I know they won't be playing for me, but at least they won't be playing against me any more. I'm a Notre Dame fan and I'll be rooting for them. No matter how you cut it, they're 6-10 and get the job done. That's why they're here."

At 1:03 the bus leaves for the Carlton Lodge, and in the rear, Joe is asked what he was thinking as Riley charged ahead.

"About what coach said -- that they weren't gonna be doin' this all game, they weren't gonna shoot like that. He said they were a streaky team. So I was just hoping that it was true."

Hampton chimes in: "I was thinking, Step up, rebound, go for it, play hard, drill 'em and kick their butt." He pauses. "We weren't intimidated. We were kinda goin' in half-heartedly. And coach told us to play with our heart. That's what we did."

Jon, seated with his legs stretched into the aisle, says, "Basketball is a game of control. All we had to do was get the control back. And I knew that once we got it back, we could keep it. That's what we did."

Up front, Desper points out, "We could have gotten buried if Peck hadn't come to play."

Before leaving the bus at the motel, McClure tells them he prefers that they not watch the Concord-Whitko game. "Watch the NCAA game or a movie; get some rest."

After settling his players, McClure enters the coaches' room, where Desper, lying in bed, is watching Concord-Whitko. "Whitko's down by 20," the assistant coach says matter-of-factly.

"You want to know something?" McClure responds while removing his shoes. "I'd rather play Concord. I'd rather play the best. And the kids play better."

Suddenly, Whitko goes on a tear, scoring 17 straight points before the half to go into the locker room down 37-34. The Steves and Harold Christie say nothing. On the tube, Glenn Heaton, McClure's old pal, tells an interviewer, "Sometimes hot shooting early is a curse," referring to Concord's fast start. "It looks too easy." And McClure says, "Amen."

Jim Kaltenmark arrives with sacks of Italian food from the Olive Garden restaurant. The players drift down the hallway to Room 264 and start reaching for salads and pasta -- $158 worth.

Whitko scores the opening basket of the second half, but that will be the Wildcats' last hurrah. And as Jim Hahn's Concord team takes command and pulls away, McClure, sitting on the floor and finishing off his lasagna, says, "Maybe we ought to use the 5-Jump against 'em. Can't go zone; they shoot too well. Let Brad try (Jamar) Johnson. Brad did the job on Adams -- forced him to take some bad shots."

As they watch and chat and eat -- relaxed -- McClure says, "If Joe and Jon don't make the all-stars, I'll burn the IHSAA building. I'll revert back to my teenage days."

After Concord disposes of Whitko, the coaches watch New Castle edge Richmond at Indianapolis before turning to the second-round NCAA game between Desper's alma mater, Ball State, and heavily favored Louisville. The Cardinals of BSU forge ahead of the Cardinals of Louisville, and Desper begins to live and die with his school.

At 3 o'clock, Bob and Rob Ross saunter through the open door, toting bananas and a jug of Gatorade for the team. They offer congratulations, depart quickly.

At 3:27, the Gatorade comes in handy. Hampton strolls in, says he's dehydrated and cramping up. He grabs the jug, and when he leaves, McClure says, "I'm little concerned with Brad and Peck. 'Course, Troy and Nathan have fresh legs."

Desper and Christie decide to stroll around the motel while McClure watches tape of the Concord-Whitko game, which Kaltenmark has gotten from dejected Whitko coach Bill Patrick. Lisa has delivered the family VCR.

At 5:01, McClure visits the motel lounge, where Desper has run into a friend, Keith Hipskind, formerly from Wabash. The conversation centers around coaching opportunities, but they keep an eye on the BSU-Louisville game unfolding on a large-screen television. McClure stays 14 minutes before leaving to shower for tonight's championship game. The monkey's even farther away, but McClure's nervousness shows as he says goodbye.

At 5:50, now showered and dressed, McClure lies in bed on his stomach, his feet against the headboard, and fills out his scoring book. Desper, back now, agonizes with BSU.

Soon, the room fills up with Christie, McClure's brothers, Bill and Mike, and Mike's wife and young son. The clan is wearing blue T-shirts with "McClure" in white on the back and "Northfield" in front.

"Go ahead, take the gas, guys," Desper moans as Louisville chops away at what was a 17-point Ball State lead.

Across the hall, Northfield's cheerleaders crowd into a room of their own, some having returned from the indoor pool. Cathy Christie, the coach's youngest daughter, has rejoined them after competing in another Fort Wayne contest this day: the Regional speech finals. She's qualified for state competition, and now dad's bursting with pride. There's a real family atmosphere in the air.

Bill, Mike and his family leave -- Bill taking charge of the VCR -- and at 6:08 the players start filing in, anxious.

"Turn it off," Desper says 15 minutes later. "It's killing me." With 2:28 to go, BSU is clinging to victory.

At 6:30, Scott Kunkel's told to shut the door and silence the set.

McClure talks to his team calmly, mixing mind stuff with court savvy in no particular order. "There isn't anybody in the state of Indiana who can play with you. Concord's undefeated. So what? So are we -- in the tournament. Take it to them. We tried to feel out Riley and you saw what happened.

"Look for the 1-2-2 press; the sides and middle are open.

"(Chad) Patrick and (Todd) Darley had the flu against Concord. If they hadn't, they might have beat 'em.

"Tonight is step seven, nothing more, nothing less.

"We'll start with a man. They'll hit some shots. But no new defensive principles need to be taught. You must block out, especially Johnson. Our defense is what brought us through, although we took the first five minutes off against Riley. They got 31 points the first quarter and 41 the rest of the game.

"Rebounding's the key. They got to know that when they take one shot, it's the last one.

"You'll see, they'll tighten up. They choked against Whitko and got away with it. You've come up a tougher road than they did. To be the best, you have to beat the best. So we need 32 minutes of step seven.

"Concord beat Riley 79-72 at Concord. Riley shot only 11 free throws.

"I believe you're a team of destiny.

"Take the running game and the 'threes' from them. If you do, it will be no contest.

"Anybody want to say anything?"

"Have fun," Jon says.

It is 6:36 and the sun has departed, leaving a chill in the air as the Norse board the bus for a 12-minute ride to the Coliseum.

Leisurely, noiselessly, they dress. After their stretching exercises, the tension is evident as they pace and bounce balls hard against the concrete floor.

At 7:22 Jon starts his clap, harder tonight than usual. "Let's go, guys," he says softly. "Rebounding, defense and execution."

Three minutes later, Chad Patrick pops into the locker room, wishes the Norse well, quickly departs with a look that says, "Boy, I wish I were here."

There's not much for McClure to say before his team takes the floor. But he reminds them again of all the things they've worked on -- moving their feet on defense, blocking out, making good outlet passes on the fastbreak, executing X-cuts, isolating the big men, rotating both on offense and defense. It is coaching by rote, and it has worked.

"I'd just as soon you not spot 'em 17 points tonight," he says, tongue firmly in cheek. "You go out there and get a 17-point lead. You don't look at the scoreboard.

"Man to man defense. We'll give you the matchups when we come back in."

Nine minutes remain before the bell signals them to take the floor; the ball-bouncing becomes more pronounced.

Christie reports that unbeaten Loogootee, the smallest school in the Sweet Sixteen with 346 students, has finally fallen. Evansville Bosse, a school with 944 students, has taken them out, 36-28. So now Northfield, with its 384, is the smallest of the final eight.

As the teams warm up, a relaxed Desper says, "Boy, (Jeff) Massey can really sky."

Massey is only one of Concord's weapons. Unlike two years ago, when the Minutemen were also undefeated, this year's squad is balanced, although 6-0 guard Jamar Johnson is the clear standout. In '88, Concord was mostly Shawn Kemp, the 6-11 high school All-American who, after sitting out his first year of college ball, turned professional with the Seattle Supersonics. Concord's center this season is 6-4 Bill Mutch, the team's tallest player.

In an interview with the Associated Press on Thursday, Coach Jim Hahn said, "I would give the ball to any one of them in any situation and feel comfortable. The kids are winners. That's their attitude."

Now Hahn hopes '88 doesn't repeat itself. His team, then ranked No. 2, was thrashed, 76-53, by No. 1 Muncie Central in the state championship game.

As game time nears, it becomes almost impossible to hear as another contest begins -- a cheering duel between Concord, in a sea of Kelly green, against Northfield, in a sea of royal blue.

"Let's go Blue! Let's go Blue! Let's go Blue! Let's go Blue! Let's go Blue!"

The larger Concord forces answer powerfully.

"Let's go Green! Let's go Green! Let's go Green! Let's go Green! Let's go Green!"

And this, of course, is what sport is all about to a large degree -- the excitement, the nervousness, the fun of cheering on one's team. But tonight, in this madhouse of 10,000 Hoosiers, it is something special, wrapped in its unique mystique.

It's time to decide who will go to the Final Four.

As in the opener, Joe starts the scoring at 7:37, taking a pass underneath from brother Jon. Noi follows with a short jumper. But Concord answers with seven straight points, and there's a feeling of *deja vu* in the air. Joe's bunny and a free throw, though, knot things.

McClure has assigned Peck to Johnson, with Hampton shadowing Massey in the man-to-man scheme of things. One thing is clear immediately: Concord plays a much more disciplined game than Riley.

At 3:20, Mike Swanson, a 6-3 junior, drops in a free throw to give Concord a 14-9 lead. Concord is small, but the Minutemen are getting the boards. And their defense is showing how it held opponents to 38 percent shooting during the season.

In the 25 games they have played, the Minutemen have averaged 23 points to their opponents' 12 in the first quarter. That's almost the case tonight, as Concord assumes an 18-11 advantage after the first eight minutes.

The pattern of the first quarter continues in the second, with Concord getting two, three and sometimes four shots in an offensive

231

sequence before scoring. And Peck can't get his shots to fall. So at the half, it's 26-21, Concord, in what has been a bruising 16 minutes of defense on both ends. Northfield's guards have just four points.

McClure is a tad angry. "Was that the greatest half you ever played?" he asks with sarcasm. "Why not? *Why not!?* You felt 'em out. Are they that good? Why don't you take it to 'em? They're waitin' to get hammered. They're backin' off you as much as we're backin' off of them. I don't know why on God's green earth you're holdin' back."

He points out that the Norse have run their offense from 22 to 25 feet out, instead of dribbling forward and trying to make something happen. "You gotta get the ball movin' at the basket, guys. That press? It's the soft 1-2-1-1. They aren't pressurin' you in bounds at all."

The old blackboard in the locker room is worn out, so McClure asks for his diagram clipboard. "Okay, we got a guard takin' it out. I want Jon in the middle. What we're gonna do, guys, is run 3 trap clear down the floor. Joe on one side, Brad the other. We don't need four people down here (on the defensive end). Then we can run our curls. You get behind the defense."

McClure's disgust with the lack of offensive effort inside flares into the open. "It's pathetic that as weak a team as that is underneath, we won't go to the basket. That is beyond my comprehension. It amazes me why you won't go at it inside. At least if you make a mistake, you're goin' at our basket.

"And we haven't run early once. That's what we said we were gonna do, beat the press and get the ball movin'."

Defensively, he's satisfied, and should be. "If you'll talk and work and get people to the ball's side, it's got 'em confused. How many 'threes' have they hit? Zero. They haven't even shot one. Now, if somebody dribbles at ya', don't just stand there and look. Rotate up. Shell drill -- 16 minutes. If you can do that, you're goin' to the Dome. If that doesn't excite ya, I don't know what will."

There's no doubt about the excitement in the Coliseum. This one figures to go down to the wire in barn-burner fashion.

As he has done repeatedly, Joe opens the second half by hitting in close to cut the margin to three. But Concord won't yield. The Minutemen methodically work their way to a 38-28 lead with 2:20 left as Northfield's offense can't defeat Concord's quick, agile athleticism. McClure calls time out.

"You gotta be more intense," he says, a bit exasperated. "You don't win getting outhustled."

By the end of the quarter, Northfield whittles three points off the lead. Eight minutes and seven points -- 40-33 -- to go. Noi will not be available for all eight minutes. He fouls out with 7:34 remaining and Concord ahead, 41-33. The sophomore has not been very effective. He has been illustrative of Northfield's struggle all night to catch the Minutemen, who have gone to the spread offensively.

Twenty seconds after Noi's departure, though, Northfield makes its run. Jon gets a tip and Hampton contributes two free throws, closing it to 41-37 and setting off fireworks in the Northfield section.

With 3:20 remaining, Jon gets a seven-footer to stick, and it's finally even at 43.

But Concord will not let loose. Micah Sharp hits two free throws at 1:57 to give the Minutemen another four-point margin, 49-45.

Joe and Jon -- their brilliant Northfield careers on the brink -- play with abandon -- and pick up their third and fourth fouls each in just 41 seconds.

Fifty seconds to go, and it's 50-47 as Johnson is called for his fourth foul. Peck at the line for one-and-one. Swish. Swish. 50-49, Concord.

Thirty seconds to go, and as Concord plays keep-away, Joe lunges for the ball near center court and against the sideline. Instead, he gets his fifth foul, sending Massey to the line. But first, time out, Northfield.

"If he misses and we take the lead, we don't call time out," McClure shouts, his voice barely audible. "If we get behind, we do. Try to foul 54 (Mutch) if we have to."

Massey steps to the line. Both free throws touch nothing but net. It's 52-49. Concord presses. The Norse break the press. Tick, tick, tick.

Thirteen seconds to go, and Peck feeds Hampton in front of the Northfield bench. Mutch is draped all over him. No matter. Hampton goes up for his first three-point attempt of the year. Bullseye! 52-52. Talk about hysteria.

Ten seconds to go, and Concord calls time. Play resumes with Northfield pressing full-court. Sharp takes the in-bounds pass. He feeds to Mutch at half court. Mutch dribbles down the middle of the floor, thinking he will take it right to the hole. But at the free throw line he finds Jon waiting.

Five seconds to go, and so Mutch shovels a pass to Massey on the left edge of the lane. Massey spies Jon moving in, leaps and puts up a high-arching jumper. Jon soars and swats the ball away.

A split second, then a whistle. Official Don Nester signals goaltending. 54-52, Concord. Nester comes by the scorer's table, says, "I'll bet the house on the call."

Two seconds to go, and Northfield calls timeout. McClure has to decide whether he wants Troy Miller, the former quarterback, to throw a court-length pass or have him available for a three-pointer. He opts for Miller throwing long to Jon, who was Troy's main receiver when they played football in their earlier Northfield days.

Hahn chooses not to harass Miller. He wants all of his people back. His biggest fear has to be a three-point play on a trey or a basket and free throw, which would end the Minutemen's season.

Miller throws a strike to Jon in the paint. The big guy is nearly surrounded. He spins to his right from five feet out and puts it up.

It won't fall.

He taps it back up.

It won't fall.

It's over.

Concord's folks in green have won the Fort Wayne Semistate, 54-52, on St. Patrick's Day.

Jon sinks to the floor in a four-point stance, bathed in sweat and grief. His teammates rally to his side.

The Norse move quickly through the crowd and into the locker room. McClure, his voice cracking and near tears, says, "I'll take you guys in a foxhole with me against anybody. We came here as a 12-man unit of guys, we leave here as a 12-man unit. It's easy to say we're a team of destiny when we're winnin' and it's God's will. We gotta say it when we get beat. I feel like you did everything you could to give yourselves a chance to win that ball game."

He pauses, choked up a bit, then: "Guys, I think we oughta just get dressed, get on the bus, ride home. I'd like to have ya all over at the house when we're done. Can you guys all make it?" Nods all around. "I think we will talk a bit. I don't think this is the time to do it. Let's pray ...

"Father, we just thank you for the neat times we've had and for the lessons. Father, if there is any guilt on any of these young men's minds, just erase it right now. Just shine your light on them and spread your love amongst this team as you have all season.

"Father, I just thank you for choosin' 12 good ones for us to go to war with. We've enjoyed it ... and we thank you for all the blessings, for all the trials you've given us down the road ... that we've been able to learn from. It's just gonna make us stronger people. Again, Father, just comfort these guys. Just let them know you love 'em. We feel your presence in this room. Thanks, Father, for a great season. In thy name we pray. Amen."

Jon slumps to his locker stall, weeping and perhaps replaying the final shot of his great high school career. Four stalls away, in a corner, brother Joe stares at his twin, pain etched in his face. As Bob and Andris Ross have said more than once, "When one hurts, the other hurts too." And now Joe's hurt is as much for his brother's anguish as it is for his team's heartbreaking loss.

Hampton cannot hold back. He slumps across Joe's lap in tears. Joe consoles him. Across the way, others cry, unabashedly letting their emotions flow. They are unable to shed their uniforms for several minutes.

"The difference?" Desper replies when asked outside the locker room. "It's so slight. It's hard to say when it's only two points. I felt like Concord's offensive execution was very, very good. We had some lapses on the press, which gave them probably five or six lay-ins, and we didn't get any lay-ups. And that's part of why you press. If you can get 10 points on the other team off easy hoops, then you're normally gonna win."

Is Concord the best team he's seen this year?

"Yeah, they probably are. Their execution is the best. They're certainly not the quickest. But they play with their skills probably better than any team we've played."

McClure has gone to the press room.

"They stretched themselves as far as they could," he says. "It was like a rubber band -- you just stretch it and stretch it and stretch, and, you know, it may pop. But you keep stretchin' on faith anyway."

What was the defense on the goaltending call, and did he expect Mutch to handle the ball as much as he did?

"No, not really. We just went straight man and tried to fan 'em out to the sides. We rotated around and got the block, and it was called goaltending. And it probably was."

McClure has just ensured that there will be no controversy.

235

From where he sat, did it appear as if the goaltending shot would have fallen?

"I think it would have. And there again, I have no problem with any calls that were made or not made. I feel like the kids had a chance to decide the game, and that's all we ever ask for from the officials."

Someone points out that the pass from Miller to Jon was perfect.

"Yeah, well, you know it was a tough angle, " he says of the shot, "'cause Jon caught it with his back to the basket and had somebody right under him. He kinda had to make a tough pivot 'cause there wasn't really enough time to plant his feet and get facin' the basket. He gave it his best shot. It just didn't go."

Another writer suggests that it has been sort of a Cinderella-type year, the small school marching toward a state championship.

"I don't consider these kids small in any way, shape or form," McClure responds. "Physically, you got the big kids. But I'm talkin' about the size of their heart and their ability to perform under the toughest conditions. There's nothin' small about the way they met challenges this year."

Was fatigue a big factor?

"I imagine it was. But our desire more than made up for any fatigue. You know, they were down 10 points to the number-one rated team and somehow got back in it, gave themselves a chance to win the ball game."

Speaking of the number one team, did his kids feel they could win?

"You better believe it. We feel like beatin' Marion at Marion puts ya in a position to beat anyone."

Was Hampton's three-point shot a designed play?

"Yeah," and McClure laughs.

It looked wild, in desperation, the questioner says.

"We wanted to score a quick basket and call time out. And Brad, he thinks out there. He knew he had to make somethin' happen. So he got it up."

The press conference ends with Mike Wainscott of the Marion *Chronicle*, who has followed Northfield much of the season, thanking McClure. "You run a class program, Steve," and McClure replies, "I appreciate that."

Strolling back to the locker room, McClure is asked about Jon.

"He's okay. He knows that we will always have nothing but love for him. He knows what his value has been to this team."

Meanwhile, Jim Hahn is sighing with relief. "With the big kids, they're never out of a game," he says. And with candor: "All year long we've won pretty easily and we didn't need too much luck. I guess we saved up our luck for the right time."

Asked about the winning goaltending shot, Hahn says no, the play was not designed for Massey. "We wanted to get the ball to Jamar, but when that wasn't there, our kids reacted as they've been taught."

By now, the Coliseum is almost empty. Among the few folks still seated are Bob and Andris Ross.

Andris fights back tears, unable to talk. Bob is calm. "They gave it all they had; they just couldn't do it," he says softly, his face reflecting peacefulness.

Back in the Northfield locker room, the team is composed now and ready to be escorted home.

It is 10:22 as they walk out the lobby doors and into the dark Coliseum parking lot. A gust of wind sweeps past them as they reach the bus, wordlessly.

Jon, as usual, is seated near the rear in a left-side seat. He is okay.

"Until you're in that position, you don't realize how long two seconds is," he says. "And I just didn't make a good pivot. And I didn't realize how close I was to the basket either.

"I honestly feel we are a better team. We played decent tonight. We didn't play great. That's unfortunate, but, hey, you know, we're in the final eight."

The smallest team in the final eight, he's told.

"That's something to be proud of," he responds. "I just hope Concord can win the state now. And, you know, you can't look back. There's nothin' I can do about it. Just look forward to Notre Dame and the rest of my senior year. And, hey, it was a great season."

Up front, McClure's mind mulls over how he can get his players to feel worthy about themselves, to understand how great their effort was for the 1989-90 season. He knows there is a danger of them sinking very low, questioning how they could come within two points of making the Final Four and failing.

The goaltending call is on his mind, too. He knows it was the talk of the arena as people filed out, but he's absolutely certain that

237

officiating did not beat his team. The door to victory was open, but his kids were too physically tired to go through, he reasons in all honesty.

Getting the kids back "up" won't leave his mind. And finally, he thinks, We'll just go to the house, order some pizza, get some pop, watch some wrestling and, more or less, party; that simple.

It is 11:33 as the bus rolls into the Northfield lot, which has a scattering of cars. A 100 or so fans have been waiting in the windy cold to greet the team. As each player steps down through the open doors, the small gathering cheers until everyone has left the vehicle.

They stow their gear for the last time in the locker room. It has been a year of 24 victories and three defeats, a year in which a small school has almost pulled off that most cherished of achievements in Indiana high school sports, a year in which lives have grown in more ways than one.

And it has been one of those periodic years in which a small school with a giant dream nearly made it come true in the world of Hoosier high school hoopla.

Chapter 18: The Finals

It is Saturday, March 24, and IHSAA Commissioner Gene Cato is aglow as fans flood the entrances to the Hoosier Dome.

The state championship has been played before a capacity crowd 61 straight times, and while that might not mean much to others, Indiana folks attach a great deal of symbolism to the feat. Breaking the skein would be a blow to the pride and prestige Hoosiers savor over an event that's all their own.

Nobody was more aware of this than Cato when he decided in July 1989 that the state finals would be moved from Market Square Arena, which seats about 17,000 fans, to the Hoosier Dome, which would be configurated for 41,000-plus.

Before Sectional play began, an Associated Press poll of 165 writers and broadcasters picked Bedford North Lawrence by a wide margin. The Stars received 33 votes to East Chicago's 16, while Concord, Lawrence North and Marion received 12 each. Now, though, the sentiment in the press section seems to favor Concord, ranked No. 1 for the last five weeks of the AP poll.

But if Concord is favored in the mind, Bedford North Lawrence is favored in the heart. In the 6-3 Bailey, the Stars have a legend in his own time. As an eighth grader, he drew lavish praise from Indiana coach Bob Knight, who's not known for dishing out plaudits.

Bailey made Knight look like the basketball genius he is, leading his team to the Final Four three times in his four years. Along the way, he broke Marion Pierce's all-time career scoring mark. And to cap his career, he has been named the Naismith National Player of the Year. But the honor Bailey hungers for the most is the state championship.

The first order of business for Bedford will be Southport's unranked Cardinals. For the first half, it appears as if Bailey and Bedford won't get a shot at the championship. Southport plays inspired basketball to take a 14-point lead before Bedford shaves it to nine at intermission. But Bailey, whose court presence and understanding of the game are the keys to his brilliance, rallies his squad in the final 16 minutes. Bedford North Lawrence wins, 58-55.

As Concord and Anderson warm up for the second game, a world-record attendance for a high school basketball game is announced: 41,046, including 431 writers and broadcasters. The figure far surpasses the previous mark of 24,764 set in 1981 at Rupp Arena on the University of Kentucky campus.

In the second game, No. 1 ranked Concord builds a big lead and then hangs on to defeat Anderson, 70-66.

So it's The Legend vs. No. 1 for the championship. And from the opening tip to the final whistle, it's a Hoosier classic. With less than five minutes to go, it's tied at 48. Then Concord begins to pull away, opening a six-point lead at 58-52.

But Bailey will not be denied. He scores Bedford's last 11 points, four on free throws in the final 40 seconds, to give the Stars a 63-60 victory. He finishes with 30 points on 11 of 16 from the field, 8 rebounds, 5 assists and 4 steals.

What Northfield could not do against Concord, Damon Bailey has done. The destiny that was not there for the darlings proves to be there for the darling.

Epilogue

Although their Northfield careers ended with the wrenching defeat to Concord, Joe and Jon Ross continued their season into the summer. They were chosen for the Indiana all-star team that faced Kentucky in the home-and-home series.

And numerous honors came their way.

Fort Wayne television station WPTA named them "Area Players of the Year," an award normally given to a single individual.

USA Today chose them for honorable mention on its All-USA High School Basketball Team.

Jon was named to the second team All-State squads chosen by the Associated Press and the The *Indianapolis News*. He made UPI's third team. AP and UPI chose Joe for honorable mention.

For the second straight year, Jon was named County Player of the Year, chosen by the five county coaches and *Wabash Plain Dealer* Sports Editor Phil Beebe. And Steve McClure was chosen Coach of the Year for the second straight year.

About the Author

If someone had asked Ray Moscowitz at the age of 14 what he wanted to do in life, he would have replied, "Be a sports writer." Moscowitz did become a writer, but instead of concentrating on his first love, sports, he has written on a wide range of subjects as a newspaper reporter and editor.

During a career that has spanned almost 30 years, Moscowitz has interviewed former senator and now Vice President Dan Quayle, Walter Cronkite, Sol Linowitz, Jane Pauley, Merv Griffin, Benny Goodman, and political figures that include Indiana Senator Richard Lugar, former Indiana Senator Senator Birch Bayh and former Indiana Governor Otis Bowen.

Today, Moscowitz is editorial director for Nixon Newspapers, Inc., based in Peru, Indiana.

Small School, Giant Dream is his second book. He is the author of *Stuffy: The Life of Newspaper Pioneer Basil "Stuffy" Walters*, published in 1982.

Moscowitz is a member of the American Society of Newspaper Editors, Sigma Delta Chi journalism fraternity and Blue Key honorary fraternity.

He resides in Wabash, Indiana.

Joe Ross (striped Sweater) and brother Jon sign to play for Notre Dame. Others, from left, are Coach McClure, Bob Ross, Andris Ross, Principal William Neale and Athletic Director Jim Kaltenmark.

Nate Winegardner brings the ball up.

Brad Hampton for two.

Peck Chay looks for an opening.

Noi Chay beats his man.

he Chay family in 1980. Front row, left to right: NuNu, Noi, Peck. Middle row: Pick, Bey, Pally. Back row: Edward, Vanh.

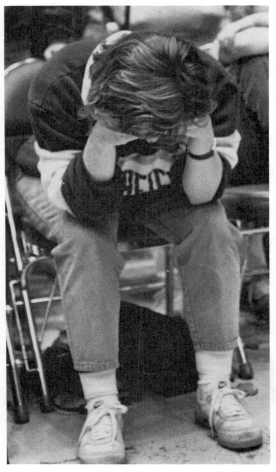

Lisa McClure has a worried
moment during a game.

Outside threat Troy Miller.

Lisa McClure has advice for husband Steve.

THE NORTHFIELD NORSEMEN

This team picture was taken after the 1990
regional championship game played at
Marion High School.